THE IMAGE OF LONDON

An exhibition at Barbican Art Gallery
from August 6th to October 18th 1987

Sponsored by 3i – Investors in Industry plc

THE IMAGE OF LONDON
Views by Travellers and Emigrés
1550-1920

Introduction and Catalogue
by Malcolm Warner

With contributions by
Brian Allen, John House, Robin Spencer and Samuel F. Clapp

Trefoil Publications, London
Rizzoli International Publications, Inc
in association with Barbican Art Gallery

Published by Trefoil Publications Ltd
7 Royal Parade, Dawes Road, London SW6

First published 1987

ISBN 0 86294 099 0

Edited by Caroline Bugler, assisted by Karen Yates and Sandrine Cholez
Designed by Elizabeth van Amerongen
Typeset by Suripace Ltd.

Distributed exclusively in the U.S.A. and Canada by Rizzoli International Publications Inc.
597 Fifth Avenue, New York, NY 10017
ISBN 0 8478 1002 X

Printed by BAS Printers Ltd, Over Wallop

CONTENTS

FOREWORD

As the chairman of 3i – Investors in Industry – a company which had its beginnings in the City of London, today has its head offices in London and retains close contact with so many of the capital's businesses, I am delighted that we chose this exhibition as our first serious venture into sponsorship of the arts.

Never before has anyone brought together a collection of this calibre, devoted exclusively to foreign artists' impressions of our capital city. Some have chosen to portray it in the stark reality of the era; others have taken a more nostalgic approach.

Whatever the subject, whatever the style, the range and scope of these paintings provides a permanent reminder of a very different London. Much of the architecture and many of the landmarks still survive today, but without the work of these artists, the life-style and the atmosphere of past centuries would be long forgotten.

Like industry, the arts will only grow if there is significant investment. Opportunities do exist to help ventures of this kind, as well as the more commercial projects in which we invest. With this in mind, I hope to see our name and resources used to support other such events in the future. Arts sponsorship reflects the 3i philosophy of helping to realise British potential in more ways than one – by investing in both industry and the arts.

John Cuckney

PREFACE

Over the centuries London has been visited by many artists from abroad and this exhibition is an attempt to illustrate how each visitor has in turn found inspiration from the city. It may seem surprising that so large a number from so many foreign countries have come to our capital to work; their reasons for visiting have been, variously, in the interests of commerce, tourism and even political survival, yet what is evident from Dr Malcolm Warner's excellent selection is that each artist has been in turn inspired by London. Some have devoted considerable time and effort to recording the culture and society of the city; others have responded by interpreting its scenery. The best cityscapes of London have been made by the foreign artists, and to some extent it is correct to say that such pictures have created the 'image' of the city in the eyes of the world.

The exhibition interprets this 'image' of London, reveals how the city has changed through four hundred years, and explores the idea of the city in the mind of the visitors and their response to it. Wyngaerde was the earlist artist to attempt to represent the city with relative accuracy. He conceived London as a great Gothic city with many towers and spires. Thomas Wyck may have witnessed the Great Fire, and he certainly painted several views of it. After the Fire, London was rapidly rebuilt and expanded. The subsequent completion of the new cathedral and the City's increasing commercial success attracted many traveller-artists. With its bustling market, Covent Garden was a favourite subject of the 18th-century artists such as Van Aken and Angillis. By contrast the serene Thames views of Canaletto and Joli recall Venice, and their interpretation of London as a city of grace and enlightenment seem more in keeping with the neo-classical order that fashioned the second half of the 18th century. In the 19th century artists began to depict the darker side of London. Focusing upon scenes of labour, poverty and suffering in an oppressive industrial environment, Géricault and Doré portrayed the Babylonian image of London. Nevertheless, Victorian London was also shown as a city of success and wealth. The river scenes of Whistler, and the busy, yet fashionable street scenes of Blanche, Tissot and De Nittis represent it as essentially a hive of activity, business and busy-ness.

Artists such as Whistler and Monet were also inspired by the atmosphere of London. Whistler's foggy and nocturnal views created an aesthetic and poetic image of the well known London fog, which became thought of as an essential ingredient in all atmospheric reconstructions of London, whether on canvas or on film, until the Clean Air Act changed its appearance irrevocably. Monet, too, with his fading eyesight, depicted the haze over the Thames which enveloped the city itself.

The exhibition also features interesting examples of the work of artists who never came to London. Rembrandt made two drawings of London based on some existing London views and played with the idea of fantastic architecture. Even a Japanese print-maker contrived to portray London: Yoshitora's print shows an imaginary view of the Thames with St. Paul's and the Monument, the view transformed into a Japanese perspective.

This exhibition would have never been realised without the generous help of lenders. We wish to thank Her Majesty Queen Elizabeth II and both private and public lenders who have enabled us to borrow such a galaxy of items from a great variety of collections. Their participation is warmly welcomed as is the assistance and collaboration of many others, in particular Dr. Malcolm Warner who has been responsible for the research and editing of the catalogue.

Finally, the Barbican Art Gallery is particularly grateful for the sponsorship that it has received from 3i Investors in Industry plc. In its advertising and its graphic profile, the company has always had a particularly bold visual identity and it is very gratifying that with the support for this exhibition – 3i's first step into major arts sponsorship – the company has committed itself also to the furtherance of an artistic awareness of the city in which it is based.

John Hoole, Curator   Tomoko Sato, Exhibition Organiser

                                                                            Barbican Art Gallery

ACKNOWLEDGMENTS

My first thanks are to John Hoole and the staff of the Barbican Art Gallery, whose cheerful support has made my work on *The Image of London* such a pleasure, and especially to Tomoko Sato, who has handled the nuts and bolts of its realisation so efficiently and reliably. Krystyna Matyjaszkiewicz worked on the exhibition before leaving the Gallery and I am grateful to her for getting the project off to a good start. I would also like to thank my very able and literate editor at Trefoil Publications, Caroline Bugler. On the scholarly side, I have benefited from the help of a number of authorities on London and on the artists who have worked here, but I would like especially to acknowledge my gratitude to Ralph Hyde, Keeper of the magnificent collection of prints, drawings and maps of London at the Guildhall Library. As a newcomer to the subject of London topography, I was extraordinarily fortunate that the specialist from whom I could learn most should be so generous with his time and expertise. The following individuals have also contributed valuable advice as I selected works for the exhibition and helped in various other ways in its preparation; their kindnesses are too many to describe in detail but none the less heartily appreciated:

Brian Allen, Alexander Apsis, Joanna Banham, Stephen Calloway, Susan Casteras, Samuel F. Clapp, Joe Earle, Rupert Faulkner, John Fisher, Jonathan Gestetner, Anne Gilbert, Anne Goldgar, Geoffrey Hindley, Rupert Hodge, Philip Hook, John House, Sarah Hyde, Mark Jones, Tania Jones, Vivien Knight, J. G. Links, Christopher Lloyd, Stefanie Maison, Michael Mason, Frederick Mulder, Harley Preston, Robert Raines, Benedict Read, Nicholas Reed, Anna Robins, Sara Ryan, Richard Shone, Jeremy Smith, Robin Spencer, MaryAnne Stevens, Richard Thomson, Rosemary Treble, Philip Ward-Jackson, David Webb, William Weston and Simon Wilson.

Lastly I would like to thank all the private collectors who have lent to the exhibition for sharing the pleasures of their pictures, drawings, prints and books with a wider audience.

M. W.

THE CITY OF THE PRESENT

MALCOLM WARNER

Day after day, at an early period, I had trodden the thronged thoroughfares, the broad, lonely squares, the lanes, alleys, and strange labyrinthine courts, the parks, the gardens and enclosures of ancient studious societies, so retired and silent amid the city uproar, the markets, the foggy streets along the river-side, the bridges, – I had sought all parts of the metropolis, in short, with an unweariable and indiscriminating curiosity; until few of the native inhabitants, I fancy, had turned so many of its corners as myself. These aimless wanderings (in which my prime purpose and achievement were to lose my way, and so find it the more surely) had brought me, at one time or another, to the sight and actual presence of almost all the objects and renowned localities that I had read about, and which had made London the dream-city of my youth... The result was, that I acquired a home-feeling there, as nowhere else in the world, – though afterwards I came to have a somewhat similar sentiment in regard to Rome; and as long as either of those two great cities shall exist, the cities of the Past and of the Present, a man's native soil may crumble beneath his feet without leaving him altogether homeless upon earth.[1]

Nathaniel Hawthorne's account of discovering London as a foreigner touches upon several of the themes of this exhibition. His list of the city's distinguishing features, the busy streets and the maze of backstreets, the markets and parks, the river, the bridges and the fog, reads like a catalogue of favourite subjects treated by foreign artists. Like all travellers, he arrives with preconceptions; he has read about London and it has become a 'dream-city' in his mind before he has ever seen the actual place. The balance between preconception and observation is one of the key issues affecting London's 'image' that we hope to explore in the exhibition and this catalogue. Hawthorne compares London with Rome, and comparison with other cities, often on a symbolic level, has been a commonplace of the view from abroad. Of course in some ways his response is typically American and typically nineteenth-century. But towards the end of our quotation he gives voice to an idea that underlies the views of artists and writers of all nationalities throughout the period with which we are concerned, an image that embraces all the others we shall be discussing, the image of London as City of the Present.

This may come as a surprise to many London visitors of today, when the point of London is so commonly understood to be its past. It may be a mecca in the very modern worlds of rock music, fashion and finance, but these are special interests. The consensus of general impressions casts London as the city of history, tradition, pomp and circumstance, royalty and Shakespeare. The picture postcards that reflect and help form tourists' impressions show stately old buildings, ceremonies such as the Changing of the Guard, beefeaters and members of the royal family, with only the occasional punk in full regalia as a jokey concession to the modern scene. Hollywood films dealing with contemporary London life are far outnumbered by those set in the past. From the sixteenth century until recent times, however, the London of the artistic and literary imagination was bound up with those features that were most particularly of the moment, its prodigious growth, its flourishing trade, its newest architecture, its power, its squalor, pollution, over-crowding, bustle and work. The modernity of London was its fascination, and the City and the docks were more essential to its image in the eyes of the world than the Tower, Westminster Abbey or any other location steeped in history.

The idea of London as the City of the Present was obviously rooted in the more significant political and economic position held by Britain through most of this period. But it was nurtured by the fact that the core of the city, and effectively its medieval past, was destroyed by the Great Fire of 1666. It was with the horrors of the Fire that London first came to be seem worthy of comparison to a great city of antiquity, to be conceived as the modern instance of something one might read about in the classics. The city was Troy, which was similarly burnt to the ground and which sprang to the educated visitor's mind all the more readily in view of the legend that Aeneas's grandson Brutus had founded London as the New Troy, 'Trinovantium'. Franciscus de Rapicani, secretary to Queen Christina of Sweden and a witness of the Fire, remembered that 'a hundred times I wished for my Virgil, for never again would I be able to impress on myself his verses on the *exidium Trojae* so well as I now could with what lay before my eyes'.[2] The destruction of London also brought forth moralising comparisons with wicked cities of the Bible that were punished by an angry God, Sodom and Gomorrah or Babylon. From this time onwards, descriptions of London that went beyond the mere recording of facts hardly seemed complete without a comparison with some ancient city of symbolic moment. In a formulation that suggested London's moral and physical similarities to cities of the past yet emphasised its status as City of the Present, it was hailed as 'the new' or 'the modern' version of some metropolis whose name had resounded down the centuries.

For most eighteenth-century observers and many in the nineteenth century too, that name was Rome, Hawthorne's City of the Past. They were thinking of ancient Rome in its prime, the power and glory of the Roman Empire, civic virtue, the classical ideal in art and architecture and its second coming in the Rome of the Renaissance. (Since Britain was a Protestant country, the Rome of the Papacy and Roman Catholicism was quietly left out of the equation.) To the neo-classical mind of the period, there could be no greater flattery than to liken a city to the very heart of classical civilisation, and no greater model to which to aspire. The London that rose Phoenix-like from the ashes of the Fire was certainly doing its best to look Roman and with some success, thanks to the chief architect of its reconstruction Sir

Fig. 1 - Antonio Joli
Capriccio with a view of the Thames and St Paul's (no 68)

12

Christopher Wren. By the time of the completion of Wren's St Paul's in 1711, it was a huge imperial metropolis, vital and powerful, full of classical architecture and dominated by a dome that echoed that of St Peter's.

Artists of the time showed London in as classical a light as possible, not only by focussing on St Paul's but also by investing their views with the classical graces of repose, clarity and order. In Antonio Joli's view of London through an architectural capriccio (fig.1), sculpted ancient Romans stand on symbolically broken columns to the left and right, making gestures that seem to express admiration on the one side and jealousy on the other at the present greatness of what, in their day, was a remote outpost of empire. Piranesi invented a Romanised version of the City Arms to place below his view of Blackfriars Bridge under construction (fig.2), modifying the Roman *SPQR* (Senatus Populusque Romanus, the Senate and People of Rome) to *SPQL*. Weighing London against Rome in the political and cultural balance, Voltaire went as far as to find Rome the one that was wanting. 'The outcome of civil wars in Rome was slavery,' he pointed out, 'and that of the troubles in England liberty.'[3] The limited power of the monarchy, the freedom of thought and the recognition of worth irrespective of background made London, for him, an ideal of social order that seemed more Greek than Roman:

Fig. 2 Giovanni Battista Piranesi
Blackfriars Bridge under construction
(no 76)

Rival of Athens, London, blest indeed
　　That with thy tyrants had the wit to chase
The prejudices civil factions breed.
　　Men speak their thoughts and worth can win its place.
In London, who has talent, he is great.[4]

But Rome was good enough for most commentators, and the London-Rome comparison continued well into the nineteenth century. 'London is the epitome of our times, and the Rome of to-day,' wrote Emerson in 1856.[5]

As industrialisation turned London into a city of grime and smog, however, the comparison could turn sour. J. D. Passavant, the German artist and connoisseur, remembered his first impression of London as a nightmare version of the traditional pilgrim's first sight of Rome:

How different are the sensations called forth on the first distant sight of St Peter's at Rome, which, with all its grand proportions of dome and pillar, stands forth clearly delineated, beneath the pure aether of an Italian sky. To the weary traveller, who is slowly toiling through the unwholesome marshes around it, the gigantic edifice is a welcome sight. Like a voice in the desert, it seems to announce the vicinity of a mighty and holy city, and to promise a sure rest and abode from the bleakness and desolation which oppresses him. On approaching London, on the contrary, the smiling fruitful country, with its enchanting villas gradually disappears; the atmosphere becomes dense and heavy of respiration – a procession-like crowd of vehicles and pedestrians bespeak the never-ending business of the city; and London itself seems the vast desert of men and houses, where a foreigner may feel himself most truly alone.[6]

London continued to be the City of the Present, a place of wealth, power and modernity – more so than ever. Yet the image of a resurrected Rome, always a positive image in the still classically oriented cultures of the west, seemed less and less tenable as the dark side of the big city became too obvious to ignore. It gave way to the image of a fallen Rome, the modern Babylon.

The Babylon invoked by St John in the Book of Revelation is not so much a place as the embodiment of vice: 'Babylon the great is fallen, is fallen, and is become the habitation of devils, and the hold of every foul spirit, and a cage of every unclean and hateful bird'; it is 'the mother of harlots and abominations of the earth'.[7] To foreign observers of the nineteenth century, overwhelmed by the vastness and corruption of the first great metropolis of the industrial age, with its labyrinthine complexity, its juxtapositions of luxury and poverty, its slums, gin palaces and pollution, drunkenness, street beggars and child prostitutes, the Babylonian comparison hardly seemed excessive. It was a reaction of amazement, moral arrogance and real fear, since London was regarded as a premonition of what industrialisation would bring to all the great cities of Europe. It was not only the City of the Present, it was the City of the Future, and a frightening prospect. Hippolyte Taine's account of a cab ride through the London streets at night is characteristic: 'A sepulchral light shone over the great, empty Babylon, casting the whiteness of a shroud upon its colossal artifacts. The dense, unwholesome air seemed still impregnated with human exhalations. From time to time we saw, beneath the dying light of a gas-jet, a belated street-woman, hungry and still hoping for a customer; or a pauper in rags, his feet tied up in more rags.'[8] The fact that this lurid conception found such potent pictorial form in the work of Gustave Doré has everything to do with his having drawn images of the visionary Babylon of St John and Isaiah for his illustrated Bible. Towards the end of *London. A Pilgrimage* Doré gives his own vision of a ruined London of the future, as if saying with St John: 'Thus with violence shall that great city Babylon be thrown down' (fig.4).[9]

Like the Roman view, the Babylonian view of London sprang from contemporary preoccupations that extended beyond London or any other particular place. Artists and writers used London to symbolise ideas, and the larger the ideas, the more pronounced their view of London became. The corollary to the romantic cult of nature was contempt for all things urban; there was much nostalgic brooding upon the city as opposed to the country, the manmade as opposed to the natural, the present as opposed to the past, and London lent itself perfectly to such contrasts, being not only long established as the City of the Present, but also surrounded by fairly unspoilt countryside – 'the smiling fruitful country, with its enchanting villas', to borrow Passavant's phrase. For some of the early socialists the city in general, and London in particular, stood for the evils of capitalism; Engels saw the crowded streets as an image of alienation and the war of all against all.[10] It was a view wholly of its time, and from the mid century onwards it retreated as another came to the fore – the image of a London beyond

Fig. 3 Théodore Géricault
Pity the sorrows of a poor old Man!
(no 96)

Fig. 4 Gustave Doré
'The New Zealander' from *London. A Pilgrimage*

good and evil, neither modern Rome nor modern Babylon but merely modern.

The origin of this view lay in the principle, set down most inspiringly by Charles Baudelaire, that art should record and celebrate those things most characteristic of the contemporary world. In his essay 'The Painter of Modern Life' and other writings on art, Baudelaire expounded an idea of the modern that was defiantly urban; his admired painter of modern life was one such as the narrator of Edgar Allan Poe's short story *The Man of the Crowd*, who watches the bustle of the London streets and 'breathes in with delight all the spores and odours of life', one for whom curiosity was an irresistible passion and the urban scene a fascinating spectacle.[11] He advocated an appreciation of the city that was neither idealising nor moralising but accepting, poetical, complex and ambiguous. 'Parisian life is rich in poetic and wonderful subjects', he wrote. 'The marvellous envelops and saturates us like the atmosphere; but we fail to see it.'[12] The challenge was as good for London as it was for Paris, and it was somewhere in the mind of all those artists aware of the ideas of the French avant-garde who crossed the Channel and addressed themselves to the London scene, including Whistler, Monet and Derain. These later nineteenth- and early twentieth-century figures paid homage to London as the City of the Present not only in their choice of modern motifs, wharves, factories, new buildings and new bridges, but also in their technical progressiveness. Derain spoke of his treatment of London as 'renewing' that achieved by Monet over the preceding years, as if only the latest style could do justice to the protean modernity of such a city.

These shifts in attitudes to London as a whole can be seen in microcosm in shifting attitudes to what is perhaps the most inseparable feature of the image of London, the fog. Though foreign writers have complained about the fog for as long as they have written about London at all, they have only portrayed it as particularly significant, or essential, since the early years of the nineteenth century, and artists ignored it altogether until that time. In the eighteenth century, the fog was a nuisance to anyone trying to understand London as the modern Rome because it conjured up all the wrong associations. If you wish to portray a place as the capital of clarity and enlightenment, its fogginess is a truth with which you tend to be economical. But as London came to seem a depressing, threatening experience, the fog, enhanced in reality by increasing pollution, began to loom larger in the imagination, suggesting both its grimness and its vast incomprehensibility, seeming to sum up the whole place. In the Babylonian view of London, the atmosphere became a funeral shroud, as with Taine, or some equally doomy image of oppression. 'Pinned down under columns of dense air, crushed by a leaden sky made twice as thick by smoke,' wrote Astolphe de Custine, 'I felt all day as if I were in a damp, dark prison cell.'[13] Finally, by the time of its canonical representative Whistler (see fig.5), the fog had come back into favour as part of the poetry of the big city, no longer a shroud but a veil. The atmosphere 'with its magnificent mystifications' seemed to Henry James to be a main ingredient of the *style* of London, because it 'flatters and superfuses, makes

Fig. 5 James McNeill Whistler
Nocturne in Grey and Gold—Picadilly (no 230)

15

everything brown, rich, dim, vague, magnifies distances and minimises details, confirms the inference of vastness by suggesting that, as the great city makes everything, it makes its own optical laws'.[14]

★   ★   ★

The desire to evoke the here and now has never shielded artists from the influence of earlier images, and the progress of the image of London has been a matter of interacting observation and preconception. It would be a very misguided assumption indeed to think that each artist or writer came with an open mind and worked wholly from direct experience. The views of and about London that we have been discussing originated partly in the look and feel of the real London, and partly in a snowball effect by which certain images became so accepted and powerful as to be difficult for any individual to throw off. During the seventeenth century up until the Fire, when topographical prints of London first began to proliferate, the prevailing view was taken from a non-existent hill in Southwark and full of anachronisms and mistakes. With comic regularity over a period of fifty years or more, dozens of different prints produced by different publishers in different parts of Europe showed a fictitious sharp northward bend in the Thames to the east of the Tower. The artists clearly copied one another, and a dock or inlet in an early view seems to have become distorted, as in a game of Chinese whispers, until it became the main course of the river. Some of the prints produced in a hurry to show the Great Fire are versions of this same erroneous view with flames and smoke added to make them topical (see fig.6). Historians of London are constantly disappointed by the failure of the visual documents to correspond to what they know, from more reliable sources, to have been fact. The diverting of the Thames and the addition of the Fire are extreme cases of something that holds for both the topographical and the emotional aspects of London in art, both the information conveyed and the moods created: the new view presents not so much a fresh image as a modification, based more or less on observation, of an old one.

Fig. 6
The Great Fire
(no 44)

Another ingredient in the making of the individual view is the stylistic identity the artist has formed before tackling London subject-matter. Canaletto was drawn to the Thames as a subject because of his experience of painting canals in Venice; Doré's illustrations to the Bible and Dante clearly prepared him for his infernal vision of the London slums. There are also factors particular to the experience of the observer from abroad. Emigrés taking refuge in London from war or revolution in their own countries are predisposed to look upon the place favourably, as Monet and Pissarro did in 1870-1 when they came and painted aspects of London, its parks and suburbs, that embodied the freedom and calm of which Paris had been bereft. The foreigner also tends to observe oddities of London life that might have become invisible to the native through familiarity, and he is apt to dwell upon those of aspects of the foreign place that are most markedly different from what he knows. The uniform of the London policeman was clearly a

I Anonymous: *London from Southwark*
See catalogue no. 30

17

II Griffier the Elder: *The Great Fire*
See catalogue no. 42

18

III Anonymous: *The Great Fire*
See catalogue no. 43

IV Vorsterman: *London from Greenwich Park*
See catalogue no. 46

20

V Hondius: *Frost Fair on the Thames at Temple Stairs*
See catalogue no. 47

VI Tillemans: *London from Greenwich Park*
See catalogue no. 56

VII van Aken: *The Old Stock Market*
See catalogue no. 62

VIII Griffier: *Frost Fair on the Thames*
See catalogue no. 59

Fig. 7 Utagawa Yoshitora
The Port of London in England
(no 160)

fascination for many foreign artists of the nineteenth century, and policemen are surely thicker on the ground in their pictures of London than they ever were in reality. The attempt to represent London by the Japanese printmaker Yoshitora (fig.7) embodies the paradoxical tendencies of the foreigner's view – to conform to the familiar yet to highlight the curious – in the way he depicts the soldiers in the foreground, their facial features quite Japanese but their uniforms as carefully copied as if they were the plumage of some exotic birds.

It comes easier to the foreign artist to simplify and generalise because he is unhampered by detailed knowledge; unless you are a fanatic, it is difficult to maintain a single pronounced response to the place where you have lived for years, simply because it accumulates too many complex and contradictory associations. It is no accident that the foreign artists who depict London as Babylon produced a more sensational image of its vices than like-minded British ones. The audience that the artist envisages also affects the view he presents. For obvious reasons, foreign artists working for a British audience, Canaletto for instance, tend to adopt a more positive view than those working for a foreign audience. On the other hand, we should remember that the most negative of all the images of London, Doré's, was addressed initially to the British audience too. This can be explained by another rule of thumb, however, which is that the image presented in prints and books (both text and illustrations) ranges to wider extremes than that presented in oil paintings. A bleak reminder of London as Babylon is all very well in words or in the relatively small form of the print, which can be kept out of daily sight on a bookshelf or in a portfolio. But oils are larger, and hardly worth possessing unless displayed for all to see, all the time, which means that the theme of abject misery is rarely a selling point.

These are only some of the factors other than the reality of London that have affected the development of its image in the eyes of the world. The image of London has had a life of its own, related to the life of the place itself but always partial, never objective. Indeed, some of the best foreign artists and writers have been the most subjective, providing historians with little or nothing in the way of reliable documentary material. One would no more wish they had been otherwise than that *Oliver Twist* contained more statistics. Each age has refashioned the image of London to some extent in its *own* image, and the result has been a succession of different Cities of the Present – which are represented by the different sections of this exhibition. But it would be simplistic to suppose that only one image had currency at any one time. Doré's and Pissarro's views of London were exactly contemporary but could hardly be less alike in mood. By the same token, it was quite possible for the nineteenth-century observer apt to see London through Doré's eyes to see it occasionally, on a sunny day, through the eyes of Canaletto. When we think of a city with as eventful a history in art as London, its latest image or images may spring to mind first only to be supplanted by others of an earlier vintage. As well as its own image of London, each age has at its disposal all those created before, and our privilege in 1987 is to have so many.

IX Angillis: *Covent Garden Market*
See catalogue no. 60

26

X Nebot: *Covent Garden Market*
See catalogue no. 66

Paying tribute to the effect of Whistler and his followers, whom he calls 'Impressionists', upon the way people saw London, Oscar Wilde wrote:

Where, if not from the Impressionists, do we get those wonderful brown fogs that come creeping down our streets, blurring the gas-lamps and changing the houses into monstrous shadows? To whom, if not to them and their master, do we owe the lovely silver mists that brood over our river, and turn to faint forms of fading grace curved bridge and swaying barge? The extraordinary change that has taken place in the climate of London during the last ten years is entirely due to a particular school of Art.[15]

With a comic flourish, Wilde points out the way the image of a place we all carry around with us in our minds, and which helps determine our actual experience of it, is formed and transformed by art – whether we are artists or not. London may no longer be the City of the Present. That conceptual metropolis has been relocated somewhere in the United States, some would say to New York, others to Los Angeles. The position of art has also changed, and in this century photography, the cinema, magazines and television have usurped paintings, prints and drawings as the means by which the image of London is disseminated. But the Cities of the Present created by Hollar, Canaletto, Géricault, Whistler, Doré, Pissarro, Monet and Derain still have the power to enrich our experience of London today.

NOTES

1. Nathaniel Hawthorne, *Our Old Home*, 1863, vol. II, pp. 82-3
2. See *Transactions of the London and Middlesex Archaeological Society*, vol. 20, part 2, p. 10
3. *Letters on England*, 1733, translated by Leonard Tancock, 1980, pp. 44-5
4. 'Verses on the Death of Adrienne Lecouvreur', *Voltaire*, translated by H. N. Brailsford, Oxford, 1947, p. 54
5. *English Traits*, 1856, p. 168
6. *Tour of a German Artist in England*, 1836, pp. 12-13
7. *Revelation* XVIII:2, XVII:5
8. *Taine's Notes on England*, translated by Edward Hyams, 1957, p. 37
9. Revelation XVIII:21
10. See *The Condition of the Working Class in England*, translated by W.O Henderson and W.H.Chaloner, Oxford, 1958, p. 31
11. 'The Painter of Modern Life', 1863, *Selected Writings on Art and Artists*, translated by P. E. Charvet, 1972, p. 397
12. 'The Salon of 1846', ibid., p. 107
13. *Mémoires et voyages*, Paris, 1830, vol. II, pp. 103-4
14. 'London', 1888, *English Hours*, 1905, p. 16
15. 'The Decay of Lying', 1889, *De Profundis and Other Writings*, 1973, pp. 78-9

TOPOGRAPHY OR ART: CANALETTO AND LONDON IN THE MID-EIGHTEENTH CENTURY

BRIAN ALLEN

When Canaletto arrived in England late in May 1746 he was one of the best known artists in Europe, his rise to fame brought about primarily by the English Grand Tourists who comprised such a sizeable portion of his patrons in his native Venice. In the early 1730s patrons such as the fourth Duke of Bedford, who commissioned a series of twenty-two canvases for Bedford House in Bloomsbury, ensured that Canaletto's prosperity in Venice was sustained.[1] However, by the early 1740s the situation had changed. The military operations in Italy in 1742 which resulted from the outbreak of the war of the Austrian Succession in the previous year curtailed the number of visitors to Venice and this in turn drastically affected Canaletto's prospects for continued success. As George Vertue, that celebrated chronicler of the London art world in the first half of the eighteenth century, put it: 'of late few persons travel to Italy from hence during the wars'.[2] In an attempt to offset these conditions Canaletto developed alternatives to views of Venice, in the form of Roman subjects, *capricci* and etchings, but the possibility of a journey to England must have seemed an increasingly attractive possible solution to his dilemma. He already had contacts in high places in London, and besides, a number of his fellow professional countrymen had already made the journey north. The Earl of Manchester had, for instance, brought back with him from Venice in 1708 the decorative history painters Giovanni Antonio Pellegrini and Marco Ricci. Three years later they were followed by Sebastiano Ricci under the same umbrella of patronage. Others like the Venetian-trained Giovanni Battista Bellucci (who stayed between 1716 and 1722) and Francesco Sleter (arrived 1719) came to meet the increasing demand for decorative history painting which resulted from the boom in country house building that followed the Glorious Revolution of 1688. Indeed, according to George Vertue, the decorative history painter Jacopo Amigoni, who spent the years 1729-1739 in England, was instrumental on his return to Venice in persuading Canaletto to move to London. No Italian landscape painter of any note had tried his professional luck in London prior to Canaletto with the exception of Antonio Joli who had come, primarily to paint scenery at the King's Theatre in the Haymarket, only a couple of years before Canaletto.[3]

When Canaletto arrived in London in 1746 the native landscape painters were beginning to enjoy a more widespread patronage. A clear indication of the continuous taste for topographical art can be seen in an important group of roundel landscapes which formed part of the decoration of the Foundling Hospital's court room, although these were donated by the artists concerned (Wale, Haytley,

XI Canaletto: *The Thames from the terrace of*
Somerset House, the City in the distance
See catalogue no. 71

XII Canaletto: *The Thames from the terrace of Somerset House, Westminster in the distance*
See catalogue no. 72

Richard Wilson and the young Thomas Gainsborough) rather than commissioned. I stress continuous taste because since the mid-seventeenth century the British had shown a particular passion for landscapes of identifiable places, whether in the form of the type of engraved views of London or other towns popularised by Hollar and the Bucks, or the fashionable country house 'portraits' of Knyff, Siberechts, Tillemans or Wootton. Until the 1720s this type of painting was almost exclusively in the hands of visiting foreign painters, usually of Dutch or Flemish extraction, but by the 1740s native born artists like George Lambert and Joseph Nickolls, to name but two, had made their mark.

Canaletto was entering an increasingly competitive market in London in the mid-1740s and his domination of the Venetian scene was not so easily transferred to London. However, he arrived in 1746 with a letter from his most prominent English patron in Venice, the British Consul Joseph Smith, to Owen McSwiney asking for the introduction to the Duke of Richmond. Whilst in Italy, where he had fled to escape his creditors, the bankrupt McSwiney had acted as an artistic agent for the Duke of Richmond and as early as 1722 had persuaded Canaletto to become involved in a series of paintings (*Tombeaux des Princes*) each designed to commemorate the deeds of a notable Englishman in a landscape and/or architectural setting.[5] A few years later, in 1727, McSwiney was arranging for the Duke of Richmond to purchase Venetian views by Canaletto, noting in a letter to his employer that Canaletto had 'more work than he can do, in any reasonable time, and well'.[6]

McSwiney apparently followed Consul Smith's instructions and persuaded Tom Hill, a former tutor to the Duke of Richmond, to write to his ex-pupil on Canaletto's behalf:

I told him the best service I thought you could do him wd be to let him draw a view of the river from yr dining-room which would give him as much reputation as any of his Venetian prospects.[7]

Nothing seems to have happened until late in the summer of 1747 when Canaletto was apparently invited to make a drawing of the Thames from a window of Richmond House.[8] The resulting paintings (figs. 8-9) are probably the greatest and best-known pictures produced by Canaletto in England.

The Thames painting, taken from a high rear window of Richmond House looking downstream to the north-east suggests that Canaletto, almost inevitably, could not suppress his Venetian mannerisms. The Thames was, after all, just as important a thoroughfare for London as the Grand Canal was for Venice, and the highly decorated state barges must have recalled for the artist the Doge's Bucintoro. The domination of the London skyline by St Paul's Cathedral may even have reminded him of the way Longhena's Santa Maria della Salute oversees the entrance to the Grand Canal. With the spires of St Mary le Strand, St Clement Danes, St Bride's and many other City Churches clearly visible, Canaletto's picture can be read as a tribute to Wren's architectural genius in resurrecting

Fig. 8   Canaletto
London: the Thames and the City of London from Richmond House
Oil on canvas, 41¾ x 46¼, Goodwood House, The Earl of March and Kinrara and the Trustees of the Goodwood Collection

Fig. 9 Canaletto
London: Whitehall and the Privy Garden from Richmond House
Oil on canvas, 43 x 47, Goodwood House, The Earl of March and Kinrara and the Trustees of the Goodwood Collection

Fig. 10 Canaletto
London: Westminster Bridge from the North on Lord Mayor's Day
Oil on canvas, 37¾ x 50¼ Yale Center for British Art, Paul Mellon Collection

London after the Great Fire.

By contrast to the crisp, clear light of the Thames picture, the Whitehall painting, its pendant, has an atmosphere and luminosity altogether more characteristic of London. Presumably taken from the same vantage point as the Thames picture, it shows in the right foreground the stables of Richmond House and the back of Montagu House. The Privy Gardens of Whitehall lead the eye towards Inigo Jones's Banqueting House flanked on the left by the Holbein Gate (demolished in 1759). Beyond can be seen a tower of Northumberland House, the spire of Gibbs's St Martin-in-the-Fields and Charing Cross with part of Le Sueur's equestrian statue of King Charles I.

When Canaletto painted Whitehall the area had just undergone considerable 'improvement' with the formation of Parliament Street, described in 1761 as 'a very handsome and spacious new built street'.[9] But, on the whole, there were few great modern public buildings in London for Canaletto to paint. Indeed, throughout the eighteenth century, complaints were made that London's public buildings were not good enough. Some, like Lord Shaftesbury, reacting against the last vestiges of the Baroque style, thought that Wren had spoilt all the great opportunities.[10] In the reign of George II the Whigs were more interested in building private fortunes than public buildings. Even the new hospitals, like the Foundling and Guy's were the result of private rather than public philanthropy. The great years of urban improvement were to follow Canaletto's departure from London in the mid-1750s.

However, one public building of major importance was under way when Canaletto arrived in London – Westminster Bridge. Remarkably, for centuries there was no bridge over the Thames between London Bridge and Kingston. The inadequacy of this situation was apparent as London grew but various attempts in the seventeenth and early eighteenth century to rectify this were frustrated either by the City, jealous of its privileges and commercial monopolies or by the Company of Watermen, who controlled river traffic and feared for the loss of their livelihood. Eventually, in 1738, the Swiss engineer Charles Labelye was engaged and building began.[11]. When Canaletto arrived in London in 1746 the Bridge was nearing completion and, given the public interest in the project, it must have seemed the most obvious of subjects for him to tackle. It has even been suggested that the completion of the bridge and its potential as subject matter was a major inducement for Canaletto to come to England.[12] Significantly, the Dukes of Richmond and Bedford, both Commissioners of the Bridge since the first Act of Parliament in 1736, were both already Canaletto patrons.

One of the earliest of Canaletto's London pictures, painted within months of his arrival, was *Westminster Bridge from the North on Lord Mayor's Day 1746* (fig. 10). The artist went to the trouble of having the picture engraved by Remigius Parr and presumed that by the time the print was published (in the Spring of 1747) the Bridge with all its shining Portland and Purbeck stone arches would be complete and opened as planned. The Bridge is shown complete with all its centres removed

XIII Canaletto: *Vauxhall Gardens, the Grand Walk about 1751*
See catalogue no. 80

XIV Canaletto: *Ranelagh, the interior of the Rotunda*
See catalogue no. 83

and the balustrade finished. Above the middle arch stand large baroque statues of the river gods, Thames and Isis, which were in fact never installed, although drawings certainly existed for them. Neither Canaletto nor the publisher of the print, John Brindley, could have foreseen that in the summer of 1747 settlement would cause the stonework of two of the arches to be dismantled, resulting in a three year delay to the opening.[13]

Accustomed to the Regattas and Ducal festivals of Venice, Canaletto no doubt felt that he could do full justice to this scene. On 29 October 1746 the Lord Mayor, William Benn, accompanied by Aldermen and various City officials, was rowed upstream in his state barge (seen here broadside) by crews of uniformed oarsmen who had the hazardous task of negotiating the arches of the new bridge before mooring their craft alongside the old King's Bridge at Westminster. Canaletto captured the bustling activity of the Thames in much the same way as he had painted the Bacino di S. Marco in Venice on numerous festive occasions.

Another nobleman originally associated with the lobby for a new bridge was Sir Hugh Smithson, who later became Earl and subsequently Duke of Northumberland. He was to become one of Canaletto's most important English patrons. The first of a number of Canaletto's works acquired by Sir Hugh was *London seen through an arch of Westminster Bridge* (fig. 11). It is not clear if this was originally commissioned by John Brindley, the publisher of the print, and later acquired by Smithson or commissioned by him direct from the artist, but it certainly resulted in further commissions. This highly original view through a single arch of the bridge was also painted in 1746 and shows the bridge still in the course of construction. The wooden centering is still in place and Canaletto introduces the picturesque device of the workman's bucket suspended from the parapet, which recalls the suspended lanterns in his Venetian *vedute* and *capricci*. In the distance, from left to right, can be seen the Water Tower, York Water Gate, Somerset House, the spires of St Clement Danes and St Bride's and, to the right, St Paul's Cathedral and St Augustine, Watling Street.

Remarkably, except for this picture, virtually nothing is known of the original buyers of the two dozen paintings and drawings by Canaletto which have survived showing Westminster Bridge in the various stages of construction.

After about a year or so in London it appeared that things were going well for Canaletto and, in addition to his views of London, he was employed, as Vertue noted in June 1749, 'in the country for the Duke of Beaufort, [painting] Views of Badminton'.[14] Other commissions for views of Warwick Castle for Lord Brooke, later Earl of Warwick, had already come his way and yet, as Vertue noted, his work was apparently not universally held in high regard:

On the whole of him something is obscure or strange, he does not produce works so well done as those of Venice or other parts of Italy. which are in Collections here. and done by him there. especially his figures in his works done here, are apparently much inferior to those done abroad. which are surprizingly well done & with great freedom & variety – his

Fig. 11 Canaletto
*London seen through an arch of
Westminster Bridge*
Oil on canvas, 22½ x 37½ The Duke of
Northumberland

water and his skys at no time excellent or with natural freedom. & what he has done here his prospects of Trees Woods or handling or pencilling of that part not various nor so skillfull as might be expected.[15]

If, as appears to be the case, the demand for Canaletto's work was declining around 1750, what are the reasons for this? It can certainly be argued that there was a falling off in the quality of his work in the later 1740s but this had already begun to happen before he left Venice in 1746. Much of his work was becoming increasingly stylised and routine, as Vertue noted, and lacking the vivacity and spontaneity which characterises so many of his earlier works, wherein the attention to detail, particularly in the handling of figures, is overwhelmingly apparent. But this relative lack of success may well be connected with the nature of Canaletto's subject matter. The fact that he was not painting his native Venice was surely a disadvantage. The success of his formula was based on the fact that the Venetian scene, with its array of exotic architecture and hedonistic atmosphere, was a constant reminder for those who bought these images of a distant Grand Tour, real or imagined. Despite its economic decay, Venice was still considered a symbol of luxury by the British in the mid-eighteenth century whilst London, despite its burgeoning commercial prosperity analogous to the great days of the Venetian Empire, was only slowly undergoing the architectural changes that would result in the spacious metropolis that emerged in the last years of the century.

The purchase of a view of Venice, albeit merely topographical, was entirely in keeping with the Grand Tour taste of the landed gentleman because it was essentially a view of the past. But the acquisition of a view of London, unless it depicted one's own property or some particular financial interest, might be seen merely to suggest an association with the mercantile views of the City.

Evidently, by the end of the 1740s, most of the great patrons already had their requirements met by Canaletto and those who still required landscapes may well have wanted a more elevated type. As Jonathan Richardson wrote in *The Connoisseur* (1719):

A History is preferable to a Landscape, Sea-piece, Animals, Fruit, Flowers or any other Still-life, pieces of Drollery, &c.; the reason is, the latter Kinds may Please, and in proportion as they do so they are Estimable . . . but they cannot Improve the Mind, they excite no Noble Sentiments.[16]

Forty years later Reynolds was still promoting similar views. In the second of his *Idler* essays, published in 1759, he criticised those painters who merely 'imitated' nature, which led to painting 'no longer being considered as a liberal art, and sister to Poetry; this imitation being merely mechanical, in which the slowest intellect is always sure to succeed best; for the Painter of genius cannot stoop to drudgery . . . The Grand style of Painting requires this minute attention to be carefully avoided'.[17] Reynolds associated the type of attention to detail which characterises Canaletto's art as consistent with the values of the Dutch school, and although he

XV Canaletto: *Westminster Abbey, with a procession of the Knights of the Bath*
See catalogue no. 73

XVI Joli: *Capriccio with a view of the Thames and St Paul's*
See catalogue no. 68

realised that natural detail was precisely what collectors admired about Dutch pictures, he considered this type of art 'certainly of a lower order, that ought to give place to a beauty of a superior kind, since one cannot be obtained but by departing from the other'.[18] Significantly, in the same essay, Reynolds referred to the Venetian school of painting as a whole as 'the Dutch part of Italian genius'.[19]

Many of the Reynolds's contemporaries, both patrons and artists, increasingly came to share these principles, which still prevailed at the beginning of the ninetenth century when Henry Fuseli, in one of his Royal Academy lectures, could describe the most uninteresting subjects for painting as:

That kind of landscape which is entirely occupied with the tame delineation of a given spot; an enumeration of hill and dale, clumps of trees, shrubs, water, meadows, cottages and houses, what is commonly called Views. These, if not assisted by nature, dictated by taste, or chosen for character, may delight the owners of the acres they enclose, the inhabitants of the spot, perhaps the antiquary or the traveller, but to every other eye they are little more than topography. The landscape of Titian, of Mola, of Salvator, of the Poussins, Claude, Rubens, Elzheimer, Rembrandt and Wilson, spurns all relation with this kind of map-work.[20]

Canaletto's work, despite his remarkable ability to handle light and shade and suggest with great subtlety the texture of buildings delineated, could not pretend, at least when dealing with English subject matter devoid of the romantic associations of Venice, to be anything other than topography. Perhaps it was legitimate for grand patrons to pay large prices for Old Master landscapes by Claude, Gaspard Dughet, Poussin or Rosa but 'inferior' topographical views could be supplied by native-born contemporaries like Samuel Scott and Francis Harding considerably cheaper than Canaletto.[21]

Horace Walpole even went as far as to make the rather ridiculous remark that he considered Samuel Scott and his pupil William Marlow 'better painters than the Venetian'.[22] Walpole, however, may have been typical of the sort of patron who did not particularly admire Canaletto's work. Apart from works by Scott and Marlow, Walpole had in his collection at Strawberry Hill a pair of pictures by Alexandre Baudin who, Vertue tells us, 'so much imitated Canaletti'.[23] A visitor to Baudin's studio in about 1740 recorded that his pictures and prints 'had so good an effect that I almost imagined myself to be once more taking a turn about Venice, which I left but three months ago'.[24]

With rivals and copyists on the London scene and his practice apparently in decline, it is not surprising to learn that Canaletto returned to his native Venice some time during September and November of 1750. By that date the War was over and visitors might be expected to return to Venice. There does not appear to be any evidence of a major commission to persuade him to undertake the arduous journey home, and he probably had decided to return for good. We know that he took back with him a number of London drawings that were subsequently acquired by his loyal patron Consul Smith, who also seems to have commissioned paintings from two of them, which were subsequently sold as part of Smith's magnificent collection to George III in 1762 and remain in the Royal Collection to this day (nos. 71-2).[25]

If Canaletto expected a fresh flow of commissions in Venice he was to be disappointed, and by mid-1751 he had apparently decided to return to London. Back in London by July 1751, as Vertue noted, Canaletto was advertising for commissions and that he had in his studio 'a large picture a View on the River Thames of Chelsea College, Ranelagh Gardens & c. an[d] parts adjacent . . . – this valud at 60 or 70 pounds'.[26]

Apart from some payments from Lord Brooke for his views of Warwick Castle, this is all we know about Canaletto's prices. Vertue's remark is not insignificant for, by comparison, even the most fashionable portrait painters in London charged far less for a whole-length canvas. In the 1740s the most expensive portraits were by Thomas Hudson, who charged 48 guineas for a whole-length.[27] Even Canaletto's fashionable compatriot, Andrea Casali, could not get £50 for a full-length portrait in the 1740s.[28] If the price of the Chelsea picture is indicative of Canaletto's normal prices, then he was charging sums that would secure good Old Masters in the London auction houses. More disturbing than Canaletto's apparently steep prices was Vertue's remark that the Chelsea view was 'not so well as some Works of Canaletti formerly brought into England, nor does it appear to be better than some painters in England can do'.[29]

Although some of his English patrons remained loyal, such as the Earl of Northumberland who commissioned views of one of his country seats, Alnwick Castle, as well as views of the Jacobean Northumberland House at Charing Cross, which had been refaced in 1752,[30] Canaletto seems not to have enjoyed any sustained patronage, with the exception of a major commission for six paintings from the wealthy radical Thomas Hollis, who had met Consul Smith (and maybe even Canaletto himself) in Venice in 1750-1. To counteract the declining demand for his work from patrons of the first rank, Canaletto seems to have turned to producing more drawings specifically for engravings.

From the moment of his arrival in London in 1746 Canaletto, as we have seen, had been aware of the potential in the print market, and before his temporary return to Venice in 1750 he probably produced the four drawings of Vauxhall Gardens which were engraved by J.S. Müller and Edward Rooker and published by Robert Sayer in December 1751 (see nos. 81-2).[31]. The print publishers were well aware that there was a market for engravings after Canaletto's work in London if the subject matter were carefully chosen.

Vauxhall Gardens was at the peak of its popularity in 1751. Although opened early in the reign of Charles II, Vauxhall had just undergone a major modernisation in the late 1740s in response to the challenge of nearby rival Ranelagh Gardens, which had opened in 1742.[32] Vauxhall's entrepreneurial proprietor, Jonathan Tyers, shrewdly realised that the opening of Westminster Bridge would make access to his popular London nightspot on the south bank of the Thames

XVII Joli: *The Thames looking towards the*
City
See catalogue no. 69

42

XVIII Joli: *The Thames looking towards*
Westminster
See catalogue no. 70

considerably easier, and invested a fortune in re-decorating to continue to attract the fashionable crowds. As John Lockman, the author of a guidebook to Vauxhall Gardens published in 1752, put it: 'all fears of perishing in the Water, in the passage to, or from *Vaux-hall* are happily remov'd, by the very fine Bridge lately built across our River at *Westminster*'.[33] Canaletto's four engraved views of Vauxhall captured all the main features of the Gardens from the 'Grand Walk', a nine hundred foot long vista lined by sycamore and elm trees, to the whimsical Chinese pavilions and the array of *trompe l'oeil* paintings that thrilled the visitors.[34] These engravings seem to have remained popular for they were re-issued by Laurie and Whittle as late as 1794. Canaletto seems to have produced only one painting of Vauxhall Gardens (fig. 12) which, like the engravings, tends to exaggerate the spaciousness of the Grand Walk.

Fig. 12 Canaletto
Vauxhall Gardens; the Grand Walk
(no 80)

The same market existed for the three views of Ranelagh Gardens, engraved by Nathaniel Parr, which were published at the same time as the Vauxhall views.[35] Although Ranelagh's success was relatively short lived, in the years immediately after its opening it enjoyed immense popularity. Horace Walpole wrote in 1744 that he was visiting Ranelagh 'every night constantly . . . which has totally beat Vauxhall . . . My Lord Chesterfield is so fond of it that he says he has ordered all his letters to be directed thither'.[36] The fashionable masquerade balls held in these Gardens must have reminded Canaletto of the Carnivals in his native Venice, and it is no surprise to learn that one of them, held in April 1749 to celebrate the Peace of Aix-la-Chapelle, was called a 'Venetian Fête'.[37]

One of the Ranelagh prints was also worked up on canvas. *Ranelagh, the interior of the Rotunda* exists in two versions. The most celebrated of these is in the National Gallery, one of the six paintings executed in 1754 for Thomas Hollis,[38] but the other version is illustrated here (fig. 13). Ranelagh's great advantage over Vauxhall, at least until 1750, was its enormous covered Rotunda, which offered greater protection from the vagaries of the unreliable English climate.[39] Designed by William Jones, later Surveyor to the East India Company, the Rotunda was a remarkable building. The internal diameter of one hundred and fifty feet was greater than both the British Museum Reading Room and the Pantheon in Rome, but it was built entirely in wood. As is so often the case with Canaletto's English pictures, the figures in the Ranelagh pictures are no more than *staffage*. In his early Venetian paintings the figures seem to be at ease with the bustle of their native environment, whilst in many of the London pictures the figures are relatively stiff and lifeless, lacking the 'freedom & variety' (as Vertue put it) of his Venetian figures.[40]

Fig. 13 Canaletto
Ranelagh, the interior of the Rotunda
(no 83)

Although Canaletto may have returned briefly for a second time to his native Venice in 1753, he was certainly back in London in 1754 and 1755.[41] It is not known exactly when he left London for good but it must have been in 1755 or 1756. His ten years in England had done little to enhance his reputation or to increase his fortune, but without his images of mid-eighteenth century London our knowledge of the City would be much diminished. Whilst a journey down the

Grand Canal in Venice today still takes us past the palaces seen by Canaletto, a contemporary ride from Lambeth to Greenwich on the Thames has changed virtually beyond recognition, since almost all the riverside buildings seen in his pictures have been demolished.

NOTES

1. They are now in the Dining Room at Woburn Abbey (see W.G. Constable (revised by J. G. Links), *Canaletto*, 2 vols (Oxford, 1976), I, p.111, II, no.4, for a full history). For studies of Canaletto in England, see Hilda F. Finberg, 'Canaletto in England', *Walpole Society*, IX (1920-21), pp.21-76; Constable and Links, *op.cit.*, I, pp.32-43, II, nos. 408-450; J.G. Links, *Canaletto and his Patrons* (London, 1977), pp.63-72; J.G. Links, 'Canaletto in England', *Journal of the Royal Society of Arts,* CXXIX (April 1981), pp.298-308, and J.G. Links, *Canaletto* (Oxford, 1982) p.145-180.
2. Vertue 'Notebooks III', *Walpole Society*, XXII (1933-34), p.132
3. For Joli, see Edward Croft-Murray, *Decorative Painting in England 1537-1837*, 2 vols (London, 1962 & 1970), II, pp.225-6
4. See Benedict Nicholson, *The Treasures of the Foundling Hospital* (Oxford, 1972), pp.20-31
5. See F.J.B. Watson, 'An Allegorical Painting by Canaletto, Piazzetta and Cimaroli', *Burlington Magazine*, XCV (November 1953), p.362
6. Finberg, *loc.cit.*, p.23. The two paintings purchased by the Duke are Constable and Links, *op.cit.*, nos.232,235.
7. Goodwood Mss. 103, f.244 (West Sussex Record Office). See also The Earl of March, *A Duke and his Friends*, 2 vols (London 1911), II, p.602
8. See Constable and Links, *op.cit.*, II, no.744, pl.138 and Links (1982), pl.141
9. [Robert Dodsley], *London and its Environs Described*, 6 vols (London, 1761), V, p.111. See also John Hayes, 'Parliament Street and Canaletto's Views of Whitehall', *Burlington Magazine*, C (October 1958), pp.341-348.
10. See Shaftesbury, *A Letter concerning the Art or Science of Design* (1712), also John Summerson, *Georgian London,* 3rd edition (London, 1978), p.113
11. For a fascinating history of Westminster Bridge, see R.J.B. Walker, *Old Wesminster Bridge. The Bridge of Fools* (London, 1979).
12. *Ibid.*, p.167
13. *Ibid.*, p. 176
14. See Vertue 'Notebooks III', *loc.cit.*, p.149
15. *Ibid.*
16. Jonathan Richardson, *The Connoisseur* (1719), pp.44-5
17. See [Joshua Reynolds], 'To the Idler', No. 79, Saturday 20 October 1759, reprinted in *The Literary Works of Sir Joshua Reynolds*, 3 vols (London, 1819), II, p.230
18. *Ibid.*, p.231
19. *Ibid.*, p.234
20. J.H. Fuseli, Lecture IV 'On Invention – Part II', *The Life and Writings of J.H. Fuseli Esq., M.A., R.A.,* ed. John Knowles, 3 vols (London, 1831), II, p.217
21. See Richard Kingzett, 'A Catalogue of the Works of Samuel Scott', *Walpole Society*, XLVIII (1980-82), pp.1-134
22. See Horace Walpole to Mann, 26 April 1771, *Yale Edition of Horace Walpole's Correspondence*, 33 (New Haven and London 1967), p.299
23. Vertue 'Notebooks V', *Walpole Society*, XXVI (1937-38) p.30. See also Col. Maurice Grant, *A Dictionary of British Landscape Painters* (Leigh-on-Sea, 1952), p.20
24. See Hilda F. Finberg, 'Joseph Baudin, imitator of Canaletto', *Burlington Magazine,* LX (April 1932), p.204
25. See Constable and Links, *op.cit.*, II, nos.428,429. For Joseph Smith, see *Canaletto Paintings and Drawings*, Queen's Gallery (1980-81), pp.11-15.
26. Vertue 'Notebooks III', *op.cit.*, p. 158 (see Links, 1982, p.160)
27. See David Mannings, 'Notes on some Eighteenth-Century Portrait Prices in Britain', *British Journal of Eighteenth Century Studies*, VI (1983), p.189

XIX van Aken: *Covent Garden Market*
See catalogue no. 63

XX Martin: *Hanover Square*
See catalogue no. 88

28. See Vertue 'Notebooks III', *loc.cit.*, p.112
29. *Ibid.*, p.158
30. Constable and Links, *op. cit.*, nos.408,419
31. *Ibid.*, II, pp.682-4
32. For the architectural history of Vauxhall Gardens, see Brian Allen, 'The Landscape' in *Vauxhall Gardens*, Yale Center for British Art (1983), pp.17-23.
33. [John Lockman], *A Sketch of Spring-Gardens, Vaux-Hall. In a Letter to a Noble Lord* (London, n.d. [1752]), p.30
34. Allen, *loc.cit.*, pp.19-21
35. Constable and Links, *op. cit.*, II, pp.683-4
36. Walpole to Henry Seymour Conway, 29 June 1744 (see *Horace Walpole's Correspondence with Henry Seymour Conway, Lady Ailesbury etc.*, ed. W.S. Lewis etc., 37 (New Haven & London, 1974), p.164
37. See Finberg, *loc. cit.*, p.61
38. Constable and Links, *op.cit.*, II, no.420
39. See Giles Worsley, '"I thought Myself in Paradise", Ranelagh and its Rotunda', *Country Life* (15 May 1986), pp.1380-1384
40. See note 15 above
41. Constable and Links, *op.cit.*, I, p.39

THE AESTHETICS OF CHANGE:
LONDON AS SEEN BY
JAMES MCNEILL WHISTLER

ROBIN SPENCER

> Still I am such a Cockney do you know, that London under all circumstances and at every season seems to me the one dwelling place possible.
>
> Whistler

Whistler lived in London for over forty years and continually made it the subject of his art. In his own statements on his work, he always preferred to emphasise purely aesthetic considerations at the expense of subject matter, but his choice of what to depict seems, in retrospect, anything but arbitrary. For the Victorians, his London scenes, although far from conventional, would have carried particular social and topographical meanings which have long been lost to us. Considered from this point of view, they tell us a great deal about the industrial and architectural development of London in the second half of the nineteenth century.

Whistler's London, stripped of its nocturnal fog and impressionist hatching, was as much of the eighteenth century and before as it was of the nineteenth. Overlooked or forgotten, generally considered intrinsically unworthy of being sanctified as a subject for art, irrelevant to ideas about the planning of the city and the needs of its inhabitants, but above all unconcerned with the monumental and the dramatic, Whistler's London equivocates between the past and the present, between permanency and change. Bridges and buildings, ancient or just old, in course of construction or imminent end, the industry of the river, new urban pleasures replacing old ones, shops and whole streets mute to the developer's hammer, fast disappearing ways of trading; all of these were reflected in Whistler's rich visual awareness of London's past and his acute perception of its rapidly changing present.

Visitors to Whistler's London will search in vain for the traditional topographer's view of the metropolis or for those new civic monuments on which the Victorians most prided themselves. Instant variations on Canaletto, the dome of St Paul's floating majestically above the City, the royal residences and the few imperial vistas inherited from the Regency period – none of these held much attraction for the artist. St Paul's is a chance excrescence on a skyline glimpsed through ships' rigging in the etching *Rotherhithe* (fig. 14); it is not intended to be recognised as such because the etching shows the scene reversed. *Windsor (Memorial)* and one of Whistler's former residences, *Chelsea (Memorial)*, both drawn on the same tiny scale, are cheekily paired as introduction and endpiece

Fig. 14 Whistler
Rotherhithe
(no 154)

XXI Whistler: *Nocturne in Blue and Gold*
See catalogue no. 228

XXII Whistler: *Nocturne in Grey and Gold –*
Piccadilly
See catalogue no. 230

respectively to the volume of *Naval Review* etchings presented to Queen Victoria on her Jubilee in 1887. An etching of *Regent's Quadrant* reveals a fragment remaining after the colonnade was demolished in 1845, with only the faintest suggestion of modern plate glass seen *across* rather than theatrically *down* what had once been London's most fashionable street. When the Houses of Parliament appear in a *Nocturne* (no. 228), they are lost to darkness, their profile nearly indistinguishable from other public buildings. The Embankment's broad perspective, a gift to the photographer, is seen in oblique *repoussoir* from a pigeon's eye view high up on the Savoy Hotel (fig. 15). Modern variations on 'Queen Anne' architecture and other advanced architectural styles are never represented, nor is the anonymous suburbia of the kind favoured by the Impressionists.

Fig. 15 Whistler
Savoy Pigeons
(no 231)

The streets he drew and painted tell us something of Whistler's liking for architecture as art, but little about buildings and even less about the people who lived in them. What he found uninteresting he either ignored or disguised. He was drawn irresistibly to trading and commerce in all its aspects, from his first river subjects to the street and market scenes of his later years. To the commerce of London he owed his livelihood as an artist, along with the attendant human and social pleasures which he enjoyed best of all.

Baedeker and other guide books advised tourists to visit the giant engineering structures of the St. Katherine's and London Docks, their vast warehouses likened to an Aladdin's cave crammed with exotic produce from distant lands and symbols of the nation's trading wealth. But Whistler preferred the dockland areas eastwards from Tower Hill to Wapping, bounded by Ratcliffe Highway north of the Thames and Bermondsey and Rotherhithe to the south. These were known to literate Londoners, but visiting such unsavoury and unsafe districts was not recommended. Regarded as a cultural novelty by the outsider and compared to darkest Africa by the early sociologists, the docks elicited excited curiosity from the English friends Whistler took there. For them, but above all to an American artist, this was a new class experience. Unlike Gustave Doré whose attempt at *déclassé* disguise and use of a police escort had failed to conceal his foreign presence, Whistler seems to have met with no difficulties of movement in the East End. He stayed at a little inn close to Wapping Steamboat Pier, probably *The Town of Ramsgate*.

With the exception of *The Limeburner* (no. 152), the occupations of individual figures in Whistler's early Thames etchings, be they coal heavers, watermen or lightermen – all scrupulously differentiated by Henry Mayhew – are imprecisely recorded. Judged by their appearance these dock-side workers assume no clearer role than being generally of the labouring classes. Yet of all his London subjects, their physical presence looms largest in relation to their surroundings. Thereafter the inhabitants of his city diminish in stature. Their street activity becomes less particularised and the premeditated repetition of adult routine as often as not gives way to the unrehearsed spontaneity of children's play.

Nevertheless, as a newcomer to London working within certain social and artistic constraints, Whistler tried to be as specific as he could. He told Fantin-Latour that in the early picture *Wapping* (fig. 16), he originally intended to give the girl so *risqué* an expression that it was clear she was telling the young sailor on the right she had already enjoyed the favours of the older man sitting between them. To emphasise this meaning he also gave her a plunging neckline, which he was obliged to repaint before submitting the picture for public exhibition. Whistler may have witnessed a similar *ménage à trois* as a criminal act of deception commonly practised in low life dives off the Ratcliffe Highway, such as that shown in one of his Thames etchings *Longshoremen*, where professional thieves preyed upon

Fig. 16 Whistler
Wapping
(no 155)

the drunken sailors whose ill luck had led them to places with whose abominations they were little acquainted. Women of the town were in league with these men; we were informed that they acted as so many decoys, and when the conversation between the sailor and the prostitute had been carried on to a certain point, the man, with whom she was in league, would come up and abuse the sailor for speaking to his wife; and after a great deal of acting, the sailor would give a sum of money to be quit of a disagreeable charge.[2]

When Whistler came to know London well he invariably chose subjects which had a special personal or professional meaning for him. For example, regular trips up to town to see his doctor brother in Wimpole Street resulted in an etching, as did the familiar view from a room in Ayr Street where he printed his etchings of Venice. The view from the window of the printer Thomas Way in Wellington Street was captured in an etching of the Gaiety, a burlesque theatre whose star attraction Whistler had once painted. For much of his work he rarely strayed far from the river near his home in Chelsea. Yet in spite of the fact that he lived in west London for the best part of forty years he was neither a suburban artist nor an artist of the suburbs – unlike French contemporaries such as Pissarro who made a speciality of the *banlieue*. The main difference lay in the fact that Chelsea had more or less ceased being a suburb when Whistler went to live there and had already become a part of London. He returned again and again to look at things within a mile's radius of his front doorstep but was responding to very different urban conditions from those which prevailed in the Paris of the Impressionists.

From the mid-eighteenth century, Chelsea's accelerating physical and social changes gradually but inexorably transformed a small village community with a rural economy into the residential extension of west London we know today. Market gardening and the river provided the principal livelihoods, and shops, inns and coffee houses catered for the influx of visitors in the summer when fashionable crowds came to the Rotunda at Ranelagh, built in 1742. Chelsea had already expanded to the east and to the west. Under Lord Cheyne and Sir Hans Sloane, whose two daughters married the Earls of Cadogan and Stanley, the succession of Chelsea's landed wealth was guaranteed well into the twentieth century. The 1770s witnessed developments from north-east of the Royal Hospital to Knightsbridge, creating Hans Town and Sloane Street. These attracted the middle and professional classes, and it was to Sloane Street that the young surgeon Francis Seymour Haden

XXIII Whistler: *Battersea Reach*
See catalogue no. 159

XXIV Daubigny: *St Paul's from the Surrey side*
See catalogue no. 162

came on his marriage to Whistler's half-sister in 1847. In spite of its rural aspects, by 1830 Chelsea was no longer a village but a medium-sized town that had already become a commuter suburb, as Thomas Carlyle found when he moved there in 1834.

Chelsea is unfashionable. It was once the resort of the Court and great, however; hence numerous old houses in it, at once cheap and excellent ... Our Row runs out upon a beautiful Parade (perhaps they call it) running along the shore of the River; shops etc., and a broad highway, with huge shady trees; boats lying moored and a smell of shipping and tar; Battersea Bridge (of wood) a few yards off; the broad River, with white-trousered, white-shirted Cockneys dashing by like arrows in their long canoes of boats; beyond, the green beautiful knolls of Surrey with their Villages; on the whole a most artificial, green-painted, yet lively, fresh, almost opera-looking business such as you can fancy.[3]

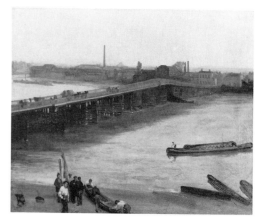

Fig. 17 Whistler
Brown and Silver: Old Battersea Bridge
Oil on canvas, 25 x 30 Addison Gallery of
American Art, Phillips Academy,
Andover Mass.

The King's Road to the north and the river to the south provided relatively easy lines of communication to London, but the building of Battersea Bridge in 1771 opened Chelsea to the competing trade of the Surrey shore. *Brown and Silver: Old Battersea Bridge* (fig. 17), painted before Whistler moved to Chelsea, shows just this: a horse drawn cart containing farm produce trundles across to Battersea and white-trousered watermen stand by the shore ready to convey goods and passengers downstream to London. Such an image was how Chelsea would have been thought of in Sloane Street and Piccadilly. For nearly half a century, while agriculture was in decline, Battersea Bridge had remained the only bridge over the Thames between Vauxhall Bridge downstream, which Whistler etched with its busy traffic in 1861, and dilapidated Putney Bridge upstream, which was also the subject of etchings in 1879 (see no. 170), made shortly before London's oldest wooden bridge was demolished.

Downstream he had already commemorated old ways of commerce and communication being superseded by new ones. The construction of new Westminster Bridge on the site of the old bridge is specifically recorded in three different stages of completion between 1859 and 1862, in two etchings and a major painting finished within months of the bridge being opened to the public in May 1862 (Museum of Fine Arts, Boston). The etching *Old Hungerford Bridge* of 1861 (no. 157) shows Brunel's pedestrian suspension bridge of 1845, a failed speculative venture intended to attract trade to Hungerford Market, which was sold in 1860 to allow for the development of Charing Cross railway station and the building of a new bridge.

A year before Whistler painted his first view of Battersea Bridge, Chelsea Suspension Bridge had been completed, directing traffic towards central London and away from Chelsea. Close by, in 1860, Grosvenor Bridge carried the first railway passengers across the Thames to a west end terminus. In 1863 Battersea Railway Bridge, linking the South Western with the Great Wetern Railway, closed off the horizon of Battersea Reach upstream of Whistler's first Chelsea home.

Fig. 18 Whistler
Nocturne: Blue and Gold
Oil on canvas 26¾ x 20 Tate Gallery, London

Fig. 19 Whistler
Nocturne: Blue and Silver – Chelsea
Oil on Panel 19¾ x 20¼ Tate Gallery,
London

Fig. 20 *Chelsea, Middlesex* Engraving published
by S. Woodburn in 1809

Fig. 21 *Progress of the Thames. Embankment at
Chelsea*
Illustrated London News 1873

Within a decade Albert Bridge appeared, its northern access slicing through Chelsea and dominating a tree lined waterfront already bristling with neo-Gothic iron and the earthworks of the new Chelsea Embankment. Faint strands of the scaffolding on Albert Bridge can just be made out in Whistler's most Japanese treatment of Battersea Bridge, the *Nocturne: Blue and Gold* (fig. 18), a composition that evolved during the last stages of the construction of Albert Bridge. The artist described poetically in his 'Ten O'Clock' lecture how, in this modern, visually inhospitable landscape, 'The sun blares, the wind blows from the east, the sky is bereft of cloud, and without, all is of iron. The windows of the Crystal Palace are seen from all points of London. The holiday-maker rejoices in the glorious day, and the painter turns aside to shut his eyes'.

Whistler shows next to nothing of these decisive intrusions which had the effect of distancing Chelsea from the trade of the river and isolating it from the rest of London. Instead he chose to paint subjects such as Battersea Reach seen from Chelsea Wharf. Here could be seen the long established livelihoods of the river where, before work on the Embankment began, millions of tons of coal were shipped downstream each year to the quays and wharves he had already etched. When the *Series of Sixteen Etchings of Scenes on the Thames and Other Subjects* (or 'Thames Set') was published in 1871, *Early Morning Battersea* (no. 168), with its busy industry clustering on the shore, would strongly contrast with a recently completed etching *Chelsea Bridge and Church* (no. 167) which shows inactive barges signalling the reduced commerce of the riverside. He depicted this subject, the heart of the old parish, on only one other occasion in "real time". It was his first "moonlight", *Nocturne: Blue and Silver – Chelsea* (fig. 19) painted in the summer of 1871, which takes its viewpoint from a boat on the river with the church tower and waterfront in a configuration favoured by countless topographical printmakers from the seventeenth and eighteenth centuries (see fig. 20).[4] Six months later, the wholesale destruction of the waterfront between Battersea Bridge and Chelsea Church would reveal by day a wasteland of chaotic rubble and unpicturable confusion.

Of all civic improvements it was the building of the last stage of the Embankment which brought the greatest change to Chelsea and finally joined it physically to the centre of London (see fig. 21). It had orginally been proposed in 1839 but the 1846 Act of Parliament for an Embankment, along with a wide road between Vauxhall and Battersea Bridge and a new suspension bridge at Chelsea, came only partly to fruition. By 1858 the cost of building Chelsea Bridge had risen and the Embankment only reached the west end of Royal Hospital Gardens. The reasons for its construction were unchallengeable. The river continued to erode its banks and the forming shoals were a hazard to both health and navigation. The Metropolitan Board of Works applied and finally obtained permission to raise the revenue by Act of Parliament in 1868. The Embankment was to be a little under a mile in length and constructed in mill stone grit, with a roadway and footpaths sixty feet wide.

XXV Tissot: *London Visitors*
See catalogue no. 218

XXVI Tissot: *A Procession descending Ludgate Hill*
See catalogue no. 217

XXVII Tissot: *Going to Business*
See catalogue no. 219

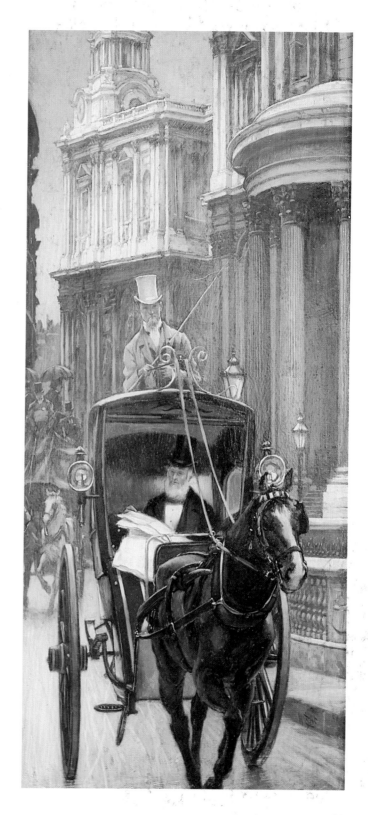

The estimated cost was £1,000,000 with a further £136 to £141,000 allocated in compensation for owners of demolished properties. The valuation of property and the compensation to be awarded presented far fewer problems than it had with the Victoria Embankment, when landowners such as the Duke of Buccleuch objected to a public right of way passing in front of their lands. Then goverment intervention had over-ruled the vested interests of the landowners and the scheme had gone ahead.[5] The Select Committee on the Thames Embankment (Chelsea) agreed with the Crown Surveyor of Works and Public Buildings that the scheme represented 'a great improvement to Lord Cadogan's Cheyne Walk' immediately to the east of Lombard and Duke Streets, the south sides of which were scheduled for demolition.

Lord Cadogan and the Honourable M. Stanley could not object to our taking the buildings, with their staircases down to the river, where people land from their pleasure boats, and go and get a drop of beer, and then go on to the next stage.[6]

The Thames Embankment Act subsequently ordained that 'all the lands so reclaimed to the south of certain streets therein mentioned were directed to be vested in and maintained by the Metropolitan Board of Works for the use of the public as places of recreation or ornamental ground.'[7] Lord Cadogan's houses in Cheyne Walk remained unaffected by the development and retained their trees in front of the river. The Committee felt that

most of the houses are of a high class of house, and we do not want the land opposite them to become a sort of Leicester Square and playing ground for all the idle vagabonds in the neighbourhood, and all the children who may come there.[8]

In 1866 *The Builder* had deplored the absence of a coherent plan for London and enviously cited Baron Haussmann's Paris, where radical replanning was taking place. The *Building News* had once suggested that the Embankment might be 'converted into a boulevard ... lined with cafés, restaurants, little paradises and pavilions, with marble tables, coffee-stalls, and pretty paraphernalia of the kind'.[9] In *Variations in Pink and Grey: Chelsea* (fig. 22), which was probably painted during the construction of the Embankment, elegant ladies, some with Japanese parasols, promenade in anticipation of these modern pleasures. It was a view of the Battersea shore at dusk and the lights of Cremorne Gardens to the west of Chelsea which promenaders might enjoy that Whistler painted again and again in the 1870s – yet the promenaders themselves are notable for their absence.

The Battersea industries benefitting from proximity to the muddy polluted riverside (which in the 1870s was still unembanked) included ribbon, silk and glove manufacturers, sugar refiners, starch, varnish and colour makers, various chemical works, including the manufacturer of Condy's Fluid, barge and boat builders, as well as the older agriculture-related processors, distillers, maltsters and flour mills. Among the most prominent profiles in Whistler's *Nocturnes* are the graphite burning chimneys of Morgan's Patent Plumbago Crucible Company's Works, the

Fig. 22 Whistler
Variations in Pink and Grey: Chelsea
Oil on canvas, 24¾ x 16 Freer Gallery of
Art, Smithsonian Institute, Washington

world's largest crucible makers and the world's biggest importer of graphite from Ceylon. A hundred foot clock tower to the east, built in 1862 and known as 'Morgan's Folly', is shown illuminated by night in several of Whistler's paintings. Winners of prizes at the International Exhibition of 1862 and renowned for withstanding up to ninety-six pourings, Morgan's crucibles were used in mints all over the world, from India to Australia, and in the Royal Arsenals of Woolwich, Brest and Toulon. Further upstream was the great hive of industry known as Belmont Works or Price's Patent Candle Factory, the subject of drypoints in the mid-1870s. Price's was the first firm to apply to a commercial enterprise the discoveries of the French chemist Chevreul concerning the properties of oil and fat, and in 1829 patented the separation of coconut oil into solid and liquid components under pressure; they also invented the self-snuffing candle in 1840. By 1875 the factory was turning out eight and a half miles of wick and thirty-two and a half million candles each year.

The spire of St Mary's, still a recognisable landmark in the *Nocturnes*, had been surrounded within living memory only by mill buildings, orchards and country renowned for its duck and wild fowl. 'In this fast age of iron railways and steam locomotives' one recorder of the Battersea scene noted with only a slight air of regret, 'when Railway Companies scruple not by virtue of Acts of Parliament to pull down by hundreds the dwellings of the poor, it is not to be supposed for an instant that a few fruit trees however delicious their produce or delightful their shadow should prove a peculiar obstacle in the way of this March of Civilisation.'[10] Whistler's vision of this lurid world, where 'the poor buildings lose themselves in the dim sky' and the 'Tall chimneys become campinili' [sic], presented the acceptable face of the march of civilisation. Not surprisingly, it appealed very much to those leading the march, and prominent industrialists and landowners were among the first purchasers of the *Nocturnes*. They included Alfred Chapman, managing director of the long established Liverpool engineering firm of Fawcett, Preston and Co., and the Liberal M.P. Cyril Flower, later Lord Battersea, who managed the estates which bore his name and whose new wife in 1877 'was disappointed that we did not settle down in Battersea amongst the working classes.'[11]

The opening of the Embankment in 1874, planted with trees 'in imitation of the boulevards of Paris', had been eagerly awaited by Chelsea residents who felt they had been too long denied the amenities of easier communication and a modern water disposal system already enjoyed by their more fortunate London neighbours. Except for the sewer, an invisible asset, the advantages were largely illusory. The Embankment caused considerable disruption to the life of the parish and brought harsh economic and social consequences in its wake. The wharves and docks on the old waterfront Whistler had painted in the 1860s were relocated downstream of Old Battersea Bridge which, despite repeated representation, remained unembanked. The free dock in Lindsey Row, beyond Whistler's house, was oversubscribed and the narrow road leading to it congested with carts and waggons, its footways strewn with refuse and made impassable by numerous

XXVIII Tissot: *The Thames*
See catalogue no. 163

XXIX Yoshitora: *The Port of London*
See catalogue no. 160

pedestrians. Residents vigorously complained of the serious depreciation in the value of their property.

The deterioration of the neighbourhood was inextricably linked to Cremorne Gardens immediately to the west, whose proprietor erected handsome wrought iron gates at the entrance in 1870 in anticipation of the rise in the number of visitors which the Embankment would bring. It attracted an altogether less desirable clientèle than expected. The short-lived illusion of an evening's entertainment enjoyed under safe cover of darkness formed the subject of a series of views of Cremorne painted in 1875, including the *Nocturne in Black and Gold: The Falling Rocket,* the subject of Ruskin's objection to Whistler's art. Mounting complaints by residents of late night noise and a marked increase in the number of brothels in the immediate area brought an end to the Gardens in 1877.[12] In the same year Whistler commissioned E.W. Godwin to build him a new house and studio in Tite Steet.

Modernity of the streamlined metropolitan kind was of no practical use in helping to absorb the thousands of people who flooded into Chelsea every decade. Between 1871 and 1881 the population increased by an unprecedented 18,000 to a total of 88,000. The Embankment itself provided no shelter and the prediction that it would ease the flow of traffic was slow to come about. The Embankment was still a 'desert' in 1874, an oasis of loneliness in the 1880s and the traditional refuge for tramps by the end of the century, 'its brilliant lights only serving to enhance the darkness', a symbol of the city's alienation for painter and poet.[13] Whistler's art played a significant part in the development of such an iconography. In spite of claiming that art should not depend upon 'dramatic, or legendary or local interest', and declaring 'I care nothing for the past, present, or future of the black figure', his *Nocturne: Grey and Gold – Chelsea Snow* (fig. 23) presents an isolated figure of indisputable isolation trudging up Royal Hospital Road towards the lights of a tavern. Whistler left nostalgic views of the old Chelsea waterfront to his English contemporaries whose versions of the past were still being reworked by successive generations of artists and illustrators well beyond the turn of the century.[14] In just one etching he did draw a memory of the old riverside, probably from a photograph by the Chelsea photographer James Hedderly. *The 'Adam and Eve' Old Chelsea* (no. 169) of 1879 reverses what would then have been remembered of the scene in nature. It is in strong contrast to Walter Greaves' teeming celebration of *The Last Chelsea Regatta* in 1871 (another source for Whistler's etching) in which spectators converge on every vantage point and cling to every foothold to witness the last race to be rowed from London Bridge before the waterfront was swept away the following year.[15] In the 1880s Whistler only represented the Embankment wall at Chelsea in watercolour and in a slight etching.

The *'Adam and Eve'* etching made shortly before he left for Venice, foreshadows the London subjects Whistler increasingly favoured after his return. These were the remains of old Chelsea, and one part in particular, which he regularly sought out to draw and paint. The demolition of the south side of Duke and Lombard Streets in 1872 had left their north sides exposed to the wide Embankment. With his back to

Fig. 23 Whistler
Nocturne: Grey and Gold – Chelsea Snow
Oil on canvas 18½ x 24½ Fogg Art
Museum, Cambridge, Mass.

the river Whistler represented from close-up and from afar the old seventeenth century houses with their frontages converted into shops, Maunder's fish shop attracting him more than any other (see no. 171). These views were not to be available for long. Seen from the river along the Embankment, in Cadogan Square and around Sloane Square, the red brick variations on Queen Anne architecture were springing up to give Chelsea an entirely different character. In 1888 Sir Charles Dilke, M.P. for Chelsea between 1867 and 1886, regretted the

Rows of bluey-red bay windowed houses – houses fresh from a modern book of architecture, which spoil the symmetry of our older streets. Where some of the most beautiful old houses of Cheyne Walk have disappeared, the builders are replacing them – not with plain houses of the true Chelsea style, modelled on Wren's beautiful building of the hospital with bricks of indian red, or here and there scarlet and of yellow, but with these unquiet I might also say disturbing and disturbed, magenta-coloured houses of an ugly pattern, which bids fair to become the monotonous livery of the future.[16]

By 1892 the north side of Lombard Street, including Maunder's fish shop, had been demolished, effectively putting an end to Whistler's Chelsea subject matter.

However much modern architectural critics extolled the visual transformation of Chelsea by the Cadogan Estate, Whistler never represented it. With the exception of one occasion in 1896, when he mistook a 'superior industrial dwelling of quite recent date' for 'old Queen Anne',[17] he preferred the original architecture of the seventeenth century including the Royal Hospital of which he made a lithograph, to its recent derivatives which he derided. On the site of Maunder's fish shop, C.R. Ashbee designed No. 74 Cheyne Walk, 'a successful example of the disastrous effect of art upon the middle classes',[18] and the house in which Whistler was to die in 1903.

Whistler had an unerring instinct for buildings of a certain scale and proportion which exactly matched his pictorial requirements. The street scenes and the increasing number of figures and wraith-like half-suggestions of people, especially children, he introduced into these settings also reflected a different social order than had existed before the Embankment was built. Parts of Chelsea were no longer socially homogeneous. The demolition by the Cadogan Estate of poorer working class housing to make way for superior and more profitable houses and mansion blocks for the middle classes caused displacements on a large scale and produced concentrated areas of slums. In 1886 protests against Lord Cadogan's 'inhuman policy of breaking up workmen's houses to fill his own pockets' were made on the streets.[19]

Although there was no extreme poverty, Charles Booth observed by the end of the century, there were 'all signs of low life and filthy habits: broken and patched windows, open doors, drink-sodden women and dirty children'.[20] The overcrowding spills out into Whistler's old streets, into his etchings of *Justice Walk* and *Milman's Row*, where children congregate on the steps of old clothes shops. Some of the especially grubby children Whistler followed home to ask their

XXX Doré: *The Violet-Seller*
See catalogue no. 215

XXXI Hammershøi: *The British Museum and Montague Street*
See catalogue no. 240

parents' permission to have them sit for him.

It is probably no coincidence that Whistler's figure-filled street scenes date from after 1883 and become progressively more crowded. After an interval of a quarter of a century he returned to the East End in 1887 to depict the old clothes district and exchange around Houndsditch and Middlesex Street. The publication of Andrew Mearns' famous pamphlet *The Bitter Cry of Outcast London* provoked a wide and dramatic public response to the social problems of overcrowding in the East End. The campaign for government legislation and for a curb on the building speculators led to the *Royal Commission on the Housing of the Working Classes* of 1884–5 and the Housing Acts of 1885 and 1890. Fuelled by W.T. Stead's articles in the *Pall Mall Gazette*, Mearns' pleas 'echoed from one end of England to the other' and 'directed the attention of the West End to the East'.[21] Whistler intended to publish a *Little London* set of the Houndsditch etchings, no doubt with those ladies and gentlemen in mind for whom it was 'the commonest thing in the world to go down to the East End';[22] but he maintained that 'the only excuse for the masses was that they were a blot of colour to be painted'.[23]

Before the Embankment came, Chelsea offered all the human interests and pursuits which Dr Johnson had once found in the whole of London. There had been shops, the trade of the river, pleasure gardens and even a *salon* centred on Whistler's own breakfast parties. But as these social pleasures either disappeared or changed, so Whistler's interest in Chelsea as art began to wane. In the 1880s and 1890s he looked increasingly to London's West End for subjects that were no longer available to him nearer home. What he saw was a city of striking extremes and strongly contrasting experiences, both visual and aural, each district and each street distinct from the next. In his etchings he often made pairings that point up the distinction. *Wych Street*, excessively narrow and noted for its 'curious old houses' though in reality one of London's most squalidly overcrowded streets, contrasts with broad *St James's Street* at the heart of the West End with its many clubs and eighteenth century associations, thronged with people of another caste and social purpose. The same bustle and excitement is evoked in his watercolour of night life on Piccadilly (no. 230). A quite different effect is produced in the etchings of people loitering by the old clothes shops in the Jews' Quarter which was silent on Saturdays, busy on Sundays. The noisy activities of the clothes exchange counterpoints the silent buildings and courtyards of nearby Gray's Inn as described by Nathaniel Hawthorne. 'Nothing else in London is so like the effect of a spell, as to pass under one of these archways, and find yourself transported from the jumble, rush, tumult, uproar, as of an age of week days condensed into the present hour, into what seems an eternal Sabbath.'[24] Several houses, streets and churches that feature in his later London prints carried artistic and literary associations with the past. They include St Martin's Lane and York Street, where Haydon, Hazlitt and Lamb once lived. The district of Soho around the churches of St Giles in the Fields and St Anne's was still a poor one, and the centre of the French community. No doubt Whistler felt at home here, not least for its association with the subject

Fig. 24 Whistler
The Thames
(no 232)

matter of his favourite English artist, Hogarth – as he would have done in the back courts of Drury Lane, and the church of St Bartholomew's where Hogarth was baptised.

Whistler told Sidney Starr that 'only one landscape interested him, the landscape of London'.[25] Before Whistler came to London, the experience of what it was like to live in the city and the effect it had on the lives of its people had already been described by writers such as Henry Mayhew and Charles Dickens, who used sociological close-up and anthropomorphic metaphor more vividly and more compellingly than any city artist since Hogarth. By mid-century, only the photographer and social statistician could compete with the demand for verifiable immediacy of this kind. Instead Whistler's choice of subjects and his treatment of them, had to be far in retreat of such advanced competition. When, late in life, he wanted to make an image of modern London as distinct from an impression of only part of it, he chose a high panoramic viewpoint similar to those favoured by the Impressionists. From a balcony of the newly-built Savoy Hotel he made lithographic sketches of the river through an angle of 180 degrees in three different views: downstream towards St. Paul's with Waterloo Bridge, upstream to Westminster with Charing Cross Railway Bridge in spite of an 'unenviable reputation for its extreme plainness, not to say ugliness' (fig. 24)[26] and the Thames by night with its southern shore directly opposite the hotel; this last was also the subject of an oil painting, *Grey and Silver: the Thames*

It was also from the Savoy Hotel, beginning in 1899, that Claude Monet painted views of the Thames and its bridges to left and to right, adding a third group of subjects, the Palace of Westminster seen from the opposite bank. There is some evidence to suggest that Whistler may have been involved in Monet's project by keeping him informed of changes in the weather.[27] Monet's brilliantly colouristic depiction of London expressed the temporal immediacy of his visual experience and became the dominant aesthetic experience for Derain and Kokoschka, who visited the capital in the twentieth century. Whistler had more time than any other foreign artist to get to know London. But his experience of the city as a long term resident was tempered by the eyes of a visitor, unconstrained by the tradition of London topographers. He also swept aside a century-old tradition in British art of depicting the commercial and domestic activity of London life with commonplace street metaphors and well-worn moral exempla. He thus became the first London artist since Hogarth to invent a new aesthetic language to celebrate the diversity of modern urban experience, and the elusive ebb and flow of the city's past and ever-changing present.

XXXII C. Pissarro: *Fox Hill, Upper Norwood*
See catalogue no. 172

70

XXXIII C. Pissarro: *Upper Norwood, Crystal*
Palace in distance
See catalogue no. 173

NOTES

1. Whistler to Mrs F.R. Leyland, 1876, Library of Congress.
2. Thomas Beames, *The Rookeries of London*, 2nd edition, 1852, reprinted 1970, p. 99
3. Tom Pocock, *Chelsea Reach*, 1970, pp. 30-1 and *passim*.
4. Elizabeth Longford, *Images of Chelsea,* Richmond-upon-Thames, 1980, *passim*.
5. David Owen, *The Government of Victorian London 1855-1898*, Cambridge, Mass., and London, 1982, pp. 74-101
6. *Select Committee on Thames Embankment (Chelsea) Bill, Proceedings before the Select Committee of the House of Commons*, Session 1868, Wednesday 20 May 1868.
7. *Ibid*.
8. *Ibid*.
9. Owen, *op. cit.,* p.106, Donald J. Olsen, *The Growth of Victorian London*, 1976, p. 107
10. Henry S. Simmonds, *All About Battersea*, 1882, pp. 6-7 and *passim*.
11. Constance Battersea, *Reminiscences*, 1922, p. 172
12. *Report of the Vestry of the Parish of Chelsea, appointed under the Metropolis Local Management Act 1855,* 1870-79, *passim*.
13. Olsen, *op. cit.,* p. 300. Raphael Samuel, 'Comers and Goers', in H.J. Dyos and Michael Wolff, *The Victorian City*, 2 vols, 1973, I, pp. 129, 146
14. Longford, *op. cit., passim*.
15. Pocock, *op cit.,* pp. 89-90
16. Rt. Hon. Sir Charles W. Dilke Bart., *Chelsea: A Lecture delivered in the Town Hall, Chelsea, Wednesday, January 11, 1888*
17. T.R. Way, *Memories of James McNeill Whistler*, 1912, p. 129
18. E.R. & J. Pennell, *The Life of James McNeill Whistler*, 2 vols., Philadelphia and London, 1908, II, p. 277
19. Olsen, *op cit.,* pp. 147-54
20. Charles Booth, *Life and Labour of the People in London,* London and New York, 1902-04, vol. 3, *Third Series: Religious Influences*, reprinted New York, 1970, pp. 112-19
21. Andrew Mearns, *The Bitter Cry of Outcast London*, 1883, edited with an introduction by Anthony S. Wohl, Leicester, 1970, pp. 9-26 and *passim*. P.J. Keating, 'Fact and Fiction in the East End', in Dyos and Wolff, *op. cit.,* II, pp. 585-602. Anthony S. Wohl, 'Unfit for Human Habitation', *ibid.,* pp. 603-624
22. Mearns, *op. cit.,* pp. 24, 26
23. Mortimer Menpes, *Whistler as I Knew Him*, 1904, p. 63
24. Nathaniel Hawthorne, *Our Old Home, and English Note-Books*, 2 vols, 1883, II, p. 581
25. E.R. and J. Pennell, *The Life of James McNeill Whistler*, 5th edition, revised, Philadelphia, 1911, p. 398
26. Way, *op. cit.,* p. 127
27. E.R. Pennell, *Journal* (unpublished), 1 Nov. 1920, Library of Congress.

LONDON IN THE ART OF MONET AND PISSARRO

JOHN HOUSE

London was an important city for Monet and Pissarro; they each painted here, both early and late in their careers, and Pissarro developed particularly close links with the place because his eldest son Lucien came to live here. In their earlier London paintings of 1870–1, they created a novel, and distinctively French, vision of the city; but, by the time they painted here again at the end of the century, an 'Impressionist' view of the city and its effects was widely current in artistic circles in London, partly through direct influence of French ideas, and largely through the activities of another expatriate artist, Whistler. The marked differences between Monet's and Pissarro's 1870–1 pictures and their later images of London reveal much about the changes in their own art, but they also reflect wider changes in the perception of the nature of life in the great metropolis.

External circumstances brought Monet and Pissarro to London in 1870: both of them were refugees from the Franco-Prussian War. London was, of course, a safe and accessible refuge, but more positive reasons may have led them to cross the Channel, for some French artists believed that London offered a more fruitful potential market for modern painting than Paris. The most significant outcome of Monet's and Pissarro's visit was, indeed, commercial; but ironically this resulted from their meeting with a French art dealer who had himself taken refuge in London, Paul Durand-Ruel. Durand-Ruel included their work in an exhibition in his London gallery in March 1871, and bought a number of paintings from them; later he was to become their mainstay and the architect of their international reputations.[1]

The pictures which Monet and Pissarro executed in London in 1870-1 had no obvious precedents in British painting; their subjects – the river, parks and suburbs – are similar to themes they had previously treated in France. But at the same time they make a real contribution to the imagery of nineteenth-century London, for they tackle a number of the most significant aspects of the modern city, and provide a view of the city which has clear parallels with the responses of other French visitors, both painters and writers.

Among British artists at the time, urban London was primarily the province of the topographical painter and printmaker, rather than the Royal Academy exhibitor. Images of the modern city appeared often in the pages of widely-circulated magazines like the *Illustrated London News*, but in the Royal Academy the city was more often the scenario for modern genre subjects. David Roberts's Thames scenes, of which several were exhibited in 1862, were exceptional for the

XXXIV C. Pissarro: *Hyde Park*
See catalogue no. 175

XXXV C. Pissarro: *The Train, Bedford Park*
See catalogue no. 176

period in treating the modern city itself as a motif; they were treated with the crisp detail and precise drawing characteristic of the topographical tradition, but in a number of ways they presented a quite misleading image of the urban Thames: they show it as a monumental rather than a commercial river, and omit the paddle-steamers and steam barges which were already the prime means of river transport; and they ignore the shroud of mist and fog which so often veiled the details of London's architecture.

Fig. 25 Monet
The Houses of Parliament
Oil on canvas, National Gallery, London

By contrast, Monet's Thames views emphasise both commerce and atmospherics, reducing the buildings to near-silhouettes and focusing primarily on the river traffic and the busy figures beside the water. Monet chose two of the river's most celebrated sites, Westminster Bridge with the Houses of Parliament, and London Bridge with the Custom House – respectively the seats of London's government and trade. *The Houses of Parliament* (fig 25) shows a particularly modern subject; though the scene may now seem a hallowed part of old London, all its features were new when Monet painted them – the Houses of Parliament, the Victoria Embankment (opened in 1870), paddle steamers, the new Westminster Bridge (opened 1862) and, in the mists on the left, St Thomas' Hospital (only opened summer 1871). The creation of the Embankments, and the accompanying new drainage system, had completely reorientated the centre of London, turning the river into a grand ceremonial way through the heart of London, like the Seine in Paris, instead of a vast open sewer approached only by narrow alleyways. A writer in the *Art Journal* remarked in 1871 that 'the opening of the Thames Embankment . . . has for the first time convinced many of us of the claims of London to architectural beauty'. The view from Tower Stairs, which Monet showed in his two views of *The Port of London* (see fig 26), was also one of the city's most famous sites, repeatedly described in the travel literature of the time; Mr and Mrs S.C. Hall, in *The Book of the Thames* (1859), summed up its resonance: 'There are, perhaps, few sights in the world more striking – certainly none more calculated to make an Englishman proud of his country.'[2]

Fig. 26 Monet
The Port of London
Oil on canvas, National Museum of Wales, Cardiff

However, Monet's harmonious, misty effects make little of architectural beauty or national pride; they are far closer to a different view of London's river, which was current in French travel writing. Hippolyte Taine described the Houses of Parliament in *Notes sur l'Angleterre*, published late in 1871 after Monet had left London: 'The palace is magnificently reflected in the gleaming river; from a distance, its clock tower, its legion of turrets and mouldings are vaguely silhouetted in the mist'; it gives 'the idea of an entangled forest'. Duranty, whom Monet knew, had described the docks in an essay of 1867: 'Their appearance is astonishing, extraordinary, particularly in grey foggy weather which gives a special character to the perspective and completes the sense of great melancholy (*tristesse*) which accompanies all modern expressions of commerce and industry.'[3]

English accounts, like contemporary English painting, concentrated on particulars and details, on what was known to be there, and on the associations of the sites, while the French emphasised the subjective response to the overall effect of the scene – and particularly the evocative effects of London's legendary fogs. Many years later, Monet commented: 'What I like most of all in London is the fog. How could English painters of the nineteenth century have painted its houses brick by brick? Those fellows painted bricks which they didn't see, which they couldn't see . . . It is the fog which gives London its marvellous breadth. Its regular, massive blocks become grandiose in this mysterious cloak.' This vision of the metamorphic effects of fog on the buildings which lined the Thames had a long tradition in France, going back to Gautier's 1842 essay *Une Journée à Londres*: 'A forest of colossal chimneys, in the form of towers, columns, pylons and obelisks, give the horizon an Egyptian look . . . Industry, on this gigantic scale, almost attains poetry, poetry in which nature accounts for nothing . . . This smoke, spread over everything, blurs harsh angles, veils the meanness of buildings, enlarges views, gives mystery and vagueness to the most positive objects. In the smoke, a factory chimney becomes an obelisk, a warehouse of poor design takes on the airs of Babylonian terrace, a grim row of columns changes into the porticos of Palmyra. The symmetrical barrenness of civilisation and the vulgarity of the forms it adopts all become softened or disappear, thanks to this kindly veil.' Whether or not Whistler knew Gautier's essay, the tenor of his ideas clearly lies behind Whistler's definitive verbal formulation of the poetry of the Thames in his *Ten O'Clock* lecture of 1885: 'And when the evening mist clothes the riverside with poetry, as with a veil, and the poor buildings lose themselves in the dim sky, and the tall chimneys become campanili, and the warehouses are palaces in the night, and the whole city hangs in the heavens, and fairyland is before us – then the wayfarer hastens home; the working man and the cultured one, the wise man and the one of pleasure, cease to understand, as they have ceased to see, and Nature, who, for once, has sung in tune, sings her exquisite song to the artist alone.'[4]

Whistler had begun to paint the Thames in mist before 1870, but it remains uncertain how much Monet knew of his work. We do not know whether the two men met in London in 1870–1, though they had contacts in common. However, the simple, liquid sweeps of paint in the background of *The Houses of Parliament* , which recur in several of Monet's other paintings of 1870-2, notably *Impression, Sunrise* (Musée Marmottan, Paris), suggest parallels with Whistler's recent work.[5] Monet's vision of the misty Thames may also owe something to the London canvases of Daubigny. Daubigny had first painted the Houses of Parliament in 1866, during the construction of the Embankment (fig 27), and was in London again in 1870–1, when he introduced Monet to Durand-Ruel. Like Monet, Daubigny handled London's mists with breadth and simplicity, and treated its celebrated monuments as just another element in the panorama of the industrial and commercial river, as in *St Paul's from the Surrey Side* (no 162).

Monet's other two London scenes show the parks, with small figures spread across wide spaces in informal groupings characteristic of the open-air scenes that Monet and his friends had painted in and around Paris in the previous past few years. Urban parks seem not to appear in English Academy painting at this date,

Fig. 27 Daubigny
The Victoria Embankment under Construction
Pushkin Museum, Moscow

XXXVI De Nittis: *Westminster*
See catalogue no. 233

XXXVII Monet: *The Houses of Parliament:*
effect of sunlight
See catalogue no. 254

but they often supplied the setting for fashionable gatherings shown in magazines such as the *Graphic* and the *Illustrated London News*. John Ritchie's paintings of the late 1850s of *A Summer Day in Hyde Park* (Museum of London) and *A Winter Day in St James's Park* were not shown at the Academy, perhaps because such subjects were felt to belong to a 'lower', more popular genre of art. Ritchie's paintings, like the magazine illustrations, have prominent figures, with clear points of psychological interest and hints at narrative storytelling, quite unlike the detached manikins which people Monet's open spaces. Yet Monet's figures, too, show a close observation of social types, deftly differentiated and succinctly characterised by a shorthand of coloured touches, which even pick out figures as small as the nursemaids and children on the path in the right middle distance of *Green Park* (fig 28). This picture also shows a close study of London's topography: the strange silhouette seen through the mist in the left background is the equestrian statue of the Duke of Wellington which stood atop the Constitution Arch at Hyde Park Corner from 1846 until 1883.[6]

Fig. 28 Monet
Green Park, London
Oil on canvas, 13½ x 28½ Philadelphia
Museum of Art

In contrast to Monet's pictures of celebrated central London sites, Pissarro in 1870–1 painted only around the area of Upper Norwood where he was living. This part of London's southern suburbs was in a process of transformation. After the Crystal Palace had been moved there from Hyde Park in 1854, it became the focus of a large suburban development, which gradually absorbed the remains of the local villages and cut into the surrounding countryside. Some of Pissarro's paintings of the area emphasise these oppositions: in *Lordship Lane Station* (fig 29), open country surrounds the rows of new suburban houses and the railway line with its train – this line had been opened as recently as 1865 to cater for crowds coming to the Palace. As a whole, Pissarro's Norwood canvases reveal the many facets of the place. In some pictures the countryside is virtually intact; some emphasise the surviving cottages from the old villages; some show new suburban streets; and two focus on the palace itself, but in very different ways: in one, it is the focus for groups of fashionable visitors, in the other, the palace and the developing suburb lie beyond unbuilt fenced-in ground, a wasteland awaiting building.

Fig. 29 Pissarro
Lordship Lane Station
Oil on canvas 17½ x 28½ Courtauld
Institute of Art, London

However, it is misleading to treat these paintings as a homogeneous group, and to view them as a comprehensive anatomy of suburban change; for they were never seen together, and they were sold piecemeal, through different outlets and at different times. Viewed separately, they show Pissarro exploring many different types of landscape – some explicitly modern, technological and specific to London, and some more generic, closer to the types of picture Pissarro had produced in the Louveciennes area, on the outer western fringes of Paris, in the two years before the war. *Fox Hill, Upper Norwood* (fig 30) is similar to some Louveciennes paintings in its juxtaposition of bushes and gardens with older cottages and newer houses. Morever, one at least of Pissarro's Norwood paintings was originally exhibited with the very inexplicit title *Effet de neige*, which would further have conditioned how it was seen; the topographically exact titles which *Lordship Lane Station* and

Fox Hill, Upper Norwood now bear are the results of recent detailed research into the sites depicted; this information would not have been available to their original viewers, of whom few if any would have had precise knowledge of this locale. The diverse subjects of Pissarro's Norwood paintings may reflect an interest in the diversity of the place, but – probably more relevantly – they provided Pissarro with a range of saleable canvases belonging to different genres of landscape, ranging from rural through suburban to distinctively contemporary. Like Monet's London pictures, Pissarro's have no parallels in contemporary British painting; these types of subject were essentially French, and the pictures' potential market lay in Paris.

Similarly, the paintings' ancestry was French in handling and treatment. A few of Pissarro's paintings contain less fully finished areas, such as the bushes on the extreme right of *Fox Hill, Upper Norwood*, which are laid in very broadly with little suggestion of their form; but the majority of them, and all five of Monet's London scenes, show a consistent degree of finish throughout the canvas, indicating foreground forms in a crisp representational shorthand of coloured touches, which evoke the features in the scene, but quite without precise and illusionistic detail. This sort of treatment is characteristic of the type of pictures which painters in France were selling to art dealers in the late 1860s – smaller and more informal than the ambitious one-off pictures generally shown at the annual Salon exhibition, but more resolved and thoroughly finished than their more rapid sketches. Both Pissarro and Monet had been finding a market for such paintings in Paris, and they were already the stock-in-trade of painters such as Boudin and Jongkind – both close associates of Monet.

When Durand-Ruel came to London in the autumn of 1870, he brought a substantial part of his dealer's stock with him, and the exhibitions he mounted in his New Bond Street gallery, together with other displays of modern French painting in London at the time, allowed critics to focus on the essential differences between British and French art. *The Times* summed up the characteristics of French landscape in reviewing Durand-Ruel's first exhibition in December 1870: '...always the broadest possible expression of some dominant sentiment – this seems the aim of the French landscape painter. In comparison with most of our landscape work his almost always seems slight, and sometimes unfinished to rudeness, and starved in colour.' Reporting on an exhibition at the French Gallery at the same time as this, the *Saturday Review* characterised current British landscape painting, 'of the school which dates from Creswick': 'a school of green, woody pastoral, placid as a summer's evening; peaceful and uneventful as a cotter's life. This average English landscape, often composed of little more than trees and a trout stream, cares not for grandeur on earth or in the elements.' And in April 1871, discussing Durand-Ruel's second exhibition, the *Saturday Review* enlarged on the differences between English and French artists: 'The French believe themselves the greatest landscape-painters on the face of the earth; and yet their ideas about nature are all but unintelligible to the average run of Englishmen. Certain

Fig. 30 Pissarro
Fox Hill, Upper Norwood
(no 172)

XXXVIII Monet: *Waterloo Bridge: effect of sunlight*
See catalogue no. 253

XXXIX Monet: *Waterloo Bridge*
See catalogue no. 257

distinctions between the two national schools are evident. Our English painters, it may be said, hold the mirror up to nature; their transcripts are photographic, uncoloured by emotion; hard, tangible facts are wrought out literally, even mechanically. On the other hand, French landscape-painters approach nature with passion, their eye kindles with the fire of frenzy, and is sometimes shaded with melancholy.'[7] Pissarro's and Monet's paintings of London differed from the mass of French landscapes seen in London by dint of the modernity of their subjects; but the artists were in line with their compatriots in their concentration on the overall effects of their scenes, rather than their details; their fascination with light, atmosphere and weather subordinated the elements in the scene to its overall mood.

Discussion of Monet's and Pissarro's first visit to London has often raised the question of the influence on them of Turner and Constable. In later years, Pissarro acknowledged that they had admired the work of the English artists, but on another occasion he denied that they had influenced his and Monet's 'conception of light.'[8] Certainly, their paintings show little sign of such influences. The flexible handling and varied greens of Constable's smaller paintings from nature bear a generic similarity to their work, but these Constables were not on view in 1870-1. Their relationship to Monet's and Pissarro's work is, rather, indirect. As most French critics acknowledged in the 1860s, Constable had been a formative influence on the French landscape 'School of 1830', particularly through his paintings shown at the 1824 Salon, among them *The Hay Wain*; but French artists had had little chance to see his work since then, and had independently developed further the study of open air effects of which he had been a pioneer. Artists such as Monet and Pissarro, who had learned their outdoor painting in the orbit of Corot, Daubigny and Boudin, would have had little to learn, by 1870, from seeing Constable's finished oil paintings. Turner's reputation was less well established in France at that date, but Monet's and Pissarro's London paintings, with their economical, controlled brushwork and their delicate, comparatively subdued colour schemes, have little in common with the lavish effects of paintwork and surface of the Turners they would have seen. Turner's broadly brushed sketches like *Norham Castle* had not been catalogued and put on display by his executor John Ruskin; only after Ruskin's death in 1900, and in the aftermath of Impressionism itself, were such unfinished colour-beginnings considered worthy of presentation to the public.[9]

The support of Paul Durand-Ruel was of central importance to Monet and Pissarro in London and during the two years after they returned home; his purchases from them fully justified their decision to treat the scenery of London in paintings of a type suitable for the French dealer market. He bought four London canvases from Pissarro in London, and soon afterwards purchased four of Monet's five London views; Monet sold the fifth, one of the port scenes, to Hecht in January 1873. However, as far as we can tell from the surviving records, Durand-Ruel did not buy any of Pissarro's most overtly modern subjects at this date.[10] Moreover, he was able to sell few of the paintings which he had bought from the Impressionists-to-be, and in 1874 he was forced to suspend his purchases from them; only from 1881 onwards was he able to resume his support for their art.

Pissarro did not paint again in London until 1890, Monet not until 1899, but they retained contacts with London in the intervening years. From 1883 Pissarro's son Lucien was mainly based in London, and the few canvases Pissarro painted here in later years were executed during visits to see him. Monet next crossed the Channel in 1887, to see Whistler, who, later in the same year, put some of his paintings on show at the Royal Society of British Artists. Throughout the 1880s, he hoped to be able to paint the Thames, but he did not work here during several brief visits in the late 1880s and early 1890s; only in 1899, when his son Michel was studying English in London, did he begin his late series of paintings of the Thames.[11]

Both Monet's and Pissarro's art underwent crucial changes in the years before they returned to work in London, but at the same time there were major shifts in the artistic climate in England. Whereas in 1870 their work would have seemed distinctively French, and far from the main currents of English art, by 1890 what were loosely described as 'Impressionist' ideas had gained a wide currency in London, and many critics were, in theory at least, predisposed to support their art. However, as in 1870–1, neither Monet nor Pissarro found a real public and market for their work in England outside a small artistic coterie, and their late London pictures also found their main outlet in Paris.

As we have seen, their paintings of 1870–1, for all their abbreviated treatment, were very responsive to the particularity and diversity of the elements in the scene, in the ways in which figures, buildings and natural textures were notated. During the 1870s, a major change took place in both Monet's and Pissarro's brushwork, towards a more uniform handling, in smaller, comparatively evenly weighted touches of colour, which subordinated the individual features of the scene to the overall play of coloured light.[12] To English viewers in 1870–1, French landscape already showed a concern for effects rather than details in its breadth of treatment that was so different from the minutiae of English painting; but this further development during the 1870s marked a decisive further stage away from particularisation.

These changes are in line with a broader shift which historians of literature have noted in the characterisation of the urban crowd, away from the notion of a crowd as an aggregate of individuals – complex maybe, but able to be disentangled – to an anonymous mass. This change appears in the verbal formulations, the descriptive strategies, which writers adopted in dealing with the crowd. Through the middle of the century, crowds were analysed by identifying and classifying the types who made them up, by anatomising their ingredients, and thereby controlling their diversity by making it intelligible. The new crowd, by contrast, could not be broken down into its constituent parts, but remained a resistant, intractable mass, anonymous and potentially threatening. In literary descriptions of London, as

Raymond Williams has pointed out, this shift can be seen in the difference between the ways in which crowds are characterised in the novels of Dickens and George Gissing.[13]

Gissing's vision of London shares much with the vision of the city which was being developed at the same time, in the 1880s, by artists and writers in the circle of Whistler and Oscar Wilde. The river, with its details swathed in fog, became the prime scenario in paintings which took their inspiration from Whistler's *Nocturnes*, and in poems where the river is generally used as the context for evocations of human sorrow and isolation. Wilde's 'Impression du matin' (1881) used the image of 'the Thames nocturne of blue and gold', and the changing colours in the fog, as the setting for a love-lorn woman; the river is used in a comparable way in poems of the 1880s and 1890s by writers such as W.E. Henley, Arthur Symons and John Davidson. In Wilde's 'Symphony in Yellow' of 1889 the sense-experiences of the river in fog are the sole theme of the poem. In his essay 'The Decay of Lying', published the same year, he elaborated on the paradox which Whistler had expressed in his *Ten O'Clock* lecture, that 'it might almost be said that Nature is usually wrong'; Wilde argued that nature imitates art, and that London's fogs were caused by the Impressionists: 'The extraordinary change that has taken place in the climate of London during the last ten years is entirely due to this particular school of Art ... One does not see anything until one sees its beauty. Then, and only then, does it come into existence. At present, people see fogs, not because there are fogs, but because poets and painters have taught them the mysterious loveliness of such effects.'[14] For all his paradoxical phrasing, Wilde was here making a crucial point, that we can only understand what we see through frameworks of expectation and classification: the earlier English view of London saw a scene as the sum of its details, of the parts that made it up, whereas an aesthetic of the 'effect' could treat London's fogs as something worthy of being seen in themselves, and not just as an impediment to seeing the objects which lay behind them. The roots of this aesthetic, as we have seen, lay in France, but it reached its full realisation in London in the work of Whistler and Wilde.

In one important respect, the Whistlerian vision of London differed from that in Monet's and Pissarro's later works: his was essentially tonal, while theirs was lavishly coloured. In 'The Decay of Lying', Wilde predicted that a coloured version of Nature, imitating Monet and Pissarro, would supplant the modish Whistlerian tonal fogs, and in March 1899 (before Monet began his London series) an imaginary dialogue in the *Artist* presented an artist enthusing over the colours of a sunset seen from the Victoria Embankment: 'There's nothing to be seen like it ever – in any town in Europe. They say it's due to the smoke and it may be; but just look at it. Look at the purple and crimson, the scarlet and gold ... And see how it all dies back and dies back, until with just the tiniest fleck of pink it sinks into the palest green.' It was these constant changes in colour which tormented Monet as he worked on his London series around 1900; he told an interviewer in 1901: 'The fog in London assumes all sorts of colours; there are black, brown, yellow, green, purple fogs, and the interest in painting is to get the objects as seen through all these fogs. My practiced eye has found that objects change in appearance in a London fog more and quicker than in any other atmosphere, and the difficulty is to get every change down on canvas.'[15]

Pissarro painted in London on three occasions in the 1890s: in spring 1890 he turned to the sites which Monet had favoured in 1870–1, and undertook two views of the Thames looking upstream from Waterloo Bridge, with the Houses of Parliament in the background, and two canvases of Hyde Park (see no 175) and Kensington Gardens; in 1892 he painted in and around Kew Gardens, and in 1897 he executed a few canvases in the fashionable 'aesthetic' suburb of Bedford Park (see no 176), where his son Lucien lived. In most of these paintings Pissarro focused on open urban spaces, treating them with the loosely structured compositions and casually disposed figures which characterised the Impressionists' treatment of such themes; yet, in contrast to his and Monet's earlier London canvases, his brushwork was much more fragmented: figures, foliage and buildings alike were treated in a small, fleck-like brushstroke in the paintings of 1890–2, which break the whole scene up into quite evenly weighted touches of colour, rather than itemising the distinct ingredients in the scene; his brushwork was generally broader in 1897, but still emphatic and broken. In these years, Pissarro himself lamented the difficulties of painting in London without having the time to select his sites and work on them over an extended period, and in 1894 he considered moving his base to London, although this project came to nothing. It was by his paintings of Rouen and Paris, not those of London, that Pissarro made his major contribution to the art of cityscape in the 1890s.[16]

By contrast, Monet's late views of London were the most ambitious sequence of urban views of his career. He worked in London for extended spells in 1899, 1900 and 1901, staying at the Savoy Hotel and painting from its fifth floor balcony and from a window in St Thomas's Hospital. He focused on only three subjects, two from the Savoy – one east over Waterloo Bridge (see nos 252, 253, 257), one south, past Charing Cross Bridge to the Houses of Parliament (fig 31) – and the third from St Thomas's Hospital looking across the river to the Houses of Parliament (see nos 154, 155, 156). He did not paint in London after 1901, but his London paintings were not ready for exhibition until 1904, after he had reworked and elaborated them extensively in his studio at Giverny. While he was in London, Monet multiplied canvases in an attempt to keep pace with the rapidly changing effects of light and atmosphere: 'At the Savoy Hotel, or at St Thomas's Hospital, from where I took my viewpoints, I had up to a hundred canvases on the go – for a single subject. By searching feverishly through these sketches I would choose one which was not too far away from what I could see; in spite of everything, I would change it completely. When I'd stopped work, shuffling through my canvases I would notice that I had overlooked precisely the one which would have suited me best and which was at my fingertips. Wasn't it stupid!' Thirty-seven London pictures were ready for exhibition in 1904, and he completed others later, but many

Fig. 31 Monet
Charing Cross Bridge
Oil on canvas, 25½ x 32 National
Museum of Wales

more remain unfinished, and he may well have destroyed others; around a hundred in all survive today, of the three subjects together.[17]

At the outset, each of Monet's canvases was a rapidly brushed notation of an atmospheric effect, but by 1900 he did not regard such rapidly sketched pictures as adequately finished. As he explained to a friend in 1890, he was 'more than ever disgusted at things that come easily, at the first attempt;' he said in 1892 that it was 'only a long continued effort that satisfied him, and it must be an important motif, one that is sufficiently absorbing'. And yet, the central subject in his art was, as he put it, ' "instantaneity", above all the enveloping atmosphere, the same light spread over everything.'[18] These seemingly conflicting concerns led to the paradox that Monet's canvases of nature's most fleeting atmospheric effects could only be finished after a prolonged period of reworking, and inevitably this generally took place in the studio, for the original effect rarely lasted for long enough, or returned often enough, for him to bring a painting to a satisfactory conclusion in front of its subject.

The resulting canvases were improvisations which took London's atmospherics as their starting point, rather than direct notations of observed effects. Much of the final effect of the finished paintings is achieved by delicate reworking, in quite thin layers of richly varied colour, across broader, dense layers of dry paint. The effect is of a sequence of fluctuating coloured screens, with the soft forms of bridges, buildings and boats looming out of the network of pastel coloured nuances which convey sky, air and water; these are punctuated by occasional gashes of light, where the sun, and its reflections in the river, break through the veils of mist. Details are almost entirely suppressed; in some of the Waterloo Bridge paintings, the bridge is busy with passing traffic, but this becomes just a pretext for a lavish display of coloured flecks of paint. In a sense, this is an archetypal image of the new, anonymous crowd, but it wholly lacks any dimension of social analysis: the crowd, like the fog and the sunbursts, is just one element in the optical spectacle which Monet recreated in these elaborate picture surfaces. Morever, Monet was prepared to manipulate observed reality in the interest of his effects. In all the finished versions of his Charing Cross Bridge subject, he omitted the crisp form of Cleopatra's Needle, which would have cut into the foreground space; it appears in two canvases that he left incomplete.[19]

It was in the rich colour schemes that Monet evolved after 1890, rather than his paintings of 1870-1, that the example of Turner became relevant. As he focused on the overriding unity which the enveloping atmosphere gives to nature, Monet came to appreciate Turner, not as a simple painter of nature, but as the architect of richly coloured ensembles which evoked the overall effects of light.[20] If Turner's lesson played little or no part in the initial development of the Impressionist vision of London, it came into its own in Monet's London series, which culminated this development.

Monet's and Pissarro's London paintings of 1870–1 actively explored the diversity and complexity of London and its inhabitants. Adopting an aesthetic and

XL Le Sidaner: *St Paul's from the River,*
Morning Sun in Winter
See catalogue no. 242

XLI De Nittis: *The National Gallery and
St-Martin-in-the-Fields*
See catalogue no. 220

XLII Lund: *The Heart of the Empire*
See catalogue no. 224

XLIII Sala: *Ludgate Circus*
See catalogue no. 223

XLIV Blanche: *Holborn*
See catalogue no. 225

XLV Derain: *Houses of Parliament by Night*
See catalogue no. 259

XLVI Derain: *The Thames and Tower Bridge*
See catalogue no. 261

XLVII Derain: *Waterloo Bridge*
See catalogue no. 258

96

social viewpoint which had evolved among Parisian artists, they viewed the public spaces of the city and its suburbs with a studied detachment, but remained alert to the different ways in which figures engaged with their surroundings. In his late series, Monet ignored the experiences of London's inhabitants, concentrating on atmospheric mood alone; like Whistler, he had come to believe that, in the final analysis, art was independent of the everyday experiences of living, and offered a release from their mundanities. This shift of emphasis, from the social to the aesthetic, represents a decisive change in the relationship between art and nature, and marks the emergence of what has come to be known as Modernism, in which the pictorial organisation of the painting, its two-dimensional qualities, are regarded as the prime criteria for its significance. And yet it was London itself – the almost tangible atmosphere of its legendary fogs – which permitted Monet to concentrate so exclusively on lavish pictorial surfaces. The fogs, which in the adventures of Sherlock Holmes veiled the crimes of the metropolis from all but the all-seeing eyes of the master detective, were for Monet a cloak which allowed him to distance the aesthetic from the social. Echoes of this vision of London remained far into the present century; it finally died when the Clean Air Acts removed the fogs which inspired it.

NOTES

1. For biographical details of Monet, see D. Wildenstein, *Monet, biographie et catalogue raisonné*, Lausanne and Paris, I, 1974; II and II, 1979; I 1985; for Pissarro, see in particular London, Hayward Gallery, *Pissarro*, exhibition catalogue, 1980–1; on their visits to London, see also London, Hayward Gallery, *The Impressionists in London*, exhibiton catalogue, 1973; J. House, 'New Material on Monet and Pissaro in London in 1870–71', *Burlington Magazine*, October 1978; M. Reid, 'Camille Pissarro: three paintings of London. What do they represent?', *Burlington Magazine*, April 1977, and 'The Pissarro family in the Norwood area of London 1870–1: where did they live?', in *Studies on Camille Pissarro*, ed. C. Lloyd, London 1986. For hopes of finding a market in London, see letter from Manet to Zola, summer 1868, in New York, Metropolitan Museum of Art, *Manet*, exhibition catalogue, 1983, p.521 (letter no.10); for Durand-Ruel, see also his reminiscences in L. Venturi, *Les Archives de l'impressionnisme*, Paris, 1939, II; since the publication of House 1978 (cited above), it has become clear that neither Monet nor Pissarro featured in the first hanging of Durand-Ruel's first exhibition in London, which opened on 10 December 1870, but both appeared in the rehanging of this show, which opened on 6 March 1871 (typescripts of the contents of both hangings are in the Archives Durand-Ruel).
2. *Art Journal*, January 1871, p.21; Mr and Mrs S.C. Hall, *The Book of the Thames*, 1859, pp.469–70.
3. H. Taine, *Notes sur l'Angleterre*, Paris, 1871, pp.241–2; Duranty, 'Aspects de Londres', *Revue libérale*, 10 May 1867, p.433.
4. Monet, quoted in R. Gimpel, *Journal d'un collectionneur*, Paris, 1963, pp.88, 156 (diary for 28 November 1918 and 1 February 1920); Gautier, 'Une Journée à Londres', *Revue des Deux-Mondes*, 15 April 1842, based on a visit to London in March 1842, quoted from *Zigzags*, Paris, 1845, pp.135, 159; *Mr. Whistler's "Ten O'Clock"*, 1888, p.15 (reprinted in *The Gentle Art of Making Enemies*, 1890).
5. For discussion of the problems about Monet's possible contacts with Whistler in 1870–1, see House 1978 (cited in note 1), pp.641–2.
6. For Ritchie's paintings, see London, The Fine Art Society, *Great Cities in the 19th Century*, exhibition catalogue, 1985, pp.30–1, 66–7; two characteristic examples of contemporary magazine illustrations of London park scenes are 'A Summer Afternoon in Kew Gardens', *Illustrated London News*, 27 August 1870, and 'Hyde Park in the Season', the *Graphic*, 6 August 1870; for the Duke of Wellington statue, see *The Impressionists in London* (cited in note 1), p.34.
7. 'Exhibition of French Pictures', *The Times*, 19 December 1870, p.4; 'Winter Exhibitions', *Saturday Review*, 10 December 1870, p.751; 'The Parisian Gallery, New Bond Street', *Saturday Review*, 29 April 1871, p.532.
8. Both letters quoted in *The Impressionists in London* (cited in note 1), p.14.

9. For discussion of the question of Turner's influence, see J. Gage, *Turner: Rain, Steam and Speed*, 1972, and J. House, *Monet: Nature into Art*, 1986, p.113.

10. For Durand-Ruel's purchases, see House 1978 (cited in note 1), p.638; since publication of this, access to Monet's account books has shown that Durand-Ruel bought one of Monet's port scenes in 1872, and Hecht the other in January 1873; for Hecht, see A. Distel, 'Albert Hecht, collectionneur (1842–1889)', *Bulletin de la Société de l'Histoire de l'Art français, 1981*, 1983.

11. Biographical details of Monet from Wildenstein 1974–85 (cited in note 1), who publishes Monet's letters to Duret, 9 December 1880 and 7 November 1887 (letter nos.203, 799), about his plans to work in London.

12. For discussion of this change in Impressionist brushwork, see House 1986 (cited in note 9), pp.79–85.

13. R. Williams, *The Country and the City*, 1973, especially pp.267ff.; for discussion of related changes in perception of the crowd in France, see S. Barrows, *Distorting Mirrors, Visions of the Crowd in Late Nineteenth Century France*, New Haven and London, 1981.

14. 'The Decay of Lying', first published in *Nineteenth Century*, January 1889, here quoted from revised version in *Intentions*, London 1891, p.40; 'Impression du matin', first published in *World*, 2 March 1881, 'Symphony in Yellow', *Centennial Magazine*, 5 February 1889, both reprinted in *Poems*, 1908. For further discussion of Whistler's vision of the Thames, and its influence, see Robin Spencer's essay in the present catalogue, and J. House, 'The Impressionist Vision of London', in *Victorian Artists and the City*, ed. I.B. Nadel and F.S. Schwarzbach, New York and Oxford, 1980.

15. 'The Decay of Lying' (cited in note 14), p.41; Vox, 'Talks by Three, V. – On the Victoria Embankment', *The Artist*, March 1899, p.166; Monet, quoted in E. Bullet, 'Macmonnies, the sculptor, working hard as a painter', *The Eagle* (Brooklyn), 8 September 1901.

16. For Pissarro's 1894 plans, see his letter to Lucien, 23 February 1894, in C. Pissarro, *Lettres à son fils Lucien*, Paris, 1950, p.335; on his visits to London, see *Pissarro* and *The Impressionists in London* (both cited in note 1); on his cityscapes of the 1890s, see K. Adler, 'Camille Pissarro: City and Country in the 1890s', in *Studies on Camille Pissarro*, ed. C. Lloyd, 1986.

17. Monet, quoted in Trévise, 'Le Pèlerinage de Giverny', *Revue de l'art ancien et moderne*, February 1927, p.126; for his series, and his letters from London, see Wildenstein 1985 (cited in note 1).

18. Letter from Monet to Geffroy, 7 October 1890, in Wildenstein 1979 (cited in note 1), letter no. 1076; Monet, quoted in the diary of Theodore Robinson, 3 June 1892 (MS Frick Art Reference Library, New York); for further discussion of these comments, see House 1986 (cited in note 9), pp.165, 220ff.

19. For the omission of Cleopatra's Needle, see House 1986, pp.59-61; for the brushwork and paint textures in his paintings of this period, see House 1986, pp.102–6.

20. See above, note 9.

CATALOGUE

The catalogue is divided into fifteen thematic sections, within which entries for individual works, and groups of entries for works by the same artist, are arranged chronologically. Sizes are given in inches, height before width. The place of publication for books is London unless otherwise indicated. Quotations are given in English; where no other translator is named, the translations are by the present author. The quotations that head the sections are from the following sources:

Samuel Sorbière, *Relation d'un voyage en Angleterre*, Paris, 1664, pp. 36-7
Isaac de Benserade, 'Sur l'embrasement de la ville de Londres', quoted from Georges Ascoli, *La Grande-Bretagne devant l'opinion française au XVIIe siècle*, Paris, 1930, vol. I, p. 141
Guy Miège, *The New State of England,* 1691, part I, p. 285
César de Saussure, *Lettres et Voyages*, ed. Berthold van Muyden, Lausanne, 1903, p. 169
Baron Pöllnitz, *The Memoirs of Charles-Lewis, Baron de Pöllnitz*, translated by Stephen Whatley, Dublin, 1738, vol. III, p. 263
Madame Du Bocage, 'Verses upon Ranelagh', *Letters concerning England, Holland and Italy*, 1770, vol. I, pp. 20-1
Heinrich Heine, *Autobiographie nach seinen Werken, Briefen und Gesprächen*, ed. Gustav Karpeles, Berlin, 1888, p. 209
Elisée Reclus, *Guide du voyageur à Londres et aux environs*, Paris, 1860, p. vii
Hippolyte Taine, *Taine's Notes on England*, translated by Edward Hyams, 1957, p. 8
Louis Blanc, *Letters on England*, translated by James Hutton, 1866, vol. I, p.111
Joris-Karl Huysmans, *Against Nature*, translated by Robert Baldick, 1959, pp. 133-4
Henry James, 'London', *English Hours*, 1905, p. 40
James McNeill Whistler, *Mr Whistler's "Ten O'Clock"*, 1888, p. 15
Octave Mirbeau, 'Claude Monet', *Vues de la Tamise à Londres*, exhibition catalogue, Galeries Durand-Ruel, Paris, 1904, p. 5
Letter from Derain to the President of the Royal Academy, quoted from Ronald Alley, *Tate Gallery Catalogues: Foreign Paintings, Drawings and Sculpture*, 1959, pp. 64-5

Only general works are listed. References to works of special relevance to the London views of individual artists will be found under their entries in the catalogue. The place of publication is London unless otherwise stated.

Bernard Adams, *London Illustrated 1604–1851. A survey and index of topographical books and their plates*, 1983

Arts Council of Great Britain (Hayward Gallery), *The Impressionists in London*, exhibition catalogue, 1973

Georges Ascoli, *La Grande-Bretagne devant l'opinion française au XVIIe siècle*, Paris, 1930

Frederick Crace, *A Catalogue of Maps, Plans and Views of London, Westminster and Southwark*, 1898

Department of the Environment (Somerset House), *London and The Thames. Paintings of Three Centuries*, exhibition catalogue, 1977

Mark Girouard, *Cities and People. A Social and Architectural History*, 1985

John Hayes, *London. A Pictorial History*, 1969

John Hayes, *Catalogue of the Oil Paintings in the London Museum, with an Introduction on Painters and the London Scene from the Fifteenth Century*, 1970

James Howgego, *Printed Maps of London circa 1553–1850*, 2nd edition, 1978

Ralph Hyde, *Printed Maps of Victorian London*, 1975

Michael Jacobs and Malcolm Warner, *The Phaidon Companion to Art and Artists in the British Isles*, Oxford, 1980

Andrew Lees, *Cities Perceived. Urban Society in European and American Thought, 1820–1940*, Manchester, 1985

Malcolm Letts, *As the Foreigner Saw Us*, 1935

J. G. Links, *Townscape Painting and Drawing*, 1972

Burton Pike, *The Image of the City in Modern Literature*, Princeton, 1981

David Piper, *Artists' London*, 1982

W. D. Robson-Scott, *German Travellers in England 1400–1800*, Oxford, 1953

Carl E. Schorske, 'The Idea of the City in European Thought: Voltaire to Spengler', *The Historian and the City*, ed. Oscar Handlin and John Burchard, 1966

Irene Scouloudi, *Panoramic Views of London 1600–1666, with some later adaptations: an annotated list*, 1953

Victorian Artists and the City. A Collection of Critical Essays, ed. Ira Bruce Nadel and F. S. Schwarzbach, New York, 1980

David Webb, *Guide Books to London before 1900: a History and Bibliography*, thesis submitted for Fellowship of the Library Association, 1974 (unpublished)

David Webb, 'For Inns a Hint, for Routes a Chart: The Nineteenth-century London Guidebook', *London Journal*, vol. 6, 1980, pp. 207–14

Francesca M. Wilson, *Strange Island. Britain through Foreign Eyes, 1395–1940*, 1953

Yale Center for British Art, *Gilded Scenes and Shining Prospects. Panoramic Views of British Towns 1575–1900*, exhibition catalogue, 1985

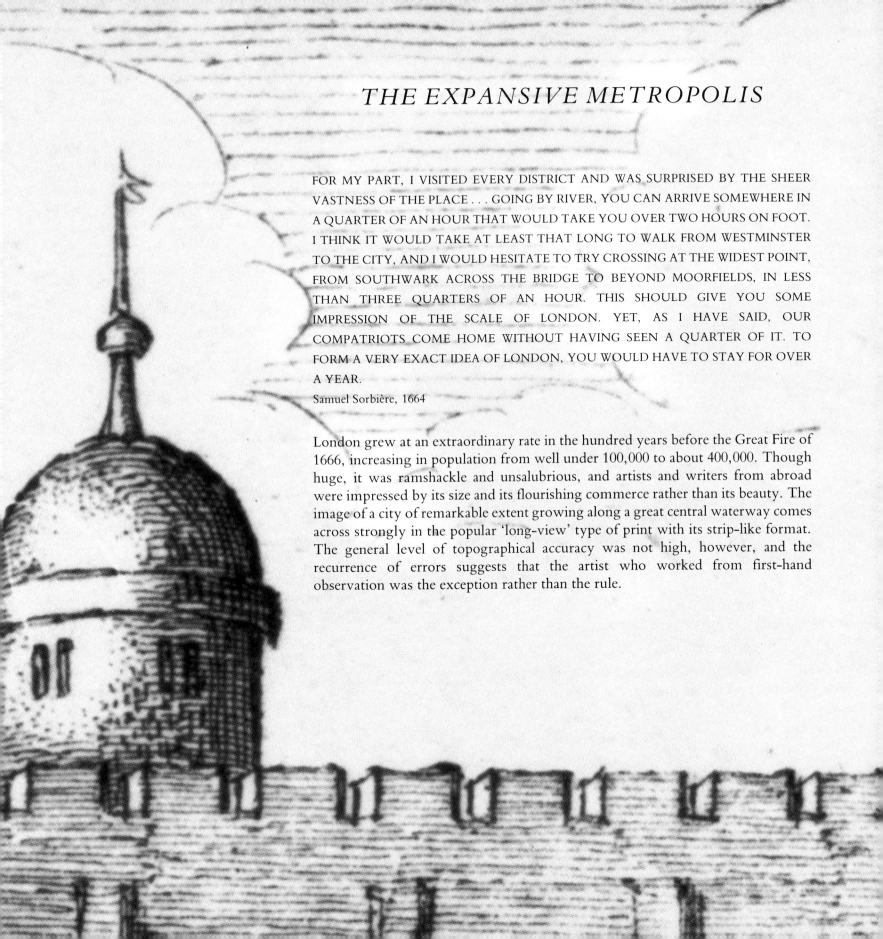

THE EXPANSIVE METROPOLIS

FOR MY PART, I VISITED EVERY DISTRICT AND WAS SURPRISED BY THE SHEER VASTNESS OF THE PLACE . . . GOING BY RIVER, YOU CAN ARRIVE SOMEWHERE IN A QUARTER OF AN HOUR THAT WOULD TAKE YOU OVER TWO HOURS ON FOOT. I THINK IT WOULD TAKE AT LEAST THAT LONG TO WALK FROM WESTMINSTER TO THE CITY, AND I WOULD HESITATE TO TRY CROSSING AT THE WIDEST POINT, FROM SOUTHWARK ACROSS THE BRIDGE TO BEYOND MOORFIELDS, IN LESS THAN THREE QUARTERS OF AN HOUR. THIS SHOULD GIVE YOU SOME IMPRESSION OF THE SCALE OF LONDON. YET, AS I HAVE SAID, OUR COMPATRIOTS COME HOME WITHOUT HAVING SEEN A QUARTER OF IT. TO FORM A VERY EXACT IDEA OF LONDON, YOU WOULD HAVE TO STAY FOR OVER A YEAR.

Samuel Sorbière, 1664

London grew at an extraordinary rate in the hundred years before the Great Fire of 1666, increasing in population from well under 100,000 to about 400,000. Though huge, it was ramshackle and unsalubrious, and artists and writers from abroad were impressed by its size and its flourishing commerce rather than its beauty. The image of a city of remarkable extent growing along a great central waterway comes across strongly in the popular 'long-view' type of print with its strip-like format. The general level of topographical accuracy was not high, however, and the recurrence of errors suggests that the artist who worked from first-hand observation was the exception rather than the rule.

ANTHONIS VAN DEN WYNGAERDE
Flemish, active about 1510-70

A topographical draughtsman and engraver, Wyngaerde seems to have been based in Antwerp but travelled and worked all over Europe. In England he made a series of drawings of royal palaces and may have been working to a particular commission. Towards the end of his career he was employed by Philip II of Spain.

1. London about 1550

Pen and sepia ink over black chalk, 9 ½ x 116
Lent by the Visitors of the Ashmolean Musem, Oxford

This is the upper row of seven sheets from a view of London from Westminster to Greenwich covering fourteen sheets, which are extensively annotated by the artist with the names of the principal buildings; the lower part of the view is far less full and detailed. The importance of the work lies less in its artistic merits than in the fact that it is the the earliest attempt to represent the city that has the flavour of direct observation; previous views are either highly stylised or mere ciphers. It is also the first of the wide bird's-eye-view panoramas or 'long-views' of London from the south and, as such, the forerunner of influential prints by Visscher and Hollar (q.v.).

FRANZ HOGENBERG
Flemish, before 1540 - about 1590

Hogenberg was born in Malines, and seems to have been in England for a period in the 1560s, but he spent most of his career in Cologne, where he engraved his most important work, the plates of the famous *Civitates orbis terrarum* (Cities of the World).

2. London 1572

Engraving, 12 ¾ x 19
Lent by the Guildhall Library

The model for innumerable books of engraved views of the cities of the world, the *Civitates orbis terrarum* was published in Cologne in five volumes from 1572 to 1598, with a sixth added in 1617. It was edited by Georg Braun and the

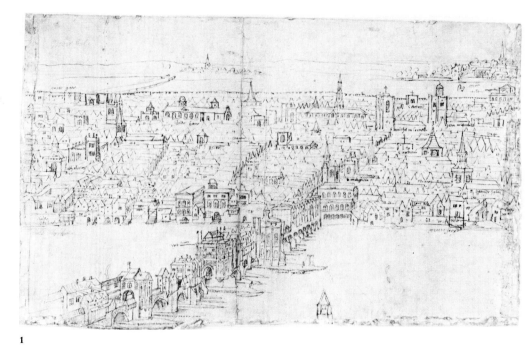

1

plates were engrad by Hogenberg, sometimes from existing plans and prospects, sometimes from drawings made specially by contributing artists, notably Joris Hoefnagel. The London plate, included near the beginning of the first volume, is one of the earliest reasonably reliable representations of the city and the first to be widely disseminated. The details of its authorship are unknown, although it is probably not after Hoefnagel – but the combination of map and bird's-eye view with elegant figures in the foreground is typical of the book as a whole. In the upper corners are the Tudor Royal Arms and the City Arms to indicate the presence in London of both royal and municipal authorities. Between them appears the title *LONDINUM FERACISSIMI ANGLIAE REGNI METROPOLIS* (London, Metropolis of the Most Fruitful Kingdom of England). The inscriptions in the lower corners, also in Latin, concern London in general and the Steelyard in particular. The Steelyard, near Dowgate, was the residence and headquarters of London's community of Hanseatic merchants and therefore of particular interest in Germany where Braun and Hogenberg's book was published. As so often in the early views, London is looked at from the commercial point of view, as a trading centre. The couple with a

pair of servants standing on the fictitious hilltop in the foreground are presumably intended to show English dress and to suggest the courtly sophistication of London society.

CLAES JANSZ. VISSCHER
Dutch, 1587-1652

The son of a ship's carpenter, Visscher became an etcher and one of the most important publishers of views and maps of his time. He lived and worked in Amsterdam, which was the centre for topographical printmaking for most of the seventeenth century. After his death the business was taken over by his son Nicolaes.

3. London 1616

Etching, 16 ¾ x 85 ¼
Signed 'C J Visscher Delineavit' (lower l.)
Lent by the Guildhall Library

Published in Amsterdam by Jodocus Hondius, no. 3 was the first major 'long-view' made abroad, and was copied as a source for other views throughout the rest of the century. It shows the city largely as it would have appeared about 1600 and was probably compiled by Visscher from existing topographical prints,

4

such as John Norden's, along with on-the-spot drawings by himself or another artist. The vantage point is similar to that of the Hogenberg print (no.2), i.e. somewhere in mid air over Southwark, although the position is much lower and the result unmistakably a view rather than a map. There was never a hill in Southwark that would provide such a view and Visscher's print, like many subsequent examples, is an ingenious piece of artifice simulating a god-like perspective. The best actual vantage point south of the river was the tower of St Mary Overy (Southwark Cathedral); although this is shown in the right foreground of Visscher's print, it was probably the place from which he or the artist on whose work he depended made his preparatory sketches. Like Hogenberg, Visscher wished to draw attention to the commercial importance of London, stressing the breadth of the great central thoroughfare of the Thames, filling it with a compendious array of shipping and heading his print with the Latin inscription *LONDINUM FLORENTISSIMA BRIT-ANNIAE URBS EMPORIUMQUE TOTO ORBE CELEBERRIMUM* (London, Most Flourishing City of Britain and Marketplace Celebrated throughout the World). (This is unfortunately missing from the example exhibited but can be seen on the derivative by Valeggio and Salmincio, no.6.) In the cartouches in the upper corners is a Latin eulogy of London by Ludovicus Hondius, perhaps the son of the publisher. From the trumpets of Fame blown by the angels hang banners bearing the Stuart Royal Arms on the left and the City Arms on the right, an idea that again echoes the Hogenberg view. Another pair of angels hold up a ribbon with the title *LONDON*.

About 1620 an amended version of no.3 appeared with Visscher's name then 'excudit' instead of 'delineavit', indicating that he himself rather than Hondius was the publisher. The most important new feature of this later print, which survives in only one copy at the Folger

Library, is that it introduces a fictitious sharp northward bend in the river just east of St Katherine's-by-the-Tower. It seems likely that whoever made the print was working from the 1616 view without reference the actual appearance of London and mistranslated the dock on the extreme right as the river's main course. Whatever the reason for it, the error was persistent, cropping up in the influential Merian view of 1638 (no.8) and countless derivatives.

CLAUDE DE JONGH
Dutch, about 1600 - 1663

De Jongh is recorded as a member of the Utrecht painters' guild in 1627 and mentioned periodically in Utrecht documents until his death, although he seems also to have worked in Haarlem. He was an occasional visitor to England, and his first wife Adriana Carpenter may well have been of English origin, but there is no evidence of his ever having settled.

4. London Bridge 1627

Pen and sepia ink and grey wash, 8 ¾ x 39
Dated 'London the 18 off / Aprill 1627' (lower r.)
Lent by the Guildhall Library

5. London Bridge 1650

Oil on panel, 16 ¾ x 39 ½
Signed and dated 'C de Jongh / 1650' (on building, lower l.)
Lent by a private collector

With its carefully judged tones and lines delicately rippled to convey atmosphere, no.4 is hardly a casual sketch. The artist may well have intended it as the basis for a painting or paintings from the outset; it certainly appears to have served as such, and the derived works span a considerable period of time. The earliest is the luminous and sparkling version of the scene by the light of early evening now in the Iveagh Bequest, Kenwood, which is dated 1630. Painted twenty years later, no.5 is more silvery, with the bridge shown against a morning sky with high, thin clouds, and some barges and a ferry creating pronounced silhouettes in the lower left part of the composition. It follows the drawing in showing the arches of the bridge as rounded and regular when in fact they were pointed and irregular; it includes a block of houses at the north end of the bridge that were destroyed by fire in 1632-3, and there is a general tendency to elongate the buildings to make them appear more elegant. A similar version also dated 1650 is in the collection of the Victoria and Albert Museum (see *London and the Thames*, exhibition catalogue, Somerset House, 1977, no. 1).

5

FRANCESCO VALEGGIO
Italian, born 1560
and
GIORGIO SALMINCIO
Italian, dates unknown

Valeggio was a painter, engraver and art dealer of Bologna. Nothing certain is known about Salmincio, although an Andrea Salmincio is said to have studied engraving under a Giovanni Valesio [sic] in Bologna, so perhaps the two men came from Bolognese artist families that were somehow related.

6. London 1629

Engraving, 17 ½ x 83
Signed 'Fran.co Valeggio f.' (lower l.)
Lent by the Guildhall Library

The view is a coarse adaptation of the Visscher view of 1616 (no.3), with even the ships on the Thames left more or less the same. The only significant differences are in the inscriptions: the cartouche in the upper left corner has been commandeered by the new authors for a dedication, and some of the names of buildings have been Italianised, as with 'la sala di Piombo' for Leadenhall. The work was published in Venice by Nicolò Misserini thirteen years after the appearance of Visscher's print in Amsterdam, and typifies the way out-of-date views were shamelessly recycled in this early period.

NICOLAS BRIOT
French, about 1579 - 1646

Briot held a post at the Paris Mint from 1606, made medals celebrating royal occasions for Louis XIII and became *Fermier Général* of all the French mints in 1617. After a scandal over corruption and mismanagement, he left for Britain in 1625, where he settled, working as an engraver at the Royal Mint in London and then from 1635 at the Scottish Mint in Edinburgh.

7. The Return of Charles I to London 1633

Medal, gold, 1 ⅝ diameter
Lent by the Trustees of the British Museum

No.7 commemorates the King's return from Edinburgh after his coronation. The obverse bears an equestrian portrait of him, the reverse a view of London. Within the limitations of the medal form, and those of Briot's technique, London takes on a naively stylised appearance, the buildings apart from London Bridge and St Paul's recalling a shanty-town. As usual, the view is taken from Southwark. It may have been based on one of the engravings of Visscher (q.v.), although there are differences in the skyline, and Briot's version of the Thames is too narrow to accommodate anything but small craft and the occasional swan. The sun, positioned impossibly in the northern sky, serves a symbolic function, representing the radiant influence of the monarch as it does in many French royal medals. The Latin inscription *SOL ORBEM REDIENS SIC REX ILLUMINAT URBEM* means 'as the sun illumines the world, the returning King illumines the city'.

MATTHAEUS MERIAN
Swiss, 1593-1650

After training as an engraver in Zurich, Merian worked for short periods in cities all over Europe before entering the print publishing firm of De Bry in Oppenheim, Germany, in 1617. He married De Bry's daughter and in 1619 returned to his native Basel to establish himself independently. In 1623 De Bry died and Merian took over his business, which by this time had moved to Frankfurt. There he ran one of the best-known and most prolific print publishers in Europe, specialising in views and illustrated topographical books. For a time he employed the young Wenceslaus Hollar (q.v.).

8. London 1638

Engraving, 8 ¼ x 27 ¼
From the *Neue Archontologia Cosmica*, edited by Johann Ludwig Gottfried, 1638
Lent by the British Library Board

The *Neue Archontologia Cosmica* is a collection of descriptions, with maps and views, of the countries and cities of the world. Merian derived his view of London from those already published by C. J. Visscher (q.v.), following the 'Visscher excudit' version of about 1620 in showing a pronounced northward bend in the river east of St Katherine's-by-the-Tower. The common recurrence of this error in early views is probably attributable more to Merian than to the 'Visscher excudit' print in which it first appeared. Merian's work was circulated more widely and much copied by the large number of topographical artists who, like Merian himself, would borrow from existing views rather than drawing their own at first hand.

8

7

WENCESLAUS HOLLAR
Bohemian, 1607–77

Born in Prague, where his father was Registrar to the Law Court, Hollar was by 1627 training as an etcher under Matthaeus Merian (q.v.) in Frankfurt. After periods in Stuttgart and Strasbourg, he settled in 1630 in Cologne. In 1636 the Earl of Arundel passed through Cologne on an embassy to the Emperor Rudolf II in Vienna and Hollar joined his suite. The following year he was in England working for Arundel, possibly with a studio in Arundel House, and in 1641 he married Margaret Tracy, a waiting woman in the same household. He made drawings and etchings after pictures in Arundel's spectacular art collection as well as etching portraits, topographical views and book illustrations. He also held a royal appointment as drawing master to the future Charles II. But the Civil War intervened. In 1642 Arundel left England as a Royalist refugee, never to return, and by the end of 1644 Hollar had moved to Antwerp. From the time of his return to London in 1652 until his death in 1677, he worked mainly as an illustrator for English publishers, notably John Ogilby, and for the rich antiquary Sir William Dugdale. In 1665 he married his second wife Honor Roberts, and in his later years he became friendly with the English landscape draughtsman Francis Place. According to John Aubrey, 'He was a very friendly good-natured man as could be, but Shiftlesse to the World, and dyed not rich.' For full topgraphical notes on Hollar's London works, see Arthur M. Hind, *Wenceslaus Hollar and his views of London and Windsor in the seventeenth century*, 1922.

9. The Thames from Westminster Pier, with Lambeth Palace in the distance 1638

Pen and ink and grey wash, over black chalk, 2½ x 5¼
Signed and dated 'WH: 1638' (upper r.)
Lent by a private collector

No. 9 is one of a number of Hollar drawings dated 1638 and showing views along the north bank of the Thames between Westminster and the City. Unlike many of the seventeenth-century artists who depicted London, Hollar worked from direct observation, and no.9 is typical of the sketches on which he based his etchings of London views.

9

10

10. Southwark looking towards Westminster about 1640

Pen and ink over pencil, 5 x 12
Lent by the Yale Center for British Art, New Haven (Paul Mellon Collection)

This and the matching drawing of the view over Southwark towards Greenwich, now also in the collection of the Yale Center for British Art, were probably the basis for the south bank of the river in Hollar's panoramic etching of London (no.19). The high vantage point from which they were made was the tower of the church of St Mary Overy. As he converted his drawings into the etching, Hollar made shifts of viewpoint in his imagination that re-orientated streets and buildings. The angle from which we see Winchester Palace in the lower right part of the drawing, for example, is adjusted in the etching so that we see more of the sides parallel, and less of those perpendicular, to the river; it is as if we were no longer seeing the building from St Mary Overy's but from a point in mid air to the west. The same principle of swivelling streets and buildings to show them more directly from the south is used throughout. The effect of the multiple viewpoint, which has been widely used in the making of panoramas, is to string out the scene to an impressive length at the expense of its depth. With the view of London from Southwark, the result is an emphasis upon the east-west extent of the city and especially its riverfronts.

11. London from Arundel House about 1640

Etching, 3½ x 5¼
Signed 'W. Hollar fecit' (lower l.)
Lent by the Guildhall Library

The view is from the roof of the riverside home of the artist's patron, the Earl of Arundel, where Hollar himself probably lived and worked during his first period in London. We are looking eastwards and St Paul's is visible in the distance.

12. Winter 1643

Etching, 9½ x 7¼
Signed and dated 'W. Hollar fecit 1643' (lower l.)
Lent by a private collector

13. Summer 1644

Etching, 9½ x 7
Signed and dated 'W: Hollar inv: et fecit, Londini 1644' (lower l.)
Lent by a private collector

Nos.12–13 are from a set of etchings on the theme of the seasons made by Hollar in 1643-4. Posed above and in front of their London backgrounds as if on stages, the women representing *Winter* and *Summer* are both personifications and London 'types'. Female dress was a favourite subject of Hollar's and the outfits the figures wear are his main means of conveying the characteristics of the two seasons. His rendering of different textures in terms of the etched line is a *tour-de-force* of tactile suggestiveness underscored in the case of *Winter* by the reference to 'furrs and Wild beasts haire' in the erotic verses beneath. The background to *Winter* is a view of Cornhill and the Royal Exchange, a place of business and the centre of the trade that brought luxuries such as furs into the country. If winter is for business then summer is for play, and the setting of no.13 is the pleasure ground of St James's Park.

12

14. The Royal Exchange 1644

Etching, 11½ x 15½
Signed and dated 'W. Hollar fecit Londini, Anno 1644' (lower r.)
Lent by the Guildhall Library

Hollar's image of London was essentially that of a bustling, thriving commercial centre and no.14 takes us into its inner sanctum like the view from the spectators' gallery in a modern stock exchange. We see the courtyard of the Exchange looking west, with trading in full swing. A couple of Russian merchants in exotic dress on the right bear witness to the cosmopolitan nature of the place, and statues of English kings preside over the scene from niches above. The accompanying verses by Henry Peacham, a minor writer connected with the Arundel household like Hollar himself, celebrate the fame of the Exchange, its magnificence, the luxuriousness of the goods traded there - scents, silks, pearls, sables, fine linen, jewels and clothes of gold - its superiority to the Amsterdam exchange upon which it was originally modelled, and even the good looks of the merchants.

15   16

13

14

17   18

15. The Royal Exchange about 1647

Etching, 5½ x 10
Signed 'W. Hollar fecit' (lower r.)
Lent by a private collector

16 Covent Garden about 1647

Etching, 5½ x 10
Signed 'W. Hollar fecit' (lower r.)
Lent by a private collector

17. The Tower of London about 1647

Etching, 5½ x 10
Lent by a private collector

18. St Mary Overy 1647

Etching, 5½ x 10
Signed and dated 'W. Hollar fecit: 1647' (lower r.)
Lent by a private collector

Nos.15-18 clearly form a group; no.18 is dated 1647 and the others were probably made about the same time. By 1647 Hollar had left England and been based in Antwerp for some three years but was still etching London views, presumably from drawings he had brought with him. The group is balanced in subject-matter, with a pair of open spaces used respectively for commercial and social purposes, and a pair of monuments, one royal and the other ecclesiastical. No.15 shows a different view of the Exchange from that of no.14, looking south instead of west and at a time outside business hours. It is early in the morning, some children are playing games and others are apparently being chased by a man with some kind of pointed staff, a schoolmaster perhaps. Sometimes dated the earliest of the group on stylistic grounds, no.16 is an afternoon scene in Covent Garden with people sauntering and taking the air, and more children at play. No.17 may have been based on Hollar's drawing of the Tower now in the British Museum, although the etching gives a closer view of the subject and includes fewer riverfront buildings on either side. In no.18 it is late afternoon or evening and people are making their way towards the south door of the church, presumably to attend a service. St Paul's is visible in the distance to the left. It was from the tower of St Mary Overy, which is now Southwark Cathedral, that Hollar made his large panoramic view of London (no.19).

19. London 1647

Etching, 18 x 92¼
Signed and dated 'Wenceslaus Hollar delineavit et fecit Londini et Antverpiae, 1647' (lower l.)
Lent by the Guildhall Library

Hollar pieced together his magnificent 'long-view' of London from drawings such as the view of Southwark looking westwards (no.10), which he must have taken to Antwerp with him when he left England. Unable to check details at first hand, he probably also consulted earlier

views, especially those of Visscher (q.v.). The Globe theatre is identified as The Hope and vice versa, and there are other minor errors of fact, but the work remains far more topographically reliable than any previous comprehensive view of the city. Despite the attempt of Merian to divert its course sharply to the north just beyond the Tower (see no.8), the river is allowed to follow its natural course. Hollar's achievement lies not merely in his accuracy, however, but in the sense of power and glory that he imparts to the scene. Here the river no longer cuts a neat horizontal path across the city as it does in the pedestrian views of Visscher and Merian; it sweeps through on a Baroque curve, gradually swelling to reach a climactic breadth in the centre then dying away again to the right. Hollar keeps one of Visscher's trumpeting angels to represent Fame but adds further allegorical figures of his own, particularly ones representing the idea of trade. The figure in the sky gesturing towards the cartouche inscribed *LONDON* is Mercury, the classical god of Commerce, and the groups of putti floating on clouds are identifiable by their attributes as symbolising (from left to right) Africa, Commerce, Asia and America. In the lower left corner sits Britannia with various royal, legal, scholarly, agricultural, commercial and military symbols, and in the lower right Father Thames with nautical symbols; they are accompanied by Latin eulogies on the present and past magnificence of London. Some of the place-names on the view, such as 'S. Pauwls', 'Boo Church' and 'S. Lorentz', are given in obviously non-native spellings. The print was published in Amsterdam by Cornelis Danckers and dedicated to Princess Mary of Orange.

20. Westminster 1647

Etching, 5½ x 12½
Signed and dated 'W. Hollar fecit, 1647' (lower r.)
Lent by a private collector

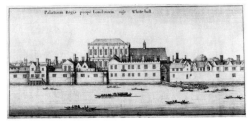

20   21

22   23

21. Lambeth Palace 1647

Etching, 5½ x 12½
Signed and dated 'W. Hollar fecit 1647' (lower l.)
Lent by a private collector

22. New Palace Yard 1647

Etching, 5½ x 12½
Signed and dated 'W. Hollar fecit 1647' (lower l.)
Lent by a private collector

23. Whitehall about 1647

Etching, 5½ x 12½
Lent by a private collector

19

A quartet of related views like nos. 15-18 above, nos.20-3 show sites in and near Westminster presented with the stately geometry that characterises Hollar's work. Three of the views are taken from the river and feature a certain amount of activity on piers to stress the importance of the Thames as a thoroughfare. No.22 is the odd one out in not being a river view but there is still an emphasis on traffic in the rows of coaches outside Westminster Hall.

24. London from Islington 1665

Etching, 3¼ x 4¾
Signed and dated 'W. Hollar delin: et sculp: 1665 (lower r.)
Lent by a private collector

25. London from Islington 1665

Etching, 3¼ x 4¾
Signed and dated 'W. Hollar delin: et sculp: 1665 (lower r.)
Lent by a private collector

Nos.24-5 are from a series of Hollar views in Islington around the Waterhouse that stood at the head of the New River, which was constructed to bring a water supply to London

24

25

from springs near Ware in Hertfordshire. They were made from points only a short distance apart and both feature the barn-like London Spa, a mineral spring and restaurant, in the middle distance; beyond is the London skyline dominated by St Paul's. The artist contrasts the raw earthworks and ditches in the foreground with the fine lines of the distant city as if to suggest the growth of civilisation from rough beginnings.

REMBRANDT VAN RIJN
Dutch, 1606-69

There is a reference in the notebooks of George Vertue to Rembrandt's having lived and worked for sixteen or eighteen months in the northern English town of Hull. But the provenance of the information is hardly auspicious, for Vertue was writing in 1713 on the basis of the recollections of the artist Marcellus Laroon, who was only sixteen when Rembrandt died. Attractive though the idea may be, Rembrandt is unlikely to have been in Hull or anywhere else in England. (The arguments for and against are fully discussed in Christopher White's article 'Did Rembrandt ever come to England ?', *Apollo*, vol. 76, May 1962, pp. 177-84.) He does, however, seem to have made at least four drawings of English places, one showing Windsor, another St Albans and the other two

26

London (nos.26-7); the Windsor and St Albans views are signed with Rembrandt's name and dated 1640, and there seems no strong reason to doubt the attribution of any of them.

26. London from the north about 1640

Pen and sepia ink and wash, 6½ x 12½; signed Rembrant' (lower r.)
Lent by the Staatliche Museen Preußischer Kulturbesitz (Kupferstichkabinett), Berlin

27. London from the north about 1640

Pen and sepia ink and wash, 6½ x 12½
Lent by the Graphische Sammlung Albertina, Vienna

If nos.26-7 were not drawn on the spot, they were presumably made from some existing London view to which the artist had access. The standard view of London prior to the Great Fire was from Southwark, however, and views from the north are rare. The print most likely to have served Rembrandt's purpose is the earliest of the engraved 'long-views', an anonymous work dating from about 1596 and showing London from a comparable position on the high ground towards Islington, which survives in a unique copy at the University of Utrecht (see Yale Center for British Art, *Gilded Scenes and Shining Prospects. Panoramic Views of British Towns 1575-1900*, exhibition catalogue, 1985, pp. 40-1). The other major possibility is that he

27

worked from an original drawing made on the spot by another artist. The view is unmistakably of London, though with some topographical quirks: the tower of old St Paul's in the centre is swivelled so that it rests diagonally on the main body of the building, and the Priory of St John of Jerusalem and the church of St Sepulchre's, immediately to the left and right respectively, are more recognisable by their positions than by their architecture. Christopher White has suggested that the Vienna drawing was made first on the grounds that it is the more elaborate of the two, and that the broader, atmospheric Berlin version is the more advanced stage in a process of refining the conjectured source. This may be true, but there is something to be said for placing the drawings the other way about. The details in the Vienna drawing are in fact fanciful enough to represent a stage further away from the source rather than closer to it; the Priory of St John of Jerusalem and the tower of St Sepulchre's show more varied contours than they ever possessed in reality, and an implausibly Dutch-looking well appears in the middle distance. Perhaps the artist made the Berlin drawing from the source first, then elaborated the composition along imaginary lines in the Vienna drawing, led by the taste that is evident throughout his work for the creation of fantastic architectural complexes. The order of Rembrandt's London drawings remains as much a matter for speculation as their genesis.

HUGUES PICART
French, 1587-1664

Little is known of this engraver beyond the fact that he was born in Châlons-sur-Marne, died in Paris and had a son, Nicolas, who followed the same profession.

28. London 1643

Engraving, 9 ½ x 31 ¼
Lent by the Guildhall Library

This 'Profil de la ville de Londre cappitalle du royaume d'Angleterre' was published by Jean Boisseau in Paris in 1643, but the view is borrowed from Visscher's of 1616 (no.3) with the addition of some strange spellings and gallicisms in the inscriptions.

ANONYMOUS
Probably Dutch

29. London from Southwark about 1650

Oil on panel, 23 ½ x 34 ½
Lent by the Trustees of the Chatsworth Settlement

30. London from Southwark about 1650

Oil on panel, 21 ¾ x 33 ¼
Lent by the London Borough of Tower Hamlets Libraries

Nos.29-30 differ in colour, the treatment of the sky and some minor points of detail; but the viewpoint, the disposition of the buildings and even the topographical errors are similar enough to suggest that one was copied from the other, or that they were both copied from an earlier original. They have much in common with the widely-disseminated Merian view of 1638 (no.8), including the misunderstanding of the course of the Thames east of the Tower, and it seems likely that the artist or artists worked from a copy of Merian's print, possibly without the benefit of direct observation. There is certainly an air of fantasy about the works, resulting mainly from a tendency to elongate and sharpen architectural features. Like an illustration from Pugin's *Contrasts* two centuries before its time, the vision is emphatically Gothic; both St Paul's and the church of St Mary Overy are made taller, and the city as a whole is given a dense, spiky appearance through the exaggeration of spires and pinnacles. Nos.29-30 have been attributed to both Claude de Jongh and Thomas Wyck (q.v.), though without any compelling reasons.
See Colour Plate I

28

PROFIL DE LA VILLE DE LONDRE CAPPITALLE DU ROYAVME DANGLETERRE

109

CORNELIS BOL
Flemish, 1589 - (?) 1666 or later

Bol trained and worked in Antwerp. He had connections with England by 1636, when he is recorded as a member of the Dutch Church in London, and he is said to have painted the Great Fire in 1666.

31. Lambeth Palace about 1650

Etching, 5 ¾ x 9 ¼
Signed 'C. bol fecit' (lower l.)
Lent by a private collector

This is from a series of river and harbour views etched by Bol after compositions by Abraham Casembrot and published by F. L. D. Ciartes. The inscription beneath no.31 reads 'A. Kaesembrot invent. Cornelius Bol fecit', but only Bol's signature appears in the plate. The work makes an interesting comparison with the roughly contemporary Hollar etchings of London views; by means of a lighter, discontinuous etched line, Bol achieves a greater sense of space and atmosphere.

31

32. The Thames and Somerset House about 1660

Oil on canvas, 25 x 43
Signed with the initials 'CB' and dated indecipherably (lower r.)
Lent by permission of the Governors of Dulwich College Picture Gallery

This airy panorama shows the view from mid-river looking upstream, from Old Somerset House in the right foreground as far as Lambeth Palace in the distance on the left; the skyline is punctuated (from left to right) by Westminster Hall, Westminster Abbey, the Banqueting House and the four turrets of Old Northumberland House. There is an almost identical view to no.32 in the collection of the family of the diarist John Evelyn, along with other Thames subjects by Bol featuring Arundel House and the Tower (see *The Age of Charles II*, exhibition catalogue, Royal Academy, 1960, nos. 214, 224, 230). No.32 is probably the earlier of the two versions, since it shows Somerset House before the remodelling of part of the river facade that took place around 1662 and which appears in the Evelyn picture.

32

33

PIETER HENDRICKSZ. SCHUT
Dutch, 1618 or 19 - after 1660

Schut was a pupil of C. J. Visscher (q.v.) and worked as an engraver for Visscher's publishing firm in Amsterdam.

33. London from Southwark, with huntsmen and dogs in the foreground about 1660

Engraving, 8 ¼ x 10 ¾
Signed 'P. H. Schut fecit' (lower centre)
Lent by the Guildhall Library

Schut follows the Hollar panorama of 1647 (no.19) fairly closely but with minor alterations to buildings and the addition of huntsmen and other figures on a fictitious hilltop in the foreground. He was clearly not working from direct observation, and may have assumed the existence of the hill because of the high viewpoint from which the Hollar is taken, which was in fact the tower of St Mary Overy. The publisher is given as C. J. Visscher's son Nicolaes, who took over the Visscher firm after his father's death in 1652. For a pyrotechnic version of the same view, see no.38 below.

THE GREAT FIRE

AS BURNED IN OLDEN TIMES THAT TROY OF FAME
THAT NEITHER KING NOR GOD DID E'ER OFFEND,
SO LONDON, STEM TO STERN, FALLS PREY TO FLAME,
AND SUFFERS, YET DESERVES, THE SELF-SAME END.

Isaac de Benserade, 1666

As news of the Great Fire spread, European writers and artists responded with various degrees of sympathy and censure. The destruction of a great city was a fascinating idea, suggesting a number of biblical and classical precedents, especially that of Troy. It seemed that a disaster of such magnitude could be no mere accident, and foreigners were almost as quick to ascribe it to divine vengeance as Londoners were to ascribe it to foreigners. In French eyes the British were being punished specifically for the crime of regicide, the execution of Charles I. The Dutch, who happened to be at war with Britain at the time, were pleased to blame the general wickedness of the city and its inhabitants.

WENCESLAUS HOLLAR
Bohemian, 1607-77

For a brief biography, see nos. 9-25 above.

34. Views of London before and after the Great Fire 1666

Etching, 8¾ x 26¼
Signed and dated 'Wenceslaus Hollar delin: et sculp. 1666' (lower r.)
Lent by the Guildhall Library

The print is divided in half horizontally, the upper part showing London 'in its flourishing condition before the Fire' and the lower half the same view 'as it appeareth now after the sad calamitie and destruction by fire'. Hollar probably derived his pre-Fire view from his own panorama of London published in 1647 (no.19), with a few variations and additions made from memory. The post-Fire view stands out as one of the few images of the disaster that ring true as eye-witness accounts.

FREDERICK DE WIT
Dutch, 1630-1706

De Wit was a prolific engraver and publisher based in Amsterdam.

35. London, with a view and a description of the Great Fire 1666

Engraved map, 22¼ x 21
Lent by the Guildhall Library

No.35 was as much an international news-sheet as a map, and includes a lengthy account of the Fire given in Dutch and French. The extent of the destruction is indicated on the map by a dotted line. Below is a weeping boatman, a London 'type' whose grief is used to suggest the grief of the city as a whole, and a vignette showing a well-dressed gentleman paying a man with a cart to transport his belongings to safety. The text refers critically to the large sums that changed hands in such transactions, and notes that various Dutchmen and Frenchmen in London were arrested on suspicion of arson but released after interrogation, 'everyone being already convinced that this fire was an act of divine vengeance, and that it would have been more rapidly extinguished had it not come directly from Heaven'. The inset illustration of London ablaze is a miniature version, with added flames, of the Hollar panorama of 1647 (no.19).

34

35

MARCUS WILLEMSZ. DOORNICK
Dutch, active around 1670

Doornick was another member of Amsterdam's large community of engravers and publishers of maps and views.

36. London, with a view and a description of the Great Fire 1666

Engraved map, tinted, 20 x 21¼
Lent by the Guildhall Library

Cast in much the same journalistic mould as no.35, Doornick's map is accompanied by a view derived from Merian's of 1638 (no.8) but with added flames, a plan for the rebuilding of the city on a grid pattern, and descriptions of the Fire in Dutch, French and English. In the lower right corner of the map we see refugees of

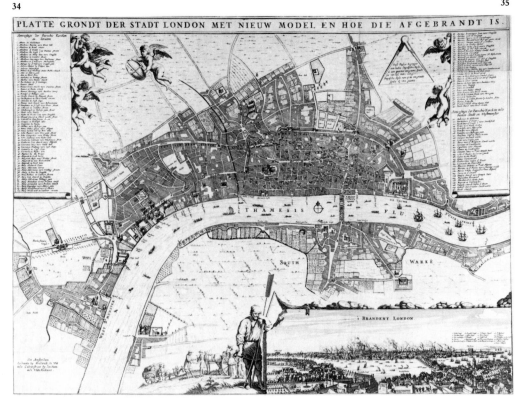

different classes, suggesting the idea that the Fire was no respecter of persons. No.36 is a good example of the dramatic effects that could be achieved by tinting. The use of yellow in the mostly dark inset view creates a vivid impression of flames lighting up the night. On the map, red is used for built-up areas and khaki for open spaces, whereas the area devastated by the Fire is left untinted as if to represent a blighted no-man's land.

ANONYMOUS
Probably Dutch

37. Sic Punit 1666

Medal, silver, 1⅜ diameter
Inscribed with the title (above) and *MDCLXVI* (below)
Lent by the Trustees of the British Museum

Sic Punit means 'Thus He Punishes'. A stylised version of London is consumed by flame on the left and bombarded by rain or hail on the right, perhaps a symbol of the plague that preceded the Fire. In the foreground a skeleton and a knight, both on horseback, clasp hands as if in greeting; they are two of the Four Horsemen of the Apocalypse representing Death and War (*Revelation* 6:4,8), the latter presumably alluding to the hostilities between Britain and the Netherlands that were taking place at the time. The Eye of Providence appears in the sky, accompanied by ominous comets. The scene is

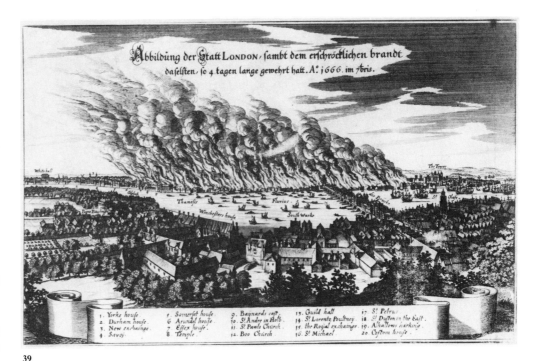

39

to be contrasted with the other side of the medal, inscribed *Mera Bonitas* (Pure Goodness) (for an illustration, see *Medallic Illustrations of the History of Great Britain and Ireland*, 1885, I, pp. 525-6). Against a heavenly landscape with a shrine and crucifix near a lake or river, flanked by a cornfield and a vineyard, St Paul is shown shaking a viper from his hand into a fire as described in *Acts* 28:1-6. The episode has normally been interpreted as symbolic of the purging of evil, and we are clearly meant to understand the Great Fire as God's way of purging the evils of London.

ANONYMOUS
Dutch

38. The Great Fire, with huntsmen and dogs in the foreground about 1666

Engraving, 8¼ x 10¾
Lent by the Guildhall Library

P. H. Schut's view of London (no.33), which was itself derived from the earlier view by Hollar, has been copied with flames added to meet the demand for views of the Fire. The publisher is identified in the lower right corner as Justus Danckerts; no engraver's name is

37

given, the 'P. H. Schut fecit' of no.33 having disappeared. Either because he lacked Schut's skill or because he was working in a hurry, Danckerts's engraver coarsens the original image. The handsome young man reclining on the right of the Schut view is transformed into a rough-featured yokel. With the major scene-change from peaceful vista to raging inferno, he and his equally relaxed companions become comically inappropriate; it is as if they were enjoying a fireworks display rather than witnessing a catastrophe. The unashamed adaptation of existing London views to represent the Fire was widespread and the original publisher of the Schut view, Nicolaes Visscher, himself brought out a version with added flames and a lengthy letterpress. For other examples of the practice, see nos.35-6, 39 and 44.

ANONYMOUS
German

39. The Great Fire about 1666

Engraving, 8½ x 13½
Lent by the Guildhall Library

Another view of the Fire contrived for the

40

occasion from the Hollar panorama of 1647 (no.19). The anonymous engraver has taken an obvious delight in the addition of particularly spectacular flames and dense clouds of smoke.

THOMAS WYCK
Dutch, about 1616 - 1677

The son of an artist, Wyck trained in Rome under Pieter van Laer and became a painter of classical harbour scenes and a variety of landscape and genre subjects. He was elected to the painters' guild of Haarlem in 1642. In about 1663 he came to London and seems to have stayed at least until 1674, although he died in Haarlem in 1677. His son Jan was also an artist, working in London and painting mainly portraits.

40. The Great Fire about 1666

Oil on canvas, 24½ x 36
Signed 'T Wyck' (lower r.)
Lent by the Duke of Beaufort

Wyck painted several views of the Fire. He may even have been in London at the time, but no.4 hardly has the qualities of an eye-witness account. London is shown as lying on a hillside crowned by a swivelled St Paul's. The high garden wall to the left is effective in making the foreground a shaded refuge that sets off the brilliance and violence of the flames in the distance; people are making their way along it towards the boats at the riverside to escape. Yet it would be more at home in one of Wyck's Italianate harbours than it is in seventeenth-century London. The burning debris in the river certainly heightens the drama, suggesting that even those taking to the river will not be free from danger, but it is hardly likely to have floated so far upstream from the blaze.

41. Old St Paul's in ruins about 1666

Pen and ink with grey wash, 5 x 7
Lent by the Guildhall Library

The view is from the north-east, and we see the remains of the south transept and parts of the nave and south nave aisle. Wyck stresses the grandeur of the building, even in its ruined state, by showing how it dwarfs the human figure and by representing his fellow observers in a sketchy manner that leaves them

41

INCENDIO DELLA GRAN CITTA DI LONDRA METROPOLI REGNO DINGHILTERRA SVCCESSO ADI 2 SETTEMBRE 1666 DAL QVALE IN 4 GIORNI FV ABBRVCCIATA LA PIV GRAN PARTE CON DANNO INESTIMABILE.

44

considerably less substantial than than the details of the architecture. The loving care with which these are delineated suggests an acute sense of loss.

JAN GRIFFIER THE ELDER
Dutch, about 1645 - 1718

This painter of landscapes, cityscapes and country house views seems to have come to England shortly after the Great Fire. He is said to have owned a yacht in which he lived with his family, sailing up and down the Thames from Windsor to Gravesend making preparatory sketches for his paintings of English views. He was once shipwrecked while attempting to sail over to Rotterdam and lost much of his stock of pictures. Griffier spent most of his career in England, enjoyed the patronage of the Duke of Beaufort, and died in London in 1718. He had two sons who also became artists, Robert and Jan 'the Younger' (q.v.).

42. The Great Fire about 1666

Oil on canvas, 35½ x 47¼
Lent by the Museum of London

No.42 was probably made by another artist after Griffier's original composition, the present whereabouts of which is unknown. It was clearly a popular work, and there are two further versions of different sizes in the same collection (see John Hayes, *Catalogue of the Oil Paintings in the London Museum*, 1970, pp. 94-6, 228-9). The work is topographically wayward, but the gateway on the left is probably meant to be Newgate. This stands out as a dramatic silhouette against the flames and, with its teeth-like portcullis, suggests the gaping mouth of hell.   *See Colour Plate II*

ANONYMOUS
Probably Dutch

43. The Great Fire about 1666

Oil on canvas, 31½ x 43¾
Lent by the Worshipful Company of Goldsmiths

No.43 recalls the work of the Dutch painter Egbert van der Poel, who specialised in conflagration subjects. It cannot be by Van der Poel himself since he died in 1664, but may well be by a pupil or follower. The view is from the east, with London Bridge on the left, St Paul's at the heart of the fire and the Tower on the right. A similar but larger and slightly more contrived composition in the Museum of London is probably by the same hand (see John Hayes, *Catalogue of the Oil Paintings in the London Museum*, 1970, pp. 78-80). In both works a fictitious wharf filled with refugees from the flames scrambling to load their belongings onto carts and boats is introduced in the foreground – a piece of artistic licence that increases the drama and helps bring home the human consequences of the spectacular blaze in the distance.
                        See Colour Plate III

ANONYMOUS
Italian

44. The Great Fire 1674

Engraving, 10½ x 35
Lent by the Guildhall Library

A plate from volume three of the *Historia di Leopoldo Cesare*, published in Vienna in 1674, no.44 represents a particularly naive example of the doctoring of an existing view to create an image of the Fire. It is taken from a now long-outdated source, the Visscher view of about 1620, and shows the conflagration extending far beyond its actual limits, all the way to Westminster in the west and well beyond the Tower in the east.

PHILIPPE-JACQUES DE LOUTHERBOURG
French, 1740-1812

The son of a miniature painter, De Loutherbourg trained in Paris and enjoyed early success after his first exhibit at the Salon in 1763 was praised by Diderot. But a marriage beset by infidelity and scandal prompted him eventually to move to London, and he was employed from 1771 to 1781 designing stage scenery for the Drury Lane Theatre. In 1774 he married his second wife, who was an Englishwoman, and lived in London for the rest of his life. In 1781 he was elected a Royal Academician and opened his 'Eidophusikon', a miniature theatre in which moving scenery evoked natural effects. After an abortive career change into medicines and faith-healing in 1788-9, he resumed painting, treating biblical and historical subjects with a particular speciality in scenes of battle and disaster.

45. The Great Fire of London about 1797

Oil on canvas, 23½ x 32
Lent by the Yale Center for British Art, New Haven (Paul Mellon Collection)

De Loutherbourg was one of the artists from whom the entrepreneur Robert Bowyer commissioned pictures of scenes from British history to be exhibited and then engraved as illustrations in his luxury edition of David Hume's *History of England*, published in 1806. No.45 is a much reduced replica (about one twelfth the size) of the vast canvas of the Great Fire that De Loutherbourg painted for Bowyer in 1797 (see *Philippe-Jacques de Loutherbourg*, exhibition catalogue Iveagh Bequest, Kenwood, 1973, no.66). It was very much his kind of subject - conflagrations were a regular attraction of the Eidophusikon - and he clearly relished the opportunities for spectacular lighting effects and life-and-death human dramas that it afforded. The action takes place under an arch of London Bridge, where distraught citizens desperately attempt to salvage some of their belongings from the blaze. Their histrionic gestures, the fancy-dress versions of seventeenth-century clothing that they wear, and the way they appear as actors in front of a set, all betray the artist's habit of working for the stage. The mixture of firelight and moonlight is also a typically theatrical effect.

45

LONDON RESTORED

IT IS A MATTER OF AMAZEMENT TO ME TO SEE HOW SOON THE ENGLISH RECOVERED THEMSELVES FROM SO GREAT A DESOLATION, AND A LOSS NOT TO BE COMPUTED. AT THREE YEARS END NEAR UPON TEN THOUSAND HOUSES WERE RAISED UP AGAIN FROM THEIR ASHES, WITH GREAT IMPROVEMENTS. AND BY THAT TIME THE FIT OF BUILDING GREW SO STRONG, THAT, BESIDES A FULL AND GLORIOUS RESTAURATION OF A CITY THAT A RAGING FIRE HAD LATELY BURIED IN ITS ASHES, THE SUBURBS HAVE BEEN INCREASED TO THAT DEGREE, THAT (TO SPEAK MODESTLY) AS MANY MORE HOUSES HAVE BEEN ADDED TO IT, WITH ALL THE ADVANTAGES THAT ABLE AND SKILFULL BUILDERS COULD INVENT, BOTH FOR CONVENIENCY AND BEAUTY.

Guy Miège, 1691

Many foreign observers were impressed by the rapidity with which London was rebuilt after the Fire, and the brand new look of the City, along with the development of the West End, created a boom in painted views, topographical illustrations and tourist literature. At long last, the ubiquitous panoramic view from Southwark began to go out of fashion as artists sought out more original vantage points from which to show the capital's extent and prosperity. The promise of political stability and artistic patronage after the Restoration of Charles II brought an influx of artists from the Low Countries, and they were to dominate the scene from the 1660s until the arrival of Canaletto in the 1740s.

JAN VORSTERMAN
Dutch, about 1643 - (?) 1699

After training in Utrecht, Vorsterman worked for a while in Paris, where he is said to have assumed a title and affected an aristocratic style of life. He moved to London in about 1675, painted country house views and occasionally received commissions from the King, but he ran into financial trouble and was eventually arrested for debt. In 1685 he set off with Sir William Soames's embassy to Constantinople; the embassy was abandoned when Soames died, and Vorsterman seems not to have returned to England. He was later in Poland, working under the patronage of the Marquis of Béthune, and is thought to have died there in 1699.

46. London from Greenwich Park about 1680

Oil on canvas, 30 x 64½
Lent by the National Maritime Museum, London

The view from One Tree Hill in Greenwich has been one of the most celebrated and most painted prospects of London, rivalled only by that from Hampstead Heath. Vorsterman's treatment of the Greenwich view shows Wren's newly-built Royal Observatory high up on the extreme left, Inigo Jones's Queen's House at the bottom of the hill, and the old Palace of Placentia behind, on the riverside site now occupied by the Royal Naval College. From there the meandering Thames, busy with shipping, leads the eye gently towards the city in the distance. The light of a glorious Baroque sunset touches the whole scene with pink, suffuses the clouds so that they look almost like brick dust, and creates a strangely intense chiaroscuro. All this is of conspicuously little interest to the group of courtly figures in the foreground, who concern themselves with their own affairs. The intriguing vignette of the man in conversation with three rather affronted-looking women has the air of a scene from a Restoration comedy.

Vorsterman and his followers produced several versions of this composition; further examples are in the collections of the Guildhall Art Gallery and the Yale Center for British Art.

See Colour Plate IV

ABRAHAM HONDIUS
Dutch, about 1630 - 1695

A native of Rotterdam, Hondius painted mainly sporting subjects. From 1659 to 1666 he lived and worked in Amsterdam, but by 1674 had moved to London, where he died in 1695.

47. Frost Fair on the Thames at Temple Stairs 1683-4

Oil on canvas, 26¾ x 44¾
Lent by the Museum of London

Because old London Bridge was a barrier that caused the Thames to flow more slowly than it does today, ice formed more readily during the winter and occasionally the river would freeze over. Londoners delighted in this novelty and ran continuous 'frost fairs' with tents, rows of market booths and even printing presses turning out personalised souvenirs of the occasion. It was clearly a fascinating sight for Hondius, and he painted frost fair subjects in 1676-7 and 1683-4; both are now in the collection of the Museum of London. Here a row of booths stretches across the river from the Old King's Barge-House to Temple Stairs on the far side. The scene is strange but jolly, and bustling with activity, with only an ominous hole in the ice in the right foreground to remind us of the potential danger of the whole enterprise. London is as cheerful when visited by ice as it was wretched when visited by fire.

See Colour Plate V

JOHANNES DE RAM
Dutch, about 1648 - before 1696

De Ram was an engraver and publisher of maps and views based in Amsterdam.

48. London, with a view and portraits of William and Mary about 1690

Engraved map, 19½ x 23
Lent by the Guildhall Library

As well as the portraits of the King and Queen, the map is decorated with putti, the City and royal arms, and a collection of emblematic objects. London's fame is represented by a trumpet, its defences by a cannon, its learning by books, its commerce by a caduceus (a wand

with intertwined snakes, the emblem of Mercury), its importance as a port by a globe and navigational instruments, and so on. The surveying instrument held by one of the putti is presumably meant to suggest the accuracy of De Ram's map. The rather vague view below is derived largely from that published about 1620 by Visscher (q.v.) but updated by the addition of Wren's St Paul's, the Monument and other landmarks of the new London.

EARLY TOURIST LITERATURE

Before the Fire, London was regarded as a place to visit for business rather than pleasure, and the number of publications devoted to its sights and amusements was tiny compared with those on Rome or Paris. With the rebuilding, and especially the completion of the new cathedral, London entered the architectural limelight, the number of visitors from abroad increased, and guides and travel books were published to meet their needs. Most took the form of observations written in a fairly leisurely style by a gentleman-traveller and illustrated with topographical engravings.

49. Henri Misson de Valbourg

Mémoires et observations faites par un voyageur en Angleterre 1698
Lent by the Guildhall Library

Misson de Valbourg's appreciative remarks on the scenery, national character, manners and customs of England were first published in French by Hendrik van Bulderen of the Hague; a Dutch translation appeared the following year and an English one in 1719. The illustrations are copied from those in Robert Morden and Philip Lea's *Prospects* of about 1687-92, many of which were themselves based on views by Hollar.

50. James Beeverell

Les Délices de la Grande Bretagne et de l'Irlande 1707
Lent by the Guildhall Library

London and the surrounding counties are the subject of the fourth of eight small volumes making up this early guide published by Pieter van der Aa in Leiden and dedicated to Queen Anne. The views of scenery and monuments were engraved from existing prints and illustrations in other works, notably Morden and Lea's *Prospects* (see no.49 above) and the first edition of the *Nouveau Théâtre de la Grande Bretagne* (see no.53). The way travellers would use such a book as a point of reference as they visited new places, comparing their impressions with those of the author, is demonstrated by the frequent mention of *Les Délices* in Zacharias Conrad von Uffenbach's account of his visit to London in 1710 (published as *London in 1710*, translated and edited by W. H. Quarrell and Margaret Mare, 1934).

51. The Foreigner's Guide (Le Guide des Etrangers) 1729

Lent by the British Library

An early example of the parallel-text guide, published in London by Joseph Pote. The text begins: 'London is the Metropolis of Great-Britain, the Seat of her Monarchs, the greatest, richest, most populous and most flourishing City in Europe.'

52. Alphonse de Serres de La Tour
Londres et ses environs, ou Guide des voyageurs, curieux et amateurs dans cette partie de l'Angleterre 1788

Lent by the British Library Board

The illustrations in this two-volume guide appear to be original but the identity of their author is unknown. They include a long fold-out view of Covent Garden with elegant figures; 'in the spring-time', the text asserts, 'this is the most pleasant sight it is possible to desire.' The work was published in Paris by Buisson.

LEENDERT KNYFF
Dutch, 1650-1721

Knyff came from a family of artists in Haarlem and came to England in the footsteps of his elder brother and fellow painter Jacob Knyff. He was in London by 1681 and stayed for the rest of his career, making only occasional visits to the Netherlands. He painted some still-lifes but specialised chiefly in country houses and parks seen from a bird's-eye view. He was also active as a picture dealer and auctioneer.

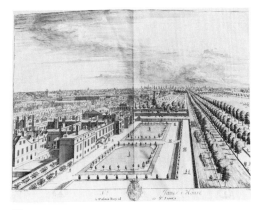

53

53. Nouveau Théâtre de la Grande Bretagne 1708

Lent by the Guildhall Library

The *Nouveau Théâtre* is a collection of engraved views of royal palaces and important country houses that was published in numerous editions from 1707 through to the middle of the eighteenth century. The first and several of the subsequent editions were published by David Mortier but others appeared under the imprint of Joseph Smith. The original work consisted entirely of views drawn by Knyff and engraved by Jan Kip (q.v.) but other artists appear in the later editions; the title was also changed occasionally to *Britannia Illustrata*. Though dating from the year after the first edition, no.53 was published by Mortier and is all the work of Knyff and Kip. The plates are double-page spreads and they include a grand vista over St James's Palace and Park towards the City, with the geometry of the French-style gardens dominating the foreground and a particularly uninformed version of St Paul's on the horizon.

54

JAN KIP
Dutch, 1653-1722

Kip was still in his native Amsterdam in 1685 but by 1697 had moved to London, where he lived for the rest of his life. A draughtsman, engraver and publisher, he is now best known for his collaboration with Leendert Knyff on the *Nouveau Théâtre de la Grande Bretagne* (no.53).

54. St James's Park from Buckingham House, with the City in the distance 1720

Engraving, 46 x 80¼
Lent by the Guildhall Library

Dedicated to the Princess of Wales, this exceptionally large and ambitious engraving was printed from twelve separate plates. In the foreground elegant ladies and gentlemen are enjoying an afternoon garden party, taking the air and playing pall-mall; orange sellers move amongst them, and on the right some milkmaids are offering refreshments straight from the cow. To the left, a couple of royal coaches are leaving the scene followed by a troop of cavalry. An emphatic linear perspective leads the eye upwards into the distance to St Paul's, establishing a central axis that symbolically connects the institutions of court and church, the authorities of earth and heaven. With the immaculately groomed park and the rectilinear streets of the West End to the fore, London appears as the very epitome of grace and order. All is well with the world, and even beggars have their place, although it is safely outside the park wall in the lower right corner of the composition.

55. Whitehall Palace 1724

Engraving, 15 x 22¾
Lent by the Guildhall Library

The view is southwards down Whitehall, with Old Horse Guards on the right, Holbein Gate in the centre and the Banqueting House on the left. It is 3.50 in the afternoon, exactly the same time as in no.54, and the street is full of courtly promenaders, vendors, soldiers on parade and guard duty, coaches, sedan chairs and booksellers' stalls.

PETER TILLEMANS
Flemish, 1684-1734

Tillemans was brought over to England from his native Antwerp in 1708 by a picture dealer named Turner. He stayed, and made his living largely as a painter of country house views and sporting subjects; he also worked occasionally for the theatre. From 1714 he enjoyed the patronage of Dr Cox Macro of Little Haugh Hall, near Bury St Edmund's, who bought pictures from him and commissioned painted decorations for his house.

56. London from Greenwich Park about 1718

Oil on canvas, 23 x 47
Lent by the Governor and Company of the Bank of England

Tillemans presents a similar view to that of Vorsterman in no.46 but from a point a little further west. With St Paul's dominating the London skyline, the Royal Observatory at the highest point on the left and the as yet unfinished Royal Naval Hospital brightly illuminated in the middle distance, the scene could hardly be a more complete tribute to Wren. It is early evening and there is a sunset glow in the western sky. On the hill Tillemans brings together a collection of figures suggesting the purposes of exercise and pleasure for which the park is used: a pair of maids in attendance on some children and a dog, a few riders, a red-coated huntsman in the foreground, some people in conversation, one of them lying on the grass, and a man on the left helping to pull his companion up the slope as she hangs on to his shoulder. A number of versions of the composition exist and it was published as an engraving, with the view updated to show the Royal Naval Hospital completed, in 1744 (see Robert Raines, 'Peter Tillemans, Life and Work, with a list of representative paintings', *Walpole Society*, vol. XLVII, 1980, p. 53).   *See Colour Plate VI*

MARCUS ABRAHAM RUPPRECHT
German, dates unknown

There was a family of artists of this name in the eighteenth century, but the identity of Marcus Abraham Rupprecht is obscure.

LONDINUM LONDEN

57

57. London from Southwark, with a coach and riders in the foreground about 1720

Engraving, 11 x 24½
Lent by the Guildhall Library

The city is seen from the time-honoured viewpoint on imaginary high ground behind St Mary Overy. Rupprecht has drawn upon previous London views by Visscher, Hollar and Kip (q.v.) but brought to them a naivety of technique and perspective that is his own; his work has a charming stylisation reminiscent of a child's picture-book. Presumably to stress its grandeur and importance, the dome of St Paul's is seen from slightly below although everything around it is seen from above. The multiplicity of City churches is stressed, and they are all identified in a key given below in Latin and German. The print was published by J. Christoph Haffner.

GUILLAUME DANET
French, dates unknown

58. London, with views of the Monument and St Mary-le-Bow 1727

Engraved map, tinted, 17½ x 24
Lent by the Guildhall Library

The choice of buildings illustrated in the corner vignettes emphasises the new, post-Fire London. Names are given in French, as with 'Rue de la Flotte' for Fleet Street.

JAN GRIFFIER THE YOUNGER
Dutch, about 1690 - about 1750

The son of Jan Griffier the Elder (q.v.) seems to have lived in London throughout his career. He painted cityscapes and decorative landscapes featuring various species of birds.

59. Frost Fair on the Thames 1739

Oil on canvas, 18½ x 25½
Signed and dated 'Jn. Griffier f. 1739' (lower l.)
Lent by the Guildhall Art Gallery

The Thames was frozen above London Bridge from Christmas Day 1739 to 1st February 1740; tents and booths were erected and a 'frost fair' was held on the ice like the one depicted by Abraham Hondius some fifty years before (see no.47). Griffier shows the scene more or less as it would have appeared from an upper window of Montagu House, which may well have been his vantage point. To the left a path across the ice stretches from Whitehall Stairs to Lambeth Marsh. On the right, sightseers take the opportunity to examine the newly-built central piers of the future Westminster Bridge, making this the first appearance in art of one of the most frequently painted London landmarks of the eighteenth century. Griffier gives the whole city a frosty appearance, delighting in the strangely cloud-like ice formations and painting his figures with the dainty touch of a miniaturist.
          See Colour Plate VIII

THE MARKET PLACE

THERE ARE COFFEE-HOUSES THAT SERVE AS MEETING-PLACES FOR LEARNED
MEN AND WITS; SOME THAT ARE FREQUENTED BY THE DANDIES; OTHERS THAT
ARE THE HAUNTS OF PROFESSIONAL NEWSMONGERS AND POLITICAL
COMMENTATORS; AND MANY THAT ARE TEMPLES OF VENUS. YOU CAN EASILY
RECOGNISE THESE LAST BECAUSE THEY SOMETIMES HAVE SIGNBOARDS WITH A
WOMAN'S ARM OR HAND HOLDING A COFFEE-POT. THERE ARE PLENTY OF
ESTABLISHMENTS OF THE KIND IN THE COVENT GARDEN AREA THAT PASS AS
CHOCOLATE HOUSES, WHERE YOU ARE SERVED BY BEAUTIFUL NYMPHS, VERY
CLEAN AND NEAT, WHO SEEM MOST FRIENDLY BUT ARE EXCEEDINGLY
DANGEROUS.

César de Saussure, 1726

There was no better place in London for admiring and meeting members of the
opposite sex than the markets, which brought together a heady mixture of
different classes of people, from fine ladies and their maids to vegetable sellers and
prostitutes, from strapping porters to suave gallants. Covent Garden had a
particularly bawdy reputation. It was also an artists' quarter, and for a number of
painters of the period a favourite source of subject-matter. They portray it
affectionately as a place for trading in amorous conversation and looks as well as
flowers, fruit and vegetables. Far in spirit from the convent garden that gave the
area its name, the market becomes an urban Garden of Love.

PETER ANGILLIS
Flemish, 1685-1734

Angillis was born in Dunkirk, settled for a time in Antwerp, moved to London about 1719 and stayed till 1727. He made a speciality of market scenes painted in a style that recalls David Teniers, and lived in the Covent Garden area. After leaving London he worked in Italy and in Rennes, where he died in 1734.

60. Covent Garden Market about 1726

Oil on copper, 18¾ x 24¾
Lent by the Yale Center for British Art, New Haven (Paul Mellon Collection)

All human life, according to Angillis, is to be found in Covent Garden. His crowds of charming, doll-like figures, from children to aged crones, from fine ladies and gentlemen to 'types', low-life and otherwise, give the place a cheerful holiday atmosphere. At centre stage in the foreground a gallant provides the picture with the love interest that was usual with this kind of subject as he approaches a couple of attractive women. Further back on the left, some baskets are toppling from the large pile carried by a market porter on his head, causing some consternation to those standing near by. Curiously for an artist so familiar with his subject, Angillis shows the light falling impossibly from the north. Another version of this composition, now in a private collection, is signed and dated 1726.   *See Colour Plate IX*

61. Vegetable Seller in Covent Garden about 1726

Oil on panel, 13½ x 10½
Lent by the Yale Center for British Art, New Haven (Paul Mellon Collection)

Everyone knew that Covent Garden was not just a market for flowers, fruit and vegetables, and the possibility gently implied by this work is that the lower-class beauty with the open features and low neckline is as available as the leeks, cabbages, turnips and carrots at her feet. Her gesture and the fact that she is looking straight out at us put us in the enviable position of someone engaged in conversation with her. In the background is the church of St Paul's Covent Garden.

61

JOSEF VAN AKEN
Flemish, 1709-49

Van Aken spent most of his career in London He painted conversation pieces and market scenes, but made his living largely as a 'drapery painter', adding the clothing in portraits by other artists.

62. The Old Stocks Market about 1730

Oil on canvas, 39½ x 49¼
Lent by the Governor and Company of the Bank of England

The Old Stocks Market was a fruit and flower market held on the site of the present Mansion House. It took its name from some stocks used for the punishment of minor criminals. Van Aken shows the view looking south, with the dome of St Stephen Walbrook prominent in the background. The equestrian statue to the left of centre originally represented John Sobieski trampling upon a Turk but had been

62

transformed into Charles II trampling upon Oliver Cromwell; it was removed in 1738 when preparations for the building of the Mansion House were begun. The setting is stage-like and the poses and gestures of the figures are almost balletic in their refinement, as if this were a scene from a comic opera rather than real life. The impression is enhanced by the curious inclusion of a Turk as one of the central characters, perhaps as a witty allusion to the original meaning of the statue and almost certainly in a spirit of bawdy fun, the Turk being a stock figure of comic lasciviousness. Beneath the statue a young man puts an amorous arm around the shoulders of a maid.

See Colour Plate VII

63. Covent Garden Market about 1730

Oil on canvas, 38 x 40
Lent by the Museum of London

No.63 is one of several versions of this view by Van Aken. We are looking eastwards across the Piazza, with the side of St Paul's Covent Garden on our left and the notorious Tom King's coffee-house in the shed on our right. The row of sheds along the centre were a fairly recent addition, erected about 1726. The willowy, elongated figures and the evident concern with the details of their dress are typical of the artist.

See Colour Plate XIX

JOHANN BAPTISTA HOMANN AND HEIRS
German
Homann was an engraver and publisher whose important mapmaking firm in Nuremberg continued under his name for some time after his death in 1724.

64. London, with a view and vignettes of Whitehall and the Royal Exchange about 1730

Engraved map, tinted, 19 x 22¾
Lent by the Guildhall Library

The engraver of the view below the map seems to have worked from the Merian view of 1638 (no.8); the north bank has been re-drawn to bring it up to date, with a naive version of St Paul's, but the south bank is full of anachronisms. Some of the names are given in a form that catered to the German audience, including 'Weest Münster' and 'Der Thems Flus'.

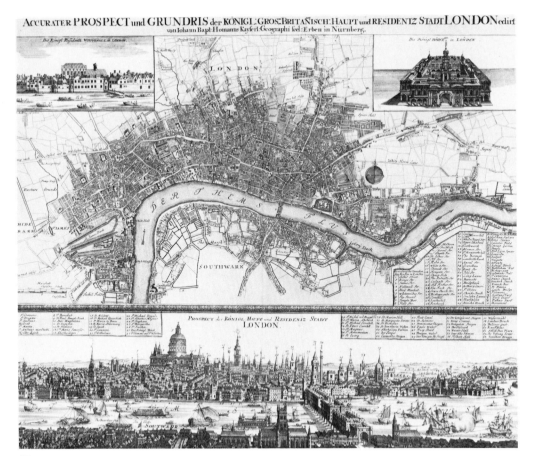

64

65. London, with views of St Paul's, St James's Square, the Custom House and the Royal Exchange about 1736

Engraved map, tinted, 19¾ x 66¼
Lent by the British Library (Map Library)

This unusually large map is accompanied not only by views of London landmarks but also by a table of German equivalents to English terms such as 'street' and 'church', and some advice on coaches and fares.

BALTHASAR NEBOT
Spanish, active about 1740

Little is known of Nebot's life. Although he is said to have been Spanish, his work looks Flemish and some of his Covent Garden scenes are virtually identical to works by Angillis (q.v.). He tackled country house views as well as genre subjects, and in 1738 painted a

remarkable series of garden scenes at Hartwell House, near Aylesbury.

66. Covent Garden Market about 1737

Oil on canvas, 31 x 48
Lent by the Guildhall Art Gallery

The view is similar to that in Angillis's Covent Garden scene (no.60), but from a point further back and a little to the north. Like Angillis, Nebot presents the market as a gathering place for all types and classes, contrasting high and low life in the well-dressed family group being approached by an old beggar whose dog is cocking its leg against the fence. With its wide open space, display of country produce and potted shrubs, the Piazza serves not only as a market but also as a kind of pleasure ground, and in the background we see some prize fighters and a children's entertainer. There is another version of no.66, signed and dated 1737, in the Tate Gallery.

See Colour Plate X

66

67

LOUIS-PHILIPPE BOITARD
French, active about 1750

Boitard's father also worked as an artist in London, and was also called Louis-Philippe. The lives and works of the two men are impossibly confused, but it seems to have been Boitard junior who made satirical prints such as no.67.

67. The Covent Garden Morning Frolick
1747

Engraving, 8¼ x 12¼
Lent by the Guildhall Library

It is 4.55 a.m. and some drunken all-night revellers frolic among the market people. The inscription *Sic Transit Gloria Mundi* (So passes the glory of the world) under the clock of St Paul's is ironic in view of the distinctly unglorious company passing in front. In the centre a man sits on top of a sedan chair waving a broken walking-stick. His lady friend inside the chair is fast asleep, in spite of the fact that the windows have been broken on three sides. The market people display a variety of reactions to the behaviour of their 'betters', from amusement to contempt, from wonder to resentment. They include vegetable sellers and London street types such as the sedan chair porters, a link-boy, a hurdy-gurdy player, a crossing-sweeper and a watchman. This last has been bashed on the head by a reveller but, as the money in his hat reveals, handsomely bribed to keep quiet. In the lower right corner a vegetable seller holds her hands up in a pose borrowed from that of Dionysius in the same position in Raphael's tapestry cartoon of *St Paul Preaching at Athens*, another touch of irony which invites us to make comic comparisons between Covent Garden and the Areopagus, between the market people and Greek philosophers, between the reveller on the sedan chair and St Paul. The modern moral message, wit and ingenuity of the print are unmistakably Hogarthian, and the idea of contrasting Covent Garden workers and upper-class revellers is borrowed specifically from the *Morning* scene of Hogarth's *Times of Day* series, published in 1738.

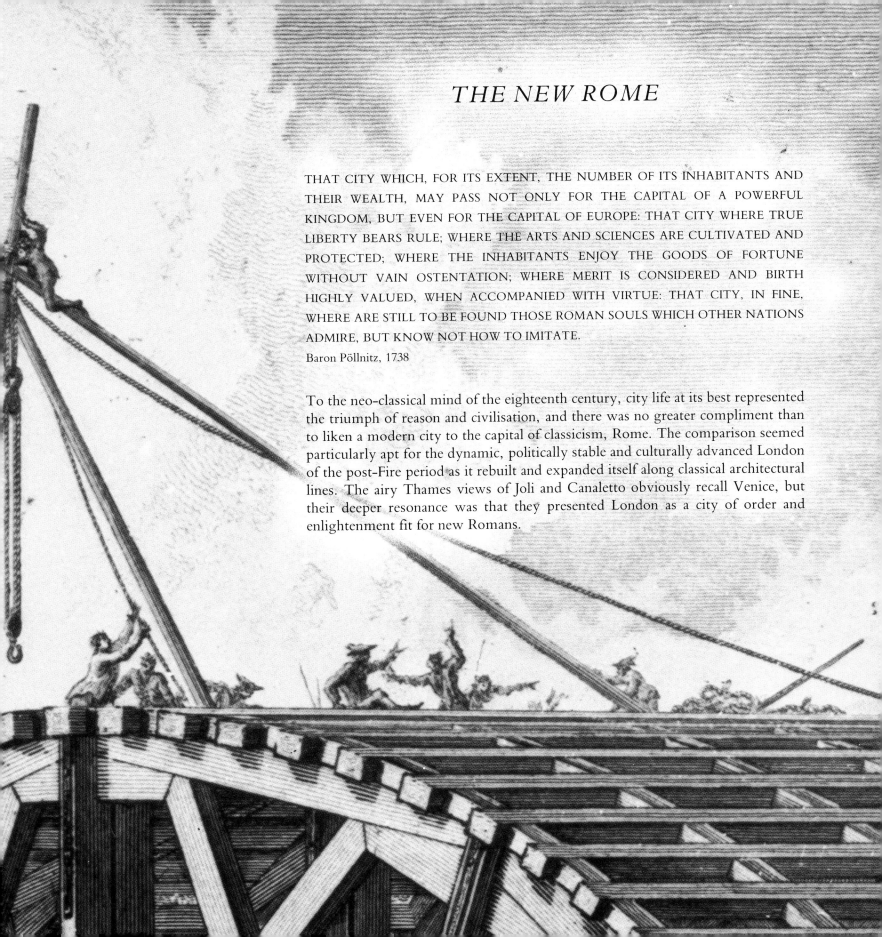

THE NEW ROME

THAT CITY WHICH, FOR ITS EXTENT, THE NUMBER OF ITS INHABITANTS AND
THEIR WEALTH, MAY PASS NOT ONLY FOR THE CAPITAL OF A POWERFUL
KINGDOM, BUT EVEN FOR THE CAPITAL OF EUROPE: THAT CITY WHERE TRUE
LIBERTY BEARS RULE; WHERE THE ARTS AND SCIENCES ARE CULTIVATED AND
PROTECTED; WHERE THE INHABITANTS ENJOY THE GOODS OF FORTUNE
WITHOUT VAIN OSTENTATION; WHERE MERIT IS CONSIDERED AND BIRTH
HIGHLY VALUED, WHEN ACCOMPANIED WITH VIRTUE: THAT CITY, IN FINE,
WHERE ARE STILL TO BE FOUND THOSE ROMAN SOULS WHICH OTHER NATIONS
ADMIRE, BUT KNOW NOT HOW TO IMITATE.

Baron Pöllnitz, 1738

To the neo-classical mind of the eighteenth century, city life at its best represented
the triumph of reason and civilisation, and there was no greater compliment than
to liken a modern city to the capital of classicism, Rome. The comparison seemed
particularly apt for the dynamic, politically stable and culturally advanced London
of the post-Fire period as it rebuilt and expanded itself along classical architectural
lines. The airy Thames views of Joli and Canaletto obviously recall Venice, but
their deeper resonance was that they presented London as a city of order and
enlightenment fit for new Romans.

ANTONIO JOLI
Italian, about 1700 - 1777

Trained as a decorative and theatrical painter, Joli had settled in Venice by 1735, where he worked for the stage and painted views of the city under the influence of Canaletto. In 1742 he left Venice, spent some time in Dresden, then came to London. From 1744 to 1748 he was scene-painter and possibly assistant manager at the King's Theatre, Haymarket, meanwhile painting *capricci* and various views on the Thames from the City to Richmond. He probably knew Canaletto, and the two men certainly had a common patron in the Duke of Richmond. By 1750 Joli was in Madrid working as scene-painter to the Court. He returned to Venice in 1754 and became a member of the Venetian Academy the following year. From 1762 he lived in Naples, where he again worked for the Court theatre, painted views and enjoyed the patronage of Sir William Hamilton.

68. Capriccio with a view of the Thames and St Paul's about 1746

Oil on canvas, 42 x 47
Lent by the Metropolitan Museum of Art, New York (Bequest of Alice Bradford Woolsey)

Courtly figures take the air along a fantastical promenade roughly in the position of the as yet undreamt-of Waterloo Bridge. The view in the background runs from the terrace of Somerset House on the left to the tower of St Mary Overy on the right. The foreground architecture is a skeletal version of the domed crossing in a Renaissance or Baroque church, yet flanked by Roman sculptures in niches as if it were in fact meant to recall an ancient interior such as that of the Roman Baths. The chipped state of the masonry and the apparent reactions of the sculpted figures on their broken columns, admiring on the left and up-in-arms on the right, are surely intended to prompt flattering comparisons between ancient Rome and London as its modern equivalent. We are looking at London from the Romans' point of view, at least that of the pair of Romans in the niches. They may have built the first London, as an outpost of the Empire, but it has risen up as a city of classical civilisation and architecture to rival and even surpass their own.

See Colour Plate XVI

69. The Thames looking towards the City about 1746

Oil on canvas, 43 x 68
Lent by the National Westminster Bank plc
See Colour Plate XVII

70. The Thames looking towards Westminster about 1746

Oil on canvas, 43 x 68
Lent by the National Westminster Bank plc

Nos.69-70 were clearly painted as pendants, like Canaletto's similar but probably later pair of views from the terrace of Somerset House (nos.71-2). No.69 may also show the view from Somerset House, though from a higher part of the terrace, but the viewpoint in no.70 seems to be some way upriver, closer to Westminster and possibly on the south bank. The focal points of the works, emphasised by the light in each case, are the chief wonders of modern London, the new Cathedral and the brand new bridge. London is presented as a city of clean lines and clear atmosphere, proud, prosperous and patriotic; there are Union Jacks flying in both works, from St Mary Overy in no.69 and St Margaret's Westminster in no.70. The influence of Canaletto is obvious, although we should remember that Joli was painting such London views some time before Canaletto arrived on the scene, and also that he was no mere imitator; his manner is distinctively earthier, stiffer, harder-edged, more shadowy and less glittering than that of his celebrated compatriot.

See Colour Plate XVIII

CANALETTO (GIOVANNI ANTONIO CANAL)
Italian, 1697-1768

Canaletto seems to have come to England because the demand for his famous views of Venice had declined as fewer Grand Tourists visited Venice following the War of Austrian Succession. He arrived late in May 1746 and stayed until 1755 or 1756, except for a couple of visits home of a few months each. His main English patron in Venice, Joseph Smith, wrote to the dealer Owen McSwiney asking him to introduce Canaletto to the Duke of Richmond, who already owned examples of his Venetian work. McSwiney complied, with the result that

his earliest and some of his best London paintings are views from Richmond House commissioned by the Duke. He also received commissions from the Earl (later Duke) of Northumberland, the Duke of Buccleuch and other noblemen, painting a total of about forty London pictures. His artistic achievement in London was considerable, and he influenced generations of townscape painters working in this country, both British and foreign. Yet professionally his stay was a disappointment. He was never to regain the popularity he had enjoyed in the 1730s and he died a poor man.

71. The Thames from the terrace of Somerset House, the City in the distance 1746-51

Oil on canvas, 41½ x 73½
Lent by Her Majesty Queen Elizabeth II
See Colour Plate XI

72. The Thames from the terrace of Somerset House, Westminster in the distance 1746-51

Oil on canvas, 42 x 73
Lent by Her Majesty Queen Elizabeth II

The views of Canaletto represent the neo-classical image of London in its canonical form. The sunlight that defines and models the city's topography suggests an ideal clarity of vision and understanding, a state of Enlightenment. Space and perspective read as metaphors of freedom and order. The mists and fogs commented upon in written descriptions by foreign visitors are cleared to reveal distant buildings in detail; there is little sense of intervening atmosphere and we see things as if through a vacuum. The basic model for Canaletto's Thames pictures was his own vision of Venice, but their finer touches and meaning are quite particular to London. He shows a special interest in distinctively English forms of dress such as that of Church of England clergymen, and, more importantly, he draws special attention to those magnificent new buildings that made the idea of London as the modern Rome virtually a commonplace - the star attractions of nos.71-2 and many other examples are London's proudest monuments of the moment, St Paul's and Westminster Bridge. With its freshness and optimism, Canaletto's style was perfectly suited to flattering a city of growing power and beauty – and arguably more attuned to London than to Venice, which was aesthetically superior but deeply in decline. Nos.71-2 were bought by Joseph Smith in Venice during the artist's brief return home of 1750-1. Canaletto may have brought them with him from England or painted them in Venice on the basis of drawings. They were bought from Smith for the Royal Collection by George III, probably in 1762. *See Colour Plate XII*

73. Westminster Abbey, with a procession of the Knights of the Bath probably 1749

Oil on canvas, 39 x 40
Lent by the Dean and Chapter of Westminster

The Knights are on their way from the Abbey, where they have attended a ceremony of installation in Henry VII's Chapel, towards the House of Lords. The work was commissioned by Joseph Wilcocks, Dean of Westminster and as such Dean of the Order of the Bath, who appears as the second-to-last member of the procession, wearing his clerical robes under the Order's crimson mantle. The event took place on 26 June 1749. The Abbey is shown spruce and intact, with no hint of the picturesque irregularity and decay that later painters were to discover in English medieval architecture. The towers at the west end of the Abbey were actually in mint condition since they were only completed about 1745, and Canaletto carefully records the carved inscription dating them to the reign of George II. *See Colour Plate XV*

74. Westminster Bridge under repair 1754

Oil on canvas, 18 x 29
Lent by a private collector

No.74 was commissioned towards the end of Canaletto's stay in London by the rich eccentric Thomas Hollis, who had met Joseph Smith in Venice and probably returned with a letter of introduction to the artist. It is one of at least eight paintings by Canaletto of Westminster Bridge in various stages of construction. This most topical landmark of the new London was opened to traffic in 1746, but one of its piers began to settle soon afterwards, necessitating a rebuilding operation that was not completed until 1750. The fact that no.74 shows this work in progress presumably indicates that it was based at least partly on an earlier drawing.

74

75

Though long out of date, the appearance of the bridge under repair allows Canaletto to suggest the idea of a city in the making, which is germane to his image of London, as well as to create interesting patterns of scaffolding. For an account of the building of the bridge and artists' views of it, see R. J. B. Walker, *Old Westminster Bridge*, 1979.

75. St Paul's 1754

Oil on canvas, 23¾ x 19¾
Lent by the Yale Center for British Art, New Haven (Paul Mellon Collection)

No.75 was also commissioned by Thomas Hollis. The sprightly lines and dots of Canaletto's technique enliven both architecture and figures. There is a grace about even the humblest of the characters that inhabit his London views, as if urban always meant urbane, and those milling around St Paul's are no exception. A man in the left foreground points towards the portico of the cathedral with his stick, no doubt drawing his companion's attention to one of Wren's subtler touches.

76

GIOVANNI BATTISTA PIRANESI
Italian, 1720-78

After training as an architect and stage-designer in Venice, Piranesi learnt the technique of etching in Rome, where he settled permanently in 1745 and soon established an international reputation with his prints of Roman antiquities. With their exaggerations of scale and theatrical lighting effects, his awe-inspired *Vedute di Roma*, published from about 1748 onwards, imbue the city with a grandeur and a drama unprecedented in the tradition of the topographical view. In 1761 he entered the contemporary debate on the achievements of Greek and Roman civilisations as an impassioned champion of Rome with his book *Della Magnificenza ed Architettura de' Romani*. He never visited Britain, but stimulated a lively response to Roman classicism amongst leading British architects such as William Chambers, Robert Adam, George Dance and John Soane.

76. Blackfriars Bridge under construction 1766

Etching, 15¼ x 23¾
Lent by the Guildhall Library

The designer of the first Blackfriars Bridge, the young Scottish architect and engineer Robert Mylne, studied in Rome in the years 1755-8 and became friendly with Piranesi, who probably assisted him in his archaeological researches into the Roman water system. Later Mylne acted on Piranesi's behalf in promoting his work among British collectors. His design for the bridge was unmistakably Piranesian, and appears even more so in Piranesi's own view of it, which typically exploits the aggrandizing effect of a low viewpoint, figures of Lilliputian proportions and a maximum of spatial complexity. Mylne sent Piranesi a description of his design and Piranesi replied, in a letter addressed to 'Roberto Mylne, Architetto Celeberrimo', on 11 November 1760: 'The account is brief to be sure but containing the most important particulars of the vast size of the structure, of the difficulty of the undertaking and of its grandeur – which will proclaim your genius to the whole world, perpetuate your fame and reflect honour upon those who have elected you to be author of one of the most glorious works of English magnificence' (see Christopher Gotch, 'The Missing Years of Robert Mylne', *Architectural Review*, CX, September 1951, pp. 179-82). He goes on to ask for a drawing, which Mylne presumably sent, and that or a later, updated version showing work on the bridge presumably formed the starting point for no.76. The bridge was begun in 1760 and opened in 1769; the inscription beneath the view gives the date of August 1764, which may be that of the stage of construction represented or of the execution of the print, and the work was published in London on 10 March 1766.

Piranesi attaches to his London view a Romanised version of the City Arms with the letters SPQL, a variation on the Roman abbreviation SPQR for *Senatus Populusque Romanus* (the Senate and the People of Rome). In no.76 he both likens London to Rome and by implication, when we remember the emphasis on crumbling ruins in his views of Rome itself, makes a typical contrast between the latter as the city of the past and London as the city of the present. Whereas the Roman magnificence he celebrates in the bulk of his work is in a state of sublime decay, the 'English magnificence' represented by Blackfriars Bridge is alive and growing.

THE PLEASURE GROUND

THERE SMILING PLEASURE, GAY DELIGHT
MIX, AND CONFOUND EACH RANK AND RIGHT;
THESE PLAINS WHICH CONSTANT JOYS SUPPLY,
DELIGHT THE TASTE, THE EAR AND EYE.
VAUNT NOT THY COMBATS OF THE FIELD,
GREECE, THOU TO *RANELAGH* MUST YIELD;
THERE VICTORS WON A LAUREL CROWN
WHICH GAVE A FLEETING, VAIN RENOWN:
A THOUSAND NYMPHS THESE PLAINS ADORN,
WHO SEEM TO CHARM ALL MANKIND BORN;
WITH HATS IN WHICH GAY FLOWERS ARE SEEN,
THEY WALK MAJESTIC O'ER THE GREEN;
THE PRIZE OF BEAUTY IS THEIR AIM,
'TIS THAT ALONE THEY JUSTLY CLAIM.

Madame Du Bocage, 1750

With its newly laid-out parks and the fashionable meeting places of Vauxhall and Ranelagh, London took over from Paris in the second half of the eighteenth century as the pleasure capital of Europe. Visitors were impressed by the opportunities it provided for socialising, and much of the work of foreign artists dwells in a typically rococo manner upon the delights of gardens, promenading and flirtation.

JACQUES RIGAUD
French, about 1681–1754

This draughtsman and engraver moved to Paris from his native Marseilles in 1720. His most important work is the series of prints of French palaces he published from 1730 under the title *Les Maisons Royales de France*. On visits to England he drew similar views of Chatsworth and other noble houses and parks.

77. St James's Park from Buckingham House about 1740

Pen and ink with grey wash, 13¼ x 29
Lent by the Guildhall Library

Rigaud views his subject very much through the eyes of an artist used to drawing views of the gardens at Versailles, which is by no means an unsympathetic response since St James's Park was itself inspired by French formal gardens. He shows the social function of the park as a place for promenades and, like many a foreign observer, notices with interest the curious mixing of fashionable ladies and gentlemen with grazing cattle. But his version of the London skyline is incomplete and inaccurate to say the least. Westminster Abbey is highly stylised and askew, St Paul's looks more like St Peter's in Rome, and the Wren City churches are represented by a solitary spire. These lapses and the impossible fall of light from the north suggest that no.77 was made at one or more removes from direct observation.

JEAN-BAPTISTE CHATELAIN
French, about 1710–about 1771

Chatelain became an artist after abandoning a military career. He worked a great deal in England, making engravings after Claude and others for the publisher John Boydell, as well as drawing his own views of English scenes, especially along the Thames.

78. St James's Park from Rosamond's Pond 1745

Engraving, 10¼ x 16¼
Lent by the Guildhall Library

Nos.78–9 were drawn by Chatelain and engraved by W.H.Toms. Here elegant strollers

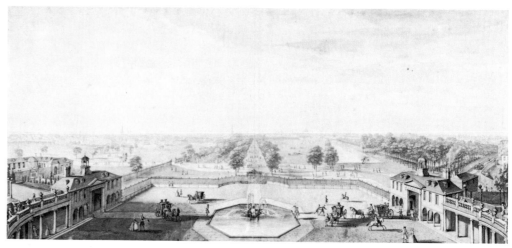

77

79

take an afternoon turn around the pond. There is an emphasis on couples, gently evoking the idea of the park as a Garden of Love, and some of the poses and gestures recall the amorous art of Watteau, especially the man holding out his hand to help a woman up an incline on the left. The view is looking eastwards, with Westminster Abbey in the distance to the right of centre.

79. The Mall 1794

Engraving, 10¼ x 16
Lent by the Guildhall Library

This is a later impression of a print originally published about the same time as no.78. It is morning and we are looking west along the Mall, which is full of promenaders, towards Buckingham House. In the foreground a soldier on guard duty looks on enviously as a well-dressed young man converses with a pair of attractive women.

130

CANALETTO
Italian, 1697–1768

For a brief biography, see nos.71–5, above.

81

82

80. Vauxhall Gardens, the Grand Walk about 1751

Oil on canvas, 20 x 30¼
Lent by Lord Trevor

This pleasure ground a short distance up and across the river from Westminster was taken over by the enterprising Jonathan Tyers in 1728 and elaborated and embellished over the following thirty years. It became the mecca of rococo decoration in England and a model for countless gardens all over Europe, many of which even borrowed its name. Visitors would approach Vauxhall by boat, usually in the late afternoon, and would spend the evening promenading, listening to music and dining by the light of 1500 oil lamps. No.80 shows the scene near the entrance to this modern Elysium, an avenue dotted with groups of pleasure-seekers, but with the Grand Walk shown grander than it actually was and the scale of the buildings exaggerated accordingly. An engraving of the same composition in reverse and with many differences of detail was published by Robert Sayer in 1751 (see nos.81-2 below). *See Colour Plate XIII*

81. The Centre Cross Walk in Vauxhall Gardens 1751

Engraving by E. Rooker, 9 x 15¼
Lent by the Guildhall Library

82. The Temple of Comus in Vauxhall Gardens 1751

Engraving by Müller, 9 x 15
Lent by the Guildhall Library

Nos.81-2 are from a set of four engravings of Vauxhall made from Canaletto's drawings and published by Robert Sayer on 2 December 1751. Canaletto embodies the gentility of the place in no.81 by showing a pair of men doffing their hats in greeting while still a considerable distance away from each other. The Temple of Comus was a nearby range of supper booths built in a style combining elements of classical, Gothic and Indian architecture, each booth resembling a side-chapel with its own altar in the form of a dining table. Comus was the classical god of revelry.

83. Ranelagh, the interior of the Rotunda
about 1751

Oil on canvas, 20 x 30
Lent by Lord Trevor

Ranelagh was opened in Chelsea in 1742 as a rival to Vauxhall Gardens. It comprised not only gardens, featuring a Chinese pagoda surrounded by a lake, but also a 150-foot Rotunda with a central fireplace, an orchestra and a circuit of supper boxes. The warmth and shelter this afforded gave Ranelagh a great advantage over Vauxhall on a damp or chilly evening. One of the many foreign visitors who were impressed by Ranelagh was Carl Philip Moritz: 'On the floor lay carpets surrounding four high black pillars containing ornate fireplaces where coffee, tea and punch were being prepared, and round all the circle tables were set with refreshments. Around these four high pillars all of fashionable London revolved like a gaily coloured distaff, sauntering in a compact throng' (*Journeys of a German in England in 1782*, translated by Reginald Nettel, 1965, p. 45). Canaletto shows this Pantheon of pleasure from the level of the first-floor gallery, rendering the fanciful lines of its architecture with evident delight. A similar view taken from the opposite side of the building is in the National Gallery.   *See Colour Plate XIV*

86

VUES D'OPTIQUE

Nos.84–7 are *vues d'optique* or 'optical views'. In the second half of the eighteenth century there was a fashion for viewing engravings through devices known as zograscopes, from the Greek *zographia* meaning picture. These come in any number of shapes and sizes but consist essentially of a large convex lens and a mirror positioned at an angle of 45 degrees. Seen through the lens and reflected in the mirror, images appear to be at some distance from the observer, which enhances the illusion of space and depth. They are also sharpened, which was an advantage in an age when many people with poor eyesight did not wear spectacles. *Vues d'optique* are prints that were made specifically for use with zograscopes. Many are city views, including a large number showing the London parks and pleasure grounds. They differ little from ordinary engravings – indeed the views

were usually copied from existing sources – but the images or inscriptions are sometimes printed in reverse to compensate for the effect of the mirror.

Zograscopes work best with emphatically perspectival compositions featuring steeply foreshortened buildings, paths and roads that draw the eye from the foreground back into the distance, and most *vues d'optique* conform to that pattern. As a result, they present very much the airy, spacious image of London favoured by the eighteenth century. Though produced all over Europe, *vues d'optique* originated mainly from Paris, London and Augsburg. Nos.84–7 were all published by Jacques Chereau in Paris around 1750. They are tinted in a typically crude manner that is none the less striking when they are viewed through the zograscopes. The zograscopes used to display them in the exhibition have been kindly lent by Mr David Robinson and the Victoria and Albert Museum.

84. St James's Park and Horse Guards

Engraving, tinted, 9 x 14¾
Lent by the Guildhall Library

85. St James's Park from Rosamond's Pond

Engraving, tinted, 10 x 15½
Lent by the Guildhall Library

A copy of Chatelain's print, no.78 above.

86. A Costume Ball in Ranelagh Gardens

Engraving, tinted, 9 x 14¾
Lent by the Guildhall Library

For a note on Ranelagh, see no.83.

87. Interior of the Rotunda, Ranelagh

Engraving, tinted, 8½ x 15
Lent by the Guildhall Library

ELIAS MARTIN
Swedish, 1739–1818

Martin was a late starter as an artist, showing talent as a draughtsman but only beginning a serious professional training in 1766, when he left Sweden for Paris to study under the marine and landscape painter Joseph Vernet. By 1768 he was in London. In 1770 he married an Englishwoman, Augusta Lee, and became an Associate of the Royal Academy, where he exhibited soft, wistful landscapes throughout the 1770s. He returned to Sweden in 1780 and painted works commemorating royal occasions for King Gustavus III. On a second stay in England in 1788–91 he lived in Bath and seems to have painted mainly *genre* subjects. He returned to Sweden for good in 1791. Hampered by ill health and a lack of public appreciation for his painting, he more or less ceased to work after 1808.

88. Hanover Square about 1770

Oil on canvas, 70½ x 83
Lent by the Count Trolle-Bonde

Laid out around 1715, Hanover Square was one of the smart new West-End developments of eighteenth-century London, the spaciousness and salubriousness of which were much admired by visitors from abroad. It was virtually on Martin's doorstep, since he had lodgings at this time in Mill Street, at the back of St George's Church, which appears in the centre of no.88. The view is looking southwards from Harewood Place; the church clock says five minutes to five and the scene is bathed in a pleasant late-afternoon light. Like so many foreign painters of London, Martin stresses the picturesque variety of the city's street life, showing a bagpipe-player, a blind beggar and a flower-girl amongst elegant ladies and gentlemen, miscellaneous children, cows, goats and horses, and a rustic cart juxtaposed with an ornate coach attended by servants. To the right a milkmaid and her swain steal away into the shadows conveniently provided by the trees. No.88 was one of Martin's first London works, ambitious in its scale and no doubt intended to make his name when shown at the Royal Academy of 1770.   *See Colour Plate XX*

90

PIERRE-FRANÇOIS TARDIEU
French, 1711–1771

Tardieu was a pupil of his uncle, the eminent engraver Nicolas-Henri Tardieu. He made maps and engravings after paintings.

89. London and Southwark about 1795

Engraved map, tinted, 12½ x 17¾
Lent by the Guildhall Library

This is a later edition of a map first published about 1765. The text provides not only a key, but also an 'Explanation of some English words'.

FRANZ JOSEF MANNSKIRSCH
German, 1768–1830

The son of an artist, this landscape painter and engraver came to London in 1796 and produced work that follows in the English landscape tradition. He remained based in London until 1819, living afterwards in Danzig (Gdansk) and Frankfurt.

90. Kensington Palace and Gardens 1798

Etching and aquatint, tinted, 12¼ x 16½
Lent by the Guildhall Library

Nos.90–1 were the first and fourth in a set of prints of London scenes made from Mannskirsch's drawings by H.Schutz and published by Ackermann. Flanked by trees and seen across a lake, Kensington Palace is presented within the time-honoured pattern of the country house view. In the foreground a lady, three children, a maid and a dog delight in the pleasures of this tamed and tidied version of nature.

91

91. Buckingham House from St James's Park 1798

Etching and aquatint, tinted, 12½ x 16½
Lent by the Guildhall Library

With a characteristic charm, Mannskirsch stresses the idea of the park as a place for promenades, conversation and meetings, carefully varying the implied social and family relationships within each little group of figures.

JOHANNES SWERTNER
Dutch, 1746–1813

As an artist, Swertner was only an accomplished amateur, his main occupation being that of preacher in the Dutch Moravian sect. He lived and worked for a period in Islington but by 1801 had moved to Bristol, where he died in 1813.

92. London from Islington 1801

Etching and aquatint, tinted with shades of green and blue, 17 x 27¾
Lent by the Guildhall Library

The darkness over the lower quarter of the composition is one of the lengthening shadows that Swertner emphasises, perhaps too much, to help evoke the feeling of a pleasant summer's evening. It is just after 7 p.m.. Some haymakers are still at work in the fields and we see different stages in the haymaking process, from cutting to raking, loading the cart, resting and taking refreshment. The artist gives us agriculture at its most picturesque, more reminiscent of comic opera than serious labour, and implies that all the pleasures of country life are on London's doorstep. Indeed his image of London shows an appreciation of suburbia, and the city as viewed from suburbia, that seems half a century ahead of its time. The waterway meandering away from us on the left is the New River and the church in the middle distance on the right is St Mary's, Islington.

92

LONDON LABOUR AND THE LONDON POOR

BUT SEND NO POETS TO LONDON ! THERE IS SUCH A BLEAK SERIOUSNESS ABOUT EVERYTHING, SUCH COLOSSAL UNIFORMITY, SUCH MACHINE-LIKE MOTION, SUCH TETCHINESS ABOUT JOY ITSELF. THIS LONDON OF EXTREMES CRUSHES THE FANCY AND TEARS AT THE HEART.
Heinrich Heine, 1827

The early nineteenth century saw the first appearance in art of the darker side of London. Visitors to the capital of what was now the most rapidly industrialising and urbanising nation in the world felt that they were seeing the future, and their response was a mixture of wonder and dismay. The clear neo-classical vision of the eighteenth century no longer seemed tenable as London's atmosphere became smog-laden and its labyrinthine vastness such as to defy comprehension in a single view. In the romantic imagination the new Rome became a grim work-place with serious social and environmental problems, a symbol no longer of man's triumph over nature but of his unnaturalness.

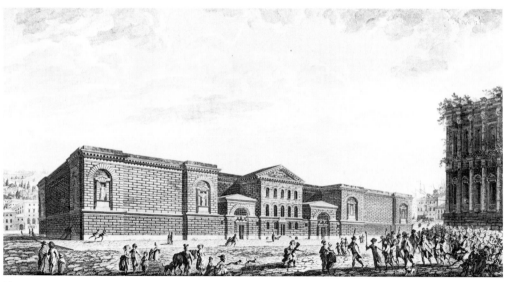

93

94. The Yard of the Spread Eagle Inn, Gracechurch Street 1814

Water-colour, 9¾ x 14¾
Signed and dated 'R B Schnebbelie 1814' (lower r.)
Lent by the Guildhall Library

The way the ostler and the coachman to the left go about their business oblivious to the demolition taking place to the right creates an air of strangeness about the scene. This is enhanced by a slightly awry perspective, especially in the underside of the balcony that swoops unsettlingly across the upper part of the composition.

94

95. The Demolition of the Guildhall Chapel 1820

Water-colour, 9½ x 10¾
Signed and dated 'Robert Blemmell Schnebbelie October 1820' (lower centre)
Lent by the Guildhall Library

Schnebbelie was much attracted by the scenes of demolition and redevelopment to be found all over London in the period following the Napoleonic Wars. Like ruins, buildings under demolition were both picturesque in appearance and romantically suggestive of the idea of transience. Here the disintegrating forms of the Guildhall Chapel are contrasted with the crisp new front of the Guildhall itself looming up behind. The rubble in the foreground is what was left of Blackwell Hall, the demolition of which Schnebbelie had recorded the previous year, and the carved wooden cartouche with the City arms held up by a couple of workers came from the tympanum over its grand entrance.

FERDINAND BOURJOT
French, 1768 - after 1838

A pupil of David, Bourjot worked as an architect as well as painting landscapes and military subjects.

93. Newgate Prison about 1792

Engraving, 11¼ x 21¼
Lent by the Guildhall Library

No.93 is datable to the period of the French Revolution from the way the printseller's address is given as 'la rue ci-devant Royale' ('the street formerly known as the rue Royale'). For obvious reasons, the rue Royale was renamed after the Revolution, becoming the rue de la Révolution in 1792 and the rue de la Concorde in 1795; it was only given back its original name in 1814. As we might expect from a pupil of David in the heat of the revolutionary moment, Bourjot conceived his print as a propaganda piece, attacking the King and Government of Britain by presenting Newgate as a symbol of repression, a British Bastille. Britain was not only reprehensible as a monarchy, but also engaged in hostilities against French revolutionary forces at the time.

In some ways George Dance's Newgate was a natural target for this kind of broadside. The most aggressive of those eighteenth-century London buildings conceived in the spirit of Roman architecture as promoted by Piranesi (q.v.), it was finished in 1778 but badly damaged by fire in the anti-Catholic Gordon Riots of 1780. Bourjot must have copied an early view of the building, since he shows the pediment that was replaced by an attic storey after the fire. Clearly his intentions were symbolic rather than topographical or historical, and he places Newgate in a fantastic setting bearing no resemblance to its actual location. To the right of the composition he introduces a ruined and overgrown version of the Banqueting House on Whitehall, the decayed grace of which serves as a foil to the prison's brutal newness and suggests a sharp contrast between Britain's past and present. In the foreground a mob is being beaten back by constables armed with cudgels as some offenders are arrested and taken off towards the prison. To reinforce the point, one of the classical statues on the facade, to the left of the entrance, is armed with a cudgel too.

ROBERT BLEMMELL SCHNEBBELIE
Swiss, about 1770-1849

The son of an artist who also lived and worked in London, Schnebbelie painted water-colour views and designed illustrations for the *Gentleman's Magazine* and Wilkinson's *Londina Illustrata*. He is said to have died in abject poverty.

95

THEODORE GERICAULT
French, 1791-1824

This seminal figure in the development of French romantic art came to England in April 1820 accompanied by the cheerful Nicolas-Toussaint Charlet (q.v.), and enjoyed great success with the exhibition of his masterpiece *The Raft of the Medusa*, living on and off in London till the end of the following year. He saw much to admire in English art, especially the work of animal painters such as James Ward and the young Landseer, and viewed London life as a detached but fascinated romantic outsider. 'I have no amusements at all, and my life is exactly the same as in Paris,' he wrote to a friend on 12 February 1821, 'working hard in my room then prowling around the streets to relax myself, where there is always such movement and variety that I'm sure you wouldn't be able to leave them' (Charles Clément, *Géricault,* Paris, 1868, pp. 192-3).

GERICAULT'S 'ENGLISH SERIES'

Nos.96-8 are from the group of Géricault lithographs published in London in 1821 under the title *Various Subjects Drawn from Life and on Stone* and now generally known as the English Series. Géricault was enthusiastic about the as yet underdeveloped printmaking technique of lithography, and especially the possibilities it offered for bold draughtsmanship and moody atmospheric effects. In 1820, taking advantage of an English vogue for prints 'drawn on stone', he secured a contract with the London firm of Rodwell and Martin to publish some examples of his work. The series was printed at the press of the well-known German lithographer Charles Joseph Hullmandel and issued from February to May 1821. The subjects treated are various, as the original title states, and most fall outside the scope of the present exhibition. In those identifiable as London scenes, Géricault exploits the heavy modelling, smudginess and smokiness to which lithography lends itself to suggest an oppressive industrial city. Dwelling upon extremes, and showing scenes of labour, poverty and suffering, he gives expression for the first time in the visual arts to that Babylonian image of London that becomes so prevalent later on in the nineteenth century.

96. Pity the sorrows of a poor old Man! Whose trembling limbs have borne him to your door 1821

Lithograph, 12½ x 14¾
Lent by the Art Institute of Chicago

A modern Lazarus slumps on the pavement in front of a baker's shop in Lambeth. Inside, a plump woman, perhaps the baker's wife, is serving a well-dressed Jewish customer. The old man is outside the shop and pitifully without the things it represents, the basic necessity of bread, the Jew's wealth and the woman's health. His figure is monumental, even heroic, but seemingly paralysed by its own weight. The presence of a coal wagon in the street on the right reminds us that this is the modern industrial world. Further away, in the smoggy distance, we see Blackfriars Bridge and the dome of St Paul's.

97. Entrance to the Adelphi Wharf 1821

Lithograph, 10 x 12¼
Signed 'Géricault' (lower l.)
Lent by the Guildhall Library

Géricault was passionately interested in horses of all kinds, and they play at least as important a part in his art as the human figure. Their bulk emphasised by the rear view, the carthorses here are the very embodiment of heavy labour. The coalmen are driving them through one of the arches that led beneath the Adelphi towards the Strand, but as they trudge into the darkness it is as if they were descending into a pit, a mine or hell itself.

98

96

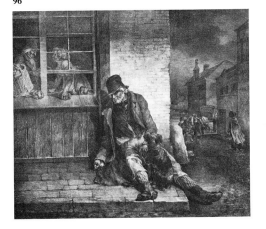

98. A Paraleytic Woman 1821

Lithograph, 8½ x 12½
Lent by the Bibliothèque Nationale, Paris

The curious spelling of 'paraleytic' appears in the title as given below the print itself. Like the poverty of the old man in no. 96, the woman's illness is accentuated symbolically by the people and things around her. The girls on the left and the hearse on the right serve as images of life and death, the position of the woman between the two symbolising her pathetic state. Her inert body is likened to the wooden toy carried by the younger girl, her chair to a coffin and, when we notice the bars on the windows of the building on the left, her paralysis to a prison.

99

forward to the drawings of Doré. The grandest buildings are made to appear bleak; the stonework on the Mansion House is visibly crumbling and Somerset House, strangely lit and uninhabited, takes on a sepulchral eeriness. Bouton and Jaime's London is very much the 'monster city' described by Flora Tristan, where 'one breathes sadness; it is in the air, it enters through every pore' (*Promenades dans Londres*, 2nd ed., 1840, p. 10).

GEORGE SCHARF
German, 1788-1860

Scharf studied at the Munich Academy from 1805 to 1810, mastering the new technique of lithography, and then moved around Europe for a few years making a living by portraiture and various forms of journeyman artistic activity. Finally he became attached to the British Army, saw action at Waterloo and decided to seek his fortune in London. He arrived in 1816 and stayed for the rest of his life. In London he drew scientific illustrations for learned bodies and journals as his bread-and-butter work, but devoted much of his time and energy to sketches of London life, which he made in large numbers and almost exclusively for his own satisfaction. He married an Englishwoman, Elizabeth Hicks, in 1820. Their son, also named George, was to become a leading figure in the art world and eventually Director of the National Portrait Gallery. Scharf Senior enjoyed no such success, was always short of money and died in poverty. For further information on Scharf and his London views, see Peter Jackson, *George Scharf's London*, 1987.

CHARLES-MARIE BOUTON
French, 1781-1853
and
?JEAN-FRANÇOIS JAIME
French, 1804 - after 1864

Bouton trained under David and painted moody architectural interiors with melancholy figures. The identity of the 'Jaime' given as the co-author of nos.99-101 is uncertain but Jean-François Jaime seems the best candidate among the known artists of that name.

99. Charing Cross and Northumberland House 1830

Lithograph, 10 x 15½
Lent by the City of Westminster Libraries

100. The Mansion House 1830

Lithograph, 10¼ x 15½
Lent by the Guildhall Library

101

101. Somerset House 1830

Lithograph, 9¾ x 15¾
Lent by the Guildhall Library

Nos.99-101 are from a series of lithographs by Bouton and Jaime entitled simply LONDRES and published in 1830 in Paris and London. They are a remarkable example of the heavy, depressing atmosphere that artists could impart to the London scene using the technique of lithography. With their down-at-heel characters on grubby streets under ominous skies, they look back to the lithographs of Géricault and

102. Crooked Lane 1830

Water-colour, 20½ x 31
Signed and dated 'G. Scharf del. London 1830' (lower r.)
Lent by the Guildhall Library

Like R. B. Schnebbelie (q.v.), Scharf was fascinated by the frenetic building activity taking place in London after the Napoleonic Wars, and scenes of demolition and construction figure prominently among his London works. In 1830 he was commissioned to record the building of the new London Bridge by the City Corporation's London Bridge Committee. He worked assiduously on the project over a period of years, making dozens of on-the-spot sketches as well as more finished water-colours and lithographs. Indeed he produced a great deal more than the Committee had bargained for; three of the water-colours were all that they would accept, and they paid him a mere £30 five years after giving him the commission. Scharf eked out his returns by selling sketches to individuals involved in the new bridge and publishing his lithographs, but was none the less sorely disappointed. Nos. 102 and 104 are two of the three water-colours accepted by the Committee. No. 102, which Scharf exhibited at the Royal Academy in 1832, shows the east side of the part of Crooked Lane that ran south off Great Eastcheap. The whole block of buildings, including the Wren church of St Michael's in the centre, was to be demolished to clear a way for the northern approach road to the new bridge. The demolition work already in progress on the right was to open a new thoroughfare leading to the Monument, which is visible in the background to the right of St Michael's. Scharf records the architectural details of the church, and every shopfront and sign along the street, with a loving care made poignant by the imminence of their destruction.

102

103

103. The Northern Approach to London Bridge under construction 1830

Lithograph, 19¼ x 59
Lent by the Guildhall Library

The most important of Scharf's London Bridge water-colours, a pair showing its northern and southern approaches and each measuring five feet across, were destroyed in 1941. No. 103 is one of the pair of lithographs he made after them. He shows the bridge swarming with busy workmen who appear ant-like in relation to the colossal structure they are erecting. By taking a view straight along the bridge's length, he stresses the fact that the church of St Michael's

lies directly, inconveniently, in its path. Like an image of the inexorability of progress, a trolley bearing a great block of masonry is being heaved forward along some tracks laid in the centre of the bridge and targeted on this doomed building like the sight of a gun. To the right are Wren buildings that will be spared, the Monument and St Magnus the Martyr.

104. Old and New London Bridges 1831

Water-colour, 19½ x 26½
Signed and dated 'G. Scharf del. London 1831' (lower l.)
Lent by the Guildhall Library

Along with no. 102, this was one of the water-colours bought from Scharf by the London Bridge Committee in 1835. The view is looking south from the bottom of Fish Street Hill, with St Magnus the Martyr on the left and Thames Street running across the foreground. We see the old bridge in the centre, still being dismantled, and the new one to the right, already busy with traffic. It is 8 a.m. and the rays of the morning sun, coming from the left of the composition, symbolically highlight the new bridge and throw its predecessor, along with St Magnus the Martyr, into the shade. **104**

OTTO, BARON VON ROSENBERG
German, dates unknown

An aristocratic traveller and amateur artist.

105. Bilder aus London 1834

Lent by the Guildhall Library

Bilder aus London (Pictures from London) was published in Leipzig by August Robert Friese with ten lithographic illustrations from the author's drawings. No.105 is Rosenberg's own interleaved copy with many pages of extra text and notes in manuscript, engraved views and original drawings, several of which were not used in the book as published. Rosenberg's speciality was comic types, and no.105 includes sketches of night watchmen, fishwives, boxers, beadles and blue-coat boys, a postman and a black crossing-sweeper with a wooden leg.

CARL HARTMANN
German, 1818 - after 1857

Born in Nuremberg, Hartmann was an engraver and genre painter who lived in London from 1839 for the rest of his life. He exhibited works at the Royal Academy from 1850 to 1857.

106

106. St James's Park and **Berkeley Street** about 1847

Pencil, water-colour and coloured chalks, on pages in a sketchbook, each 5 x 7
Lent by the Syndics of the Fitzwilliam Museum, Cambridge

St James's Park is no longer the earthly paradise of the eighteenth-century views but a place where you might see a park-keeper prodding with his cane at a vagrant, or possibly a dead body, lying on the grass. In the same realist vein, Hartmann's view of Berkeley Street shows not the high society of Mayfair but a Lascar crossing-sweeper leaning against the wall. The sketchbook also contains drawings of Pimlico near the artist's lodgings (one dated 1847), the Thames Tunnel with gypsies, London Bridge with a blind beggar and Cremorne Gardens with hot-air balloons, as well as panoramic views from the Monument and the Duke of York's column.

CARL HAAG
German, 1820-1915

London was a second home for Haag from 1847 onwards. As a young man he attended the Royal Academy Schools and showed works at the R.A. exhibitions, learning much from the English water-colour tradition. From 1853 he received commissions from Queen Victoria for paintings and prints recording the activities of royal parties at Balmoral in Scotland. In 1858 he accompanied the British painter Frederick Goodall on a trip to Cairo, the first of a number of visits he was to make to the Middle East, and he painted mainly Orientalist subjects for the rest of his long career.

107. Panorama of London from the Monument 1848

Water-colour, 7 ½ x 69
Signed and dated 'C. Haag 1848' (in a lower corner of each of the four sheets that make up the drawing)
Lent by the Guildhall Library

Haag takes us through the whole 360 degrees of the view from the Monument in a long continuous strip, beginning on the left looking eastwards towards the Tower, coming round to look southwards across London Bridge, then westwards towards St Paul's and finally northwards along Gracechurch Street on the right. The occasional thumbprint in the paint suggests that he may have executed the work at least partly on the spot while contending with the elements. Haag subtly evokes a low, cold light passing through a smoke-laden atmosphere, playing over dingy stone and brickwork, and gleaming on the surface of the river - an effect he achieves by the use of bodycolour and scraping-out. The unusually high viewpoint dwarfs and almost seems to bury the people in the streets below while giving prominence to all the chimneys, creating a sombre vision of London as a city of inhuman scale and smoky exhalations.

107

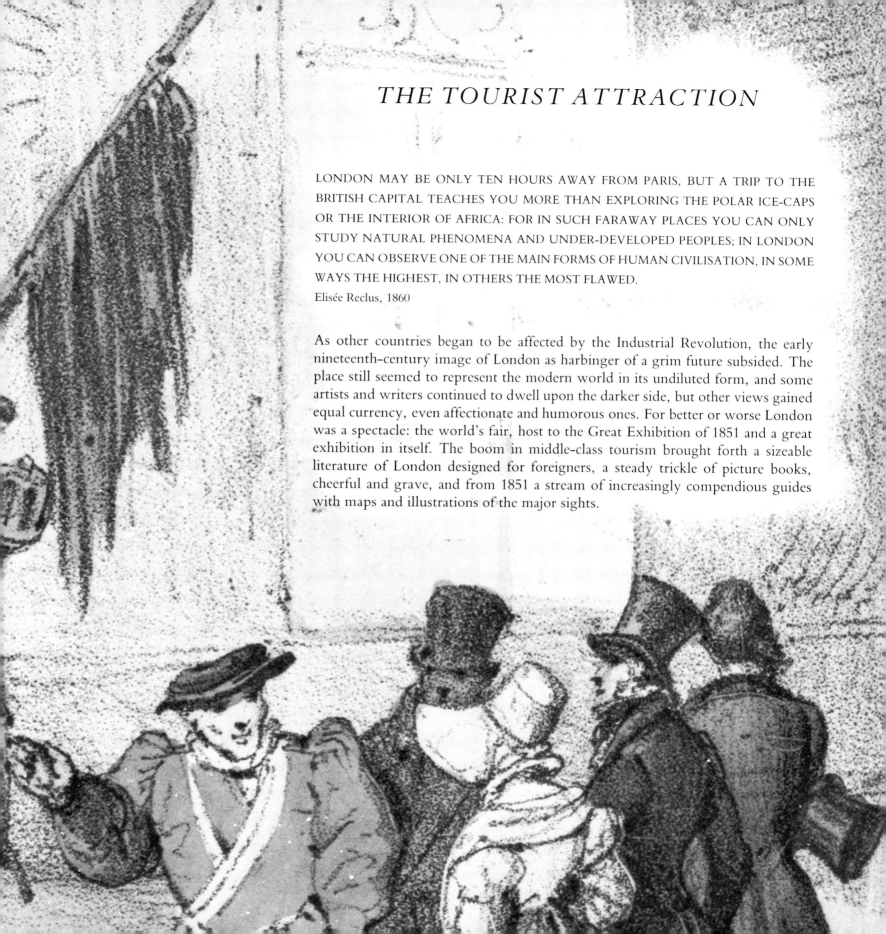

THE TOURIST ATTRACTION

LONDON MAY BE ONLY TEN HOURS AWAY FROM PARIS, BUT A TRIP TO THE BRITISH CAPITAL TEACHES YOU MORE THAN EXPLORING THE POLAR ICE-CAPS OR THE INTERIOR OF AFRICA: FOR IN SUCH FARAWAY PLACES YOU CAN ONLY STUDY NATURAL PHENOMENA AND UNDER-DEVELOPED PEOPLES; IN LONDON YOU CAN OBSERVE ONE OF THE MAIN FORMS OF HUMAN CIVILISATION, IN SOME WAYS THE HIGHEST, IN OTHERS THE MOST FLAWED.

Elisée Reclus, 1860

As other countries began to be affected by the Industrial Revolution, the early nineteenth-century image of London as harbinger of a grim future subsided. The place still seemed to represent the modern world in its undiluted form, and some artists and writers continued to dwell upon the darker side, but other views gained equal currency, even affectionate and humorous ones. For better or worse London was a spectacle: the world's fair, host to the Great Exhibition of 1851 and a great exhibition in itself. The boom in middle-class tourism brought forth a sizeable literature of London designed for foreigners, a steady trickle of picture books, cheerful and grave, and from 1851 a stream of increasingly compendious guides with maps and illustrations of the major sights.

EUGENE LAMI
French, 1800-90

Called 'the poet of official dandyism' by
Baudelaire, Lami is best known for his water-
colours of glittering social occasions. He learnt
the technique of water-colour from his friend
Bonington, who may also have inspired him to
move from Paris to London early in 1826. He
probably stayed until the spring of the following
year, making sketches of London life that were
published as lithographs in the *Souvenirs de
Londres* and *Voyage en Angleterre*. Back in
Paris, Lami cultivated aristocratic connections
and in the 1830s painted battle pictures for King
Louis-Philippe's gallery of military history at
Versailles. It was also for Louis-Philippe, from
1838 onwards, that he began to paint the high-
society water-colours that formed the mainstay
of his work for the rest of his long life. After the
fall of Louis-Philippe in the 1848 Revolution
Lami spent a second period in London, staying
until 1852.

108. Souvenirs de Londres 1826
Lent by the Guildhall Library

This volume of cheerful tinted lithographs
presents a trip to London in a dozen episodes.
We begin with a queasy crossing of the
Channel, then travel through Kent on the coach,
visit Pall Mall, Westminster Abbey and the
Tower, enjoy a hunt, some horse-racing, a
cockfight, a boxing match, a boat race and a
sermon, and return home via Dover. The plates
were printed by de Villain and published by
Lami-Denozan, the firm of the artist's brother.

109. A Fishmonger's 1830

Lithograph, tinted, 5¼ x 8
Lent by the Guildhall Library

110. People's Funeral 1830

Lithograph, 6 x 9
Lent by the Victoria and Albert Museum

Nos.109-110 are plates 21 and 23 in the set of
lithographs published by Lami and Henry
Monnier in 1829-30 as *Voyage en Angleterre*
(see no.117). The fishmongers, pushed to the
right of the composition as if to make way for
the slab on which their fish are displayed,
present comically contrasted characteristics, the

108

109

one pale and bony, the other flushed and tubby
with a drinker's nose. To the right of the fish are
some theatre bills with gallicised spelling, as in
FAVORITE DIVERTISSE[MENT]. In the funeral
scene, the coffin-bearers and mourners pass
before a grand-looking church with a classical
portico. It is a recognisable as a 'people's' funeral
because there is no hearse. The sign NEW ROAD
could indicate any number of locations in this
world or the next.

111. Ludgate Circus 1850

Water-colour and bodycolour, black chalk and
pencil, 5½ x 9½
Signed and dated 'E. L. 1850' (lower r.)
Lent by the Victoria and Albert Museum

This scene of a cart, a coach, a donkey cart
shedding its load, an omnibus and other vehicles

madly revolving around a traffic island recalls a
circus in more ways than one.

112. Hyde Park about 1850

Water-colour, bodycolour and pencil, 6 x 10¼
Signed 'EUG. LAMI' (lower r.)
Lent by the Victoria and Albert Museum

A subject pitched at an altogether higher social
level than no.111 and, as such, more
characteristic of Lami. The view is eastwards
along Rotten Row with fashionable riders to the
fore and the equestrian statue of the Duke of
Wellington in the distance. Though leaving
their faces undefined, Lami suggests a lively
interaction between the figures through their
gestures.

113. Belgrave Square about 1850

Water-colour, bodycolour and pencil, 5¾ x 9¾
Signed 'Eugene Lami' (lower r.)
Lent by the Victoria and Albert Museum

A pair of ladies in elaborate gowns step across a
pavement laid with a carpet towards a waiting
coach. There are servants in attendance, an
organ grinder near the coach and a beggar
woman on the pavement to whom one of the
ladies is handing some money. The work shows
to advantage Lami's ability to bestow glamour
on a scene through his dashing and stylish
technique and especially the white heightening
he uses to suggest the glint and sparkle of light.

142

114

114. Pall Mall and Trafalgar Square about 1850

Water-colour, bodycolour and pencil, 6 x 10
Signed 'EUGENE LAMI' (lower l.)
Lent by the Fine Art Society

The National Gallery and St Martin-in-the-Fields are visible in the background. As usual, Lami shows a special interest in horses, coaches and smart outfits - in this case military uniforms.

HENRY MONNIER
French, 1799-1877

Monnier was a playwright and actor as well as an artist. From 1822 to 1828 he more or less lived in London, spending only occasional periods in Paris. As a draughtsman and illustrator he was much influenced by the British comic tradition. He admired Hogarth and Rowlandson, and came to know Cruikshank personally during his time in London.

115. Billingsgate Market about 1827

Pen and sepia ink, pencil, and sepia and grey washes, 6½ x 10¾
Lent from a private collection

Monnier used this drawing as the basis for plate 14 in *Voyage en Angleterre*, the set of lithographs he published with Eugène Lami in 1829-30 (see no.117); the image appears in reverse in the book as a result of the printing process. A fishwife smoking a pipe gazes nonchalantly out at us, with characters moving and gesturing behind her who may be taking part in a fish auction. Individual faces are mostly

avoided in favour of an impression of massed humanity. It is one aspect of Monnier's realism that his works tend to lack obvious compositional pointers and central accents, leaving the spectator's attention to flit from one part to another, and no.115 is a case in point. The deliberately grubby appearance of his wash technique also enhances the slice-of-life effect.

EUGENE LAMI & HENRY MONNIER

For brief biographies, see nos.108-114 and 115 above.

116. A Main Road at 5 p.m. 1829

Lithograph, tinted, 9¼ x 14½
Lent by the Victoria and Albert Museum

This view across Parliament Square, difficult to match against the actual location because it has been reversed in the printing process, is the combined work of both contributors to the *Voyage en Angleterre* (see no.117), in which it appears as plate 20. Monnier seems to have been responsible for the near-caricatural figures and Lami for the rest. The print includes a variety of people and modes of transport, schoolboys, soldiers and old men, carts carrying barrels, a coach and a hearse, all flatly drawn and arranged in groups that look like cut-outs placed at different distances. The overall effect is appropriately hectic and confusing.

117. Voyage en Angleterre 1829-30

Lent from a private collection

Lami and Monnier became friends as students under Baron Gros in Paris. They met in London in 1826-7 and near the beginning of 1827 secured a commission from Colnaghi's to publish a collection of lithographs of their impressions of English life. The work was published in 1829-30 by Colnaghi's in London and Firmin-Didot and Lami-Denozan in Paris, and accompanied by notes written by Amédée Pichot. The plates comprise fourteen designs by Lami, nine by Monnier and one joint effort (no.116). Lami's are airier and smoother in style, Monnier's fussier and more caricatural. They were printed by de Villain and many sets were tinted by hand. Among the London subjects are a group of aged watchmen returning from their night's duty, a noisy street argument and a Billingsgate market scene by Monnier (see no.115), and a fishmonger's and a funeral by Lami (nos.109-110). The tone is generally one of wry humour.

115

118

ANONYMOUS
French

118. Balloon view of London from the east
probably 1830s

Etching and aquatint, 10 x 39
Lent by the City of Westminster Libraries

No.118 was copied from an English print, Robert Havell's *Aeronautical View of London*, published in 1831. It is cruder than the original and bears a French title PANORAMA DE LONDRES VU DE LA NACELLE D'UN BALLON (cropped in the copy shown here) and gallicised place-names in the lower margin, such as 'Chapelle blanche' for Whitechapel. The view is from roughly the position of the present Tower Bridge looking westwards, which gives prominence to the working end of London and relegates Westminster and the West End to the distance. The unnaturally high tonal contrasts in the design give the city a curiously jazzy appearance. For further balloon views by Jules Arnout, see nos.122-3 below.

NICOLAS-TOUSSAINT CHARLET
French, 1792-1845

After studying under Baron Gros, Charlet made his career as a painter and lithographer mainly of military subjects. He was a fervent Bonapartist and many of his works show scenes from the Napoleonic Wars, notably the *Episode from the Retreat from Russia* of 1836. From 1838 until his death he was Professor of Drawing at the Ecole Polytechnique. By nature he was humorous and fond of practical jokes. He visited London in 1820 with his friend Géricault (q.v.) but was too homesick for Paris to do any serious work.

No.119 suggests that he returned at least once but no further details are known.

119. The Bank of England, Royal Exchange and Mansion House 1844-5

Oil on canvas, 35½ x 56
Lent by the Governors and Company of the Bank of England

Charlet obviously found the overcrowding of the City streets a comic spectacle, and in no.119 takes the idea to the brink of caricature. The composition has its characters and its amusing vignettes, such as the omnibus on the left with an animated group of French soldiers on top and a fat lady attempting to squeeze in below. Yet the abbreviated technique in which most of the scene is treated betokens greater interest in the overall effect of extreme busy-ness than in particular details. Forms tend to blockiness and silhouette, faces are stylised, and the figures further back lose their individuality altogether in a mass of ditto-mark heads and hats. The view was topical in featuring the recently opened new Royal Exchange. Chantrey's statue of the Duke of Wellington was erected in front of the Exchange on 18 June 1844, and no.119 was presumably painted between that date and Charlet's premature death on 30 December 1845.

'CHAM' (AMEDEE-CHARLES-HENRI, COMTE DE NOE)
French, 1819-79

A pupil of Charlet (q.v.) then Delaroche, this artist-aristocrat abandoned high art to become a popular caricaturist, comic illustrator and parodist of his more pretentious colleagues. He published his first album of drawings under the pseudonym of 'Cham' in 1839.

120

120. Moeurs britanniques about 1850
Lent by a private collector

Published in Paris by Aubert et Cie, *Moeurs britanniques* is an album of tinted lithographs representing the thoughts of 'Cham' on the manners and customs of the British. 'Visite au Musée' shows a distraught young Frenchman outside the British Museum, searching his waistcoat pockets for a tip to give the portly beadle standing expectantly at the door. 'Pay to get in, pay to get out, you always have to pay,' he complains. 'The thing you see best in London is the bottom of your purse.'

? NICOLAS-MARIE-JOSEPH CHAPUY
French, 1790-1858

121. London about 1850

Etching and aquatint, tinted, 20¼ x 32¾
Lent by the Guildhall Library

The author of this general bird's-eye view is given in the lower margin as 'Chapuis' [sic], but it seems more likely to have been the topographical draughtsman and lithographer

Nicolas-Marie-Joseph Chapuy than any artist spelling his name in exactly that way. The high vantage point was one of the towers of Westminster Abbey; the view of the Abbey in the foreground was ingeniously fabricated rather than observed. The nineteenth-century bird's-eye view, whether taken from a building or a balloon, inevitably drew attention to London's abundance of chimneys and smoke, and a blue-grey pall of rain covers the scene beyond a line from the Tower to Euston. Otherwise no.121 promotes a hospitable image; the foreground is lit by sunshine, and the streets are full of people happily going about their business. The very French-looking red-tiled roofs in the foreground betray a foreigner's unfamiliarity with the English scene. The work is datable to some time between the opening of Waterloo Station, which is shown, and that of Queen Victoria Street, which is not - i.e. to between 1848 and 1851 - and the Houses of Parliament are in a state of completion consistent with that period. The print was published in Paris by A. Appert.

121

LOUIS-JULES ARNOUT
French, 1814-68

Following in the footsteps of his father Jean-Baptiste (q.v.), Arnout was a painter and lithographer. His pictures and prints are generally of French, Italian or English scenery.

122. Balloon view of London about 1850

Lithograph, 11 x 17½
Lent by the British Library (Map Library)

123. Balloon view of London from Greenwich about 1850

Lithograph, tinted, 11 x 17
Lent by the Guildhall Library

Nos.122-3 are from a series of *Excursions aériennes*, drawn and lithographed by Arnout, printed by Lemercier, and published by Bulla frères et Jouy in Paris and Gambart, Junin & Co. in London. In no.122 the artist's balloon is drifting over the south bank, providing a view centred on Trafalgar Square and including Westminster, Hungerford and Waterloo Bridges. No.123 is a much elevated version of

the traditional vista over London from One Tree Hill in Greenwich, which now features long railway viaducts leading towards a mass of smoking chimneys in the distance.

124

124. Fleet Street and Ludgate Hill about 1850

Lithograph, tinted, 14¼ x 11¼
Lent by the Guildhall Library

The view along Fleet Street and up Ludgate Hill afforded a kind of apotheosis of St Paul's, which rose unexpectedly high above the humdrum bustle of the streets like a misty apparition. The effect attracted Arnout and many other visiting artists.

CHARLES TRINOCQ
French, dates unknown

125. London, with vignettes of important buildings 1851

Lithographed map, 21 x 28¾
Lent by the Guildhall Library

The map has been tinted with green for parks, blue for the river and ponds, and magenta for railway lines. The Crystal Palace in Hyde Park, also picked out in magenta, is labelled BUILDING FOR THE GREAT INDUSTRAL [sic] EXHIBITION. The margins contain a directory of places of interest and a dozen vignettes of

London landmarks, all with gallicised captions such as 'Banque d'Angleterre' and 'Colonne du Duc d'York'. The work was published in Paris by Garnier Frères.

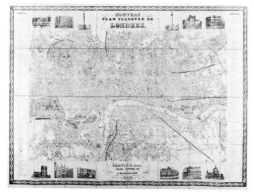

125

GUIDEBOOKS

Nos.126-34 are a selection from the large number of illustrated foreign-language guidebooks to London that appeared in the second half of the nineteenth century. Then as now, guidebooks played an important part in forming and disseminating the image of London, although the contents rarely aspired to a high literary or artistic standard and were often anonymous. They catered to the boom in middle-class tourism and, like many of the works of art produced for a middle-class audience in this period, were emphatically factual and down-to-earth. Earlier guides were aimed at the gentleman tourist with plenty of time and money; they were more stylishly written, less comprehensive in the information they contained and designed for reading at home rather than at the sights they described.

The story of the modern guidebook to London begins with the Great Exhibition of 1851. The influx of millions of visitors from abroad created a huge demand, which was met by at least 44 new guidebooks in English, including the first Murray's handbook to London, and some 36 in various foreign languages. Those brought forth by the International Exhibition of 1862 were smaller in number, but they included the first of the London Baedekers, which were

to dominate the scene well into the twentieth century. The famous Baedeker series provided more information than ever, including advice on practical matters such as hotel prices and fares, as well as details about the less obviously attractive commercial, industrial and engineering achievements of the city. Yet they helped the reader who was in a hurry by clearly indicating what was essential and what was not by means of typographical variations and starring systems. They were not meant to be read from cover to cover while sitting in an armchair, but carried in the pocket and consulted on the spot. For a fuller discussion of this subject, see David Webb, 'For Inns a Hint, for Routes a Chart: The Nineteenth-century London Guidebook', *London Journal*, vol. 6, 1980, pp. 207-14).

126. Nouveau Guide à Londres pour l'exposition de 1851 1851

Lent by the British Library Board

The Paris publishing firm of Napoléon Chaix et Cie had published a London guide in 1848 and this is an updated edition for French people coming over for the Great Exhibition. The frontispiece is a fold-out tinted lithograph by Emile Mandouce showing the Crystal Palace with crowds of visitors outside, many in exotic national dress.

127. Guide illustré du voyageur à Londres et aux environs 1851

Lent by the British Library

Although the title-page claims that all the 100 illustrations in this guide were drawn on the spot by the artists Charles-François Daubigny (q.v.) and Samuel Freeman, their authorship is only occasionally indicated and most seem in fact to be second-hand engravings from previous publications. The work was published jointly by Ernest Bourdin in Paris and W. Thomas and Churchill in London.

128. Illustrirter London-Führer 1851

Lent by the British Library Board

Issued by the firm of J. J. Weber in Leipzig, this copiously illustrated guide was by far the most detailed to appear before the advent of Baedeker.

129. Elisée Reclus
Guide du voyageur à Londres et aux environs 1860

Lent by the Guildhall Library

No.129 is from the series of guidebooks published by the firm of Hachette in Paris and known as the 'Guides-Joanne' after their general editor Adolphe Joanne; the first Guide-Joanne to London appeared in 1851. The author of this later edition was a remarkable individual of a literary ability far superior to the majority of guidebook writers. He was a curious combination of geographer and anarchist, and was to publish a nineteen-volume *Nouvelle géographie universelle* from 1875, as well as numerous pamphlets promoting libertarian ideas. In 1882 he founded the Anti-Marriage Movement.

130. Karl Baedeker
London und seine Umgebung 1862

Lent by the British Library Board

Baedeker's guidebooks brought new standards of accuracy and thoroughness to the form, dispensing with the advertisements that cluttered the pages of his rivals' publications, providing clear, up-to-date maps and laying out a wealth of information in an easily accessible manner. Published in Coblenz, no.130 was the first London Baedeker. It was followed by a French edition in 1866 (no.132) and an English edition, which catered mainly for the American market, in 1878. By 1900 there had been thirteen editions in German, ten in French and twelve in English, comprising a total output of about 175,000 books.

131. Elisée Reclus
Londres illustré 1865

Lent by the Guildhall Library

An abridged edition of no.129 with additional illustrations.

132. Karl Baedeker
Londres 1866

Lent by the Guildhall Library

The first French edition of the London Baedeker.

133. Louis Rousselet
Londres et ses environs 1879

Lent by the Guildhall Library

Though credited to Louis Rousselet, who was a traveller and editor of the *Journal de la Jeunesse*, this 'Guide diamant' in the Guides-Joanne series is in fact a revised version of Elisée Reclus's *Guide du voyageur* of 1860 (no.129). It was first published in 1874; no.133 is a later edition.

134. Londres, ses environs et les principales villes d'Angleterre, d'Ecosse et d'Irlande 1892

Lent by the British Library Board

No.134 is a new edition of a particularly detailed and comprehensive Guide-Joanne that first appeared in 1886. It contains recommended walks through London and provides maps with the routes marked in red; the '1ère Promenade' could almost be a guide to the London of Claude Monet (q.v.).

ANONYMOUS
French

135. Allegory of London probably 1850s

Wallpaper panel, colour print from woodblocks, 50 x 22½
Lent by the Whitworth Art Gallery, Manchester

London is represented as a fictive marble statue of a matronly female figure in a golden niche wreathed with flowers. She wears a castellated head-dress, symbolising the general idea of the walled city and the Tower in particular, and carries a trident like the sea-god Neptune or his wife Amphitrite; at her feet an urn spouts water and a cupid-like boy clutches an anchor, representing the Thames and shipping. The floral surround to the niche may be intended to suggest the pleasures of the London parks and suburbs, but may equally be stock decoration favoured by the designer or manufacturer concerned. Above the niche is the time-honoured combination of the City and Royal Arms.

JEAN-BAPTISTE ARNOUT
French, 1788 – after 1865

Arnout was a watercolourist and lithographer of sites in France, England, Belgium, Italy and Spain. He was the father of Louis-Jules Arnout (q.v.), who was also a topographical artist.

136. Paris et Londres 1852

Lent by a private collector

This miscellany of delicate tinted lithographic views was published in Paris by N. Leclercq and presumably designed to appeal to the large number of French people who had visited London for the Great Exhibition of 1851.

CHARLES RIVIERE
French, dates unknown

137. Vues de Londres probably 1862

Lent by a private collector

An album of double-page lithographic views, unaccompanied by any text and crudely tinted orange and pink in the areas occupied by ground and buildings, and blue in the areas of sky. The subjects include the International Exhibition of 1862 with much traffic and bustle in the foreground. The work was published in Paris by the Maison Martinet.

PAUL GAVARNI (SULPICE-GUILLAUME CHEVALIER)
French, 1804-66

Gavarni's wry and sprightly drawings of manners and customs were a popular feature of the *Charivari* and other French journals. He spent a period in London in 1847 following the break-up of his marriage.

138. Londres et les anglais probably 1862

Lent by a private collector

The fruits of Gavarni's stay in London were originally published as cartoons in the *Charivari*. They first appeared in book form in 1849 with a text in English by Albert Smith. No.138 is a later French edition; it is undated but the new text, by Emile de la Badollière, refers to the International Exhibition of 1862 as an imminent event. Indeed the book was probably aimed at French people who were travelling to London to see the exhibition. It was published in Paris by Gustave Barba.

'FAUSTIN' (FAUSTIN BETBEDER)
French, born 1847

Faustin was a student at the Ecole des Beaux-Arts when the Franco-Prussian War broke out; he made a satirical drawing of Napoleon III that revealed a talent for caricature and continued to work as a comic artist for the rest of his career, much of which he spent in London. He also designed posters and costumes for the theatre.

139. Londres pittoresque about 1872

Lent by a private collector

Though undated on the title-page, *Londres pittoresque* contains a number of illustrations signed by Faustin and dated 1872. He presents a tragi-comic view of London indebted both to Gustave Doré, whose *London. A Pilgrimage* was published in parts from January 1872, and to the cheerful English illustrator Richard Doyle. He proclaims his allegiance to his compatriot in the very first illustration, which shows a man with a sandwich-board advertising the Doré Gallery. The Doré-esque drawings include a scene of indigents queuing outside a workhouse door, with a bill for the opera *La Traviata* placed symbolically above the head of a mother with her child. The text is by Roger Dalton and the work was published in Paris by Franklin.

G. MONTBARD (CHARLES-AUGUSTE LOYE)
French, 1841-1905

Montbard was a caricaturist and comic illustrator who may have had some special British connections since he is known to have died in London in 1905.

140. Henri Bellenger
Londres pittoresque et la vie anglaise 1876

Lent by the British Library Board

The butts of Montbard's illustrations to Bellenger's jovial text include a column of policemen marching along a rainswept London street. The work was published by Georges Decaux in Paris and E. Sardou in Brussels.

AUGUSTE LANÇON
French, 1836-1887

Though best known for his prints and illustrations, especially of animal subjects, Lançon was also a painter and exhibited works at the Paris Salon. In 1871 he took part in the Commune, was almost executed and spent six months in prison.

141. Jules Vallès
La Rue à Londres 1884
Lent by the Guildhall Library

No.141 is illustrated with 28 full-page etchings by Lançon and numerous wood-engravings made from his drawings. Some are fairly amusing in tone, including a number of studies of entertainers, but the most memorable are those dealing with the grimmer side of London life. Their subjects present London as a city of contrasts and their blocky, pronounced chiaroscuro provides visual reinforcement to the point. Outside Euston Station, for example, a few sleeping vagrants are huddled together on a bench under a statue of George Stephenson striding forward as if full of strength and optimism – a juxtaposition suggestive of the best and the worst of the modern city. The work was published in Paris by Georges Charpentier.

'MARS' (MAURICE BONVOISIN)
French, born 1849

A cartoonist who contributed to the *Charivari* and the *Journal amusant*.

142. La Vie de Londres. Côtés Riants about 1890

Lent by a private collector

Mars's illustrations are comic but suave. A typical page in this album shows a handsome guardsman with a moustache sitting on the Embankment chatting to a young cockney woman, with verses about the romantic attractions of 'le guardsman' for 'les pretty girls', along with a scene of upper-class flirtation in Mayfair and a vignette of a bibulous M.P. enjoying some champagne and a cigar. The work was published by Plon in Paris.

CHARLES DANA GIBSON
American, 1867 – 1944

After training as an artist in New York and Paris, Gibson became a popular illustrator, contributing to the magazine *Life* and publishing collections of his drawings as albums such as no.143. He was influenced by the English comic draughtsmen George Du Maurier and Phil May. The favourite type ubiquitous in his work was a self-assured upper-class beauty that became known as 'the Gibson Girl'.

143. London as seen by Charles Dana Gibson 1897

Lent by the Guildhall Library

Gibson concentrates on high society, beautiful young women and men who are 'characters'. His drawings and the text he wrote to accompany them are almost fawningly anglophile. The album was published by Charles Scribner's Sons of New York.

ANONYMOUS
French

144. Guide des Plaisirs à Londres about 1910

Lent by the British Library Board

The subtitle of this guide for the playboy visitor reads 'London by day, London by night. Where to have fun, How to have fun, The underside of London'. It was published in Paris and London by the firm of Nilsson but the author is unnamed. There is a section on 'La Femme à Londres' and the illustrations are mostly photographs of the attractive women to be sought out in the London streets, theatres and bars.

141

142

143

RIVER LIFE

NOTHING HERE IS NATURAL; EVERYTHING IS TRANSFORMED – FORCED – FROM
THE EARTH AND MANKIND TO THE LIGHT AND AIR. BUT THE SHEER ENORMITY
OF SUCH HUMAN ACCRETION AND CREATION MAKES ONE FORGET THE
DISTORTION AND THE ARTIFICIALITY; INSTEAD OF A NOBLE, HEALTHY BEAUTY,
THERE IS LIFE, SWARMING AND GRANDIOSE; THE GLEAM ON THE BROWN WAVES,
THE DIFFUSION OF LIGHT TRAPPED IN VAPOUR, THE GENTLE HIGHLIGHTS AND
TRACES OF PINK PLAYING OVER THE WHOLE COLOSSAL SPECTACLE BESTOW A
SORT OF GRACE UPON THE MONSTROUS CITY, LIKE A SMILE ON THE FACE OF A
SWARTHY, BRISTLING CYCLOPS.

Hippolyte Taine, 1862

The teeming commercial thoroughfare of the Thames was a constant fascination
for visitors to Victorian London. The forest of masts and rigging, the dense flotillas
of ships, barges and ferries, the endless array of warehouses, wharves, cranes,
moorings, buoys and debris made the port of London a wonder of the industrial
world. For artists such as Whistler, it was a repository of suggestions for designs
and effects that was all the more attractive for being unhallowed by conventional
ideas of the picturesque.

JAMES McNEILL WHISTLER
American, 1834-1903

After training for the military at West Point and working for the U.S. Coast and Geodetic Survey in Washington, Whistler decided upon an artistic career and moved to Paris. He studied there from 1855 to 1858, mixing in *avant-garde* company and admiring the work of Courbet. He came to London regularly to visit his half-sister Deborah, who had married the British artist Seymour Haden, and etched and painted Thames subjects from 1859 onwards. In 1863 he moved into Lindsey Row, Chelsea, and became friendly with Rossetti and his circle. From 1871 he painted a succession of Thames night scenes or *Nocturnes*. In 1878 he moved to the White House in Tite Street, still in Chelsea, and the same year engaged in a libel action against Ruskin for his attack on a *Nocturne* exhibited at the Grosvenor Gallery. He won but was only awarded a farthing's damages without costs. In 1879 he was declared bankrupt; bailiffs took possession of the White House and Whistler moved to Venice for a year. He lived at a number of London addresses from 1880 till his death, mainly in Chelsea, although he travelled a great deal and spent long periods in Paris. Like his friend Oscar Wilde, he was a witty and determined advocate of aestheticism, or 'art for art's sake', his most celebrated exposition of the doctrine being the 'Ten O'Clock' lecture of 1885.

WHISTLER'S 'THAMES SET'

Nos.145-52, 154, 156-7 and 167-8 are from the group of etchings made in 1859-61, published in 1871 by Ellis and Green of Covent Garden as *A Series of Sixteen Etchings of Scenes on the Thames and Other Subjects,* and normally known as the 'Thames Set'. The set is dominated by scenes of working life on the ramshackle wharves along the Thames in Wapping and Rotherhithe. Whistler was probably inspired to tackle such subjects by the call of the French poet and critic Baudelaire for an art that dealt with modern city life. Baudelaire certainly admired the Thames Set when he saw it in Paris, finding in it 'the profound and complex poetry of a vast capital'. In fact, Whistler's modernity is only relative, since he concerns himself with old wharves and

145

warehouses along the riverfront rather than the newer and more severe-looking docks that lay behind them. But the images hardly look nostalgic. With a raw immediacy, they seem to reproduce not just everyday sights but an everyday way of seeing. The etched line builds up an accumulation of detail and a marvellous multiplicity of textures in areas meant to be read as in focus, while elsewhere the paper is left blank to indicate lack of focus; foreground features may be only summarily sketched while objects of attention further away are sharply defined.

The occasional reversal of the images suggests that Whistler at least sometimes drew onto the prepared etching plates on the spot, as opposed to making a drawing on paper and transferring it onto the plate back-to-front so as to print the right way round. For further discussion of the Thames Set and Whistler's etching career as a whole, see Katharine A. Lochnan, *The Etchings of James McNeill Whistler,* 1984.

145. Thames Warehouses 1859

Etching, 3 x 8
Signed and dated 'Whistler 1859' (lower r.)
Lent by the Trustees of the British Museum

The view is from the Thames Tunnel Pier in Rotherhithe, looking up-river, with St Paul's in the distance.

146. Old Westminster Bridge 1859

Etching, 3 x 8
Signed and dated 'Whistler 1859' (lower l.)
Lent by the Trustees of the British Museum

146

The Houses of Parliament and Old Westminster Bridge seen, in reverse, from the north. The bridge, which had been painted under construction by Canaletto and Joli amongst others, was at this time about to be demolished, and Whistler shows the scaffolding erected for the purpose, especially under one of the central arches. In 1862 he painted the new bridge in a picture paradoxically entitled *The Last of Old Westminster* (Museum of Fine Arts, Boston).

147

147. Limehouse 1859

Etching, 5 x 8
Signed and dated 'Whistler 1859' (lower r.)
Lent by the Trustees of the British Museum

148

149

150

151

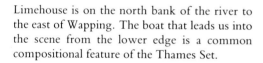

152

Limehouse is on the north bank of the river to the east of Wapping. The boat that leads us into the scene from the lower edge is a common compositional feature of the Thames Set.

148. Eagle Wharf 1859

Etching, 5¼ x 8½
Signed and dated 'Whistler 1859' (lower centre)
Lent by the Trustees of the British Museum

The view is looking down-river, i.e. eastwards, from a point on the banks of the Thames in Wapping. The fact that the face of the boy in the foreground is in shadow suggests that the light is coming from behind, and therefore that it is morning. Eagle Wharf is actually the furthest of the row of buildings on the left.

149. Black Lion Wharf 1859

Etching, 6 x 8 ¾
Signed and dated 'Whistler 1859' (lower r.)
Lent by the Trustees of the British Museum

The row of riverfront buildings from Black Lion Wharf on the right to Hoare's Wharf on the left, viewed from the Horsleydown New Stairs on the south bank of the river in Bermondsey. The foreground figure seems integrated with his

environment in a way that is typical of Whistler's river characters. With the riverfront seen largely across its breadth rather than along its length, this is the least perspectival and most decorative of the river views in the Thames Set, and as such represents a small step in the direction of the Japanese-influenced *Nocturnes* of the 1870s. The work appears in an abstracted form on the wall in Whistler's famous portrait of his mother, painted in 1871 (Musée du Louvre, Paris).

150. The Pool 1859

Etching, 5½ x 8¼
Signed and dated 'Whistler 1859' (lower l.)
Lent by the Trustees of the British Museum

The Pool, a stretch of the Thames down-river from London Bridge, was a hive of commercial activity in Whistler's time and lined with wharves, warehouses and docks. No.150 is a good example of the variety of degrees of attention the artist pays to different parts of the image: the focus is fairly sharp on the face of the shifty character in the foreground, relaxes on the barges behind him, tightens up for the buildings along the shore around St George's Wharf, then relaxes again into the distance.

151. Thames Police 1859

Etching, 6 x 9
Signed and dated 'Whistler 1859' (lower r.)
Lent by the Trustees of the British Museum

The Thames Police Station, shown on the right of this full and intricately-worked composition, stood a short distance to the east of Eagle Wharf on the north bank of the river in Wapping. If he was trying in the Thames Set to represent all aspects of the working life of the river, Whistler may have featured this building as a wry comment on the notorious criminality of the East End.

152. The Limeburner 1859

Etching, 9 ¾ x 7
Signed 'Whistler' (lower l.), and signed and dated 'Whistler 1859' (lower r.)
Lent by the Trustees of the British Museum

Here the river is only glimpsed through an alleyway. We have come 'backstage' and see the riverfront buildings in close-up, structures that have grown by accretion rather than design, where inside and outside are indistinguishable.

153. Billingsgate 1859

Etching, 6 x 9
Signed and dated 'Whistler 1859' (lower r.)
Lent by the Trustees of the British Museum

Though made at the same time as etchings in the Thames Set and showing a similarly low-life subject, no.153 was for some reason not included in the set as published in 1871. The view, which is reversed, shows the river front of Billingsgate fish market, London Bridge and the church of St Mary Overy; it was probably drawn from Custom House Stairs. The clock shows seven o'clock, which may mean five o'clock if that too is reversed. In any case, it is early in the morning and fish are being unloaded onto the crowded quayside from a row of fishing boats.

153

154. Rotherhithe 1860

Etching, 10 ¾ x 7 ¾
Signed and dated 'Whistler 1860' (lower l.)
Lent by the Trustees of the British Museum

Another reversed image, showing the view from the balcony of The Angel, a riverside inn in Rotherhithe, looking north-eastwards towards the City and including the dome of St Paul's in the distance. The grid-like division of the composition may reflect Whistler's enthusiasm for the formal properties of Japanese prints. No.154 is obviously related to, and may have served as a preliminary stage in the gestation of, the slightly later painting of *Wapping* (no.155), which is set on the same balcony though looking in a different direction.

154

155. Wapping 1860-4

Oil on canvas, 28 x 40
Signed and dated 'Whistler. 1861' (lower r.)
Lent by the National Gallery of Art, Washington

The etching *Rotherhithe* (no.154) was executed in June 1860 and *Wapping*, which is set on the same inn balcony, was under way by October that year; the artist worked on it fitfully until the spring of 1864. Almost obscured in the picture by a forest of masts and rigging, Wapping is the dockland area opposite Rotherhithe across what was one of the busiest stretches of the working river. The model for the red-haired young woman in the foreground was Whistler's mistress Joanna Hiffernan, and the bearded man next to her is a likeness of his friend and fellow artist Alphonse Legros.

The scene they are enacting with the sailor on the right is more than a little *risqué*. At one stage Whistler wrote in a letter to his friend the French painter Fantin-Latour that he had given the woman 'the air of saying to her sailor "That's all

155

very well, old fellow, but I've seen others" –
you know – winking and mocking him'. He
originally painted her neckline lower as well,
and, when warned that this might make the
picture unacceptable to the Royal Academy,
threatened to open her shirt more and more
until he was elected an Academician and could
hang the work without submitting it to the jury.
In fact, he probably altered the figure to make
her more modest before sending the work to the
Academy, and it was accepted for the exhibition
in 1864. Nevertheless, the implication remains
that she is a prostitute, the bearded man her
pimp and the sailor a prospective client. Robin
Spencer quotes a description of the kind of
trickery that was practised on unsuspecting
sailors by such shady dockland characters (see
page 53 above). The semi-comic point of
Wapping lies in the juxtaposition of different
forms of river commerce, that represented by
the figures and that represented by the shipping
in the background. One is reminded of the river
scene as described by the artist's fellow
American Nathaniel Hawthorne: 'the muddy
tide of the Thames, reflecting nothing, and
hiding a million of unclean secrets within its
breast, – a sort of guilty conscience, as it were,
unwholesome with the rivulets of sin that
constantly flow into it' (*Our Old Home*, 1863,
vol. II, p. 132), although Whistler's tone is more
amused than moralising.

156. Millbank 1861

Etching, 4 x 5
Dated '1861' on the back of a barge (lower l.),
and inscribed with an advertisement for an
exhibition of Whistler's prints at E. Thomas's
gallery in Bond Street (lower r.)
Lent by the Trustees of the British Museum

For the later etchings of the Thames Set,
Whistler moved up-river, and no. 156 shows the
view, in reverse, from Millbank looking north
towards Lambeth Palace in the distance.

157. Old Hungerford Bridge 1861

Etching, 5 1/4 x 8 1/4
Signed 'Whistler' (lower r.)
Lent by the Trustees of the British Museum

No. 157 typifies the development of Whistler's
etching technique in its delicate and wispy lines
and its enhanced effect of atmosphere; it also

stands apart from earlier river views of the
Thames Set in its high viewpoint. Again the
image is reversed. The view must have been
taken from a vantage point close to the future
site of the Savoy Hotel, from which both
Whistler and Monet were to depict the bridge
that took the place of the one shown here. Old
Hungerford Bridge was about to be dismantled
and much ominous scaffolding and debris is
shown to the left of the composition.

157

156

158

158. Grey and Silver: Old Battersea Reach
1863

Oil on canvas, 20 x 27
Signed and dated 'Whistler. 63' (lower l.)
Lent by the Art Institute of Chicago (Potter
Palmer Collection)

159. Battersea Reach about 1863

Oil on canvas, 20 x 30
Lent by the Corcoran Gallery of Art,
Washington (Bequest of James Parmelee)

Nos.158-9 show views from Whistler's house
on the river in Chelsea. Their subject is the river
as a work-place, an idea Whistler conveys by
means of a sketchy impression of movement
and busy-ness rather than by the kind of specific
ergonomic detail of, say, a landscape by
Constable. The surfaces of the pictures are
appropriately worked and rough-and-ready,
especially in comparison with Whistler's thinly
painted *Nocturnes* of the 1870s (see no.228),
and their compositions are casual-looking, with cut-
off effects at the edges and a calculatedly tenuous
sense of balance.   *See Colour Plate XXIII*

UTAGAWA YOSHITORA
Japanese, active about 1850-80

A pupil of Itagawa Kuniyoshi, Yoshitora made
'floating-world' prints showing views in
Tokyo, scenes with foreign visitors in
Yokohama, and views of foreign cities.

160. The Port of London in England 1862

Colour print from woodblocks, 14 x 28½
Lent by the Victoria and Albert Museum

The opening of Japan to the outside world from
the 1850s stimulated an interest in foreigners and
the places from which they came. Printmakers
such as Yoshitora catered to the curiosity and
the prejudices of their audience by recreating the
appearance of these 'barbarian' cities on the basis
of a little research among western engravings
and a great deal of imagination. The best-
informed part of no.160 is the central section of
the background, showing the London skyline
with St Paul's and the Monument. Elsewhere
things become fairly fantastical. The Thames is
spanned by a Japanese-looking bridge with
arches so small that the huge battleships
anchored upriver would have no chance of
reaching the open sea. The palatial architecture
of the foreground forms a setting for some
figures with western dress of the 1850s but
Japanese features, positioned inexplicably in
relation to each other and clearly copied out of

context from different sources. The inscriptions
give the names of the artist and the publisher,
Yamadaya Shojiro, the title of the print as given
above, the title of the series from which it
comes, *A Compendium of Famous Places in
Barbarian Countries*, and the following
description of London:

London, the capital city of England, lies on the River Thames.
There are a great many buildings, and the whole population is
prosperous. The river is spanned by a large bridge 1800 feet
long and 40 feet wide. There are three light towers which are
lit at night for the benefit of travellers crossing the bridge. The
bank of the river is dominated by an imposing fortress. In
various parts of the city English goods are traded with
merchants from all over the world. The mouth of the river is
so choked with ships that one would believe one was on dry
land. The population is large, and the number of students
normally at university is never less than several tens of
thousands. The women are extremely lustful and the men are
both shrewd and cunning. To fulfil their ambitions they build
large ships with which to sail the oceans of the world. They
trade in all manner of goods and make enormous profits for
themselves. They have 28,000 merchantmen with 185,000
officers on board. The monarch's ship has 40 cannons, and
there are eight hundred or more ships with 120 cannons each
(translation kindly supplied by Rupert Faulkner).

It is interesting to compare this Japanese artist's
image of London with Japanese-influenced
views by Whistler such as nos.167-8, 170, 228-9
and 232.   *See Colour Plate XXIX*

CARL FREDERICK SØRENSEN
Danish, 1818-79

Sørensen studied under Eckersberg at the
Copenhagen Academy and became a painter
largely of marine subjects. He made regular
sketching trips to seaside locations and in 1846
accompanied a Danish frigate on a voyage to the
Mediterranean. He became a member of the
Copenhagen Academy in 1856.

161. The Thames and London Bridge 1862

Oil on canvas, 36¼ x 53
Signed and dated 'C. Frederick Sørensen 1862'
(lower r.)
Lent by the Trafalgar Galleries, by courtesy of a
private collector

This characteristically luminous riverscape
shows London Bridge from the east, against the
light, with Billingsgate Market in shadow on
the right. It is late afternoon and the bridge is
busy with traffic leaving the City. By choosing
this particular stretch, with its clusters of fishing
boats and scruffy quaysides, its buoys and
moorings, Sørensen presents the Thames very
much as a commercial thoroughfare and place of
work.

CHARLES-FRANÇOIS DAUBIGNY
French, 1817-78

After an early career as a book and magazine
illustrator, Daubigny made his name as a
landscape painter in the 1850s, developing a
realist manner indebted to Courbet. He worked
at a number of favourite sites, including the
Forest of Fontainebleau, where he was
associated with the 'Barbizon School', and
Villerville on the northern coast of France. He
liked to paint outdoors, often from a studio
boat, and the controversial sketchiness of his
technique was an inspiration to the
Impressionists. Daubigny was in London in
1866 and again in 1870-1, taking refuge from the
Franco-Prussian War. He was on friendly terms
with his fellow refugees Monet and Pissarro,
and effected an important introduction for
Monet to the dealer Paul Durand-Ruel.

162. St Paul's from the Surrey Side 1873

Oil on canvas, 17½ x 32
Signed and dated 'Daubigny 1873' (lower l.)
Lent by Trustees of the the National Gallery

This was probably the painting exhibited under
the given title at Durand-Ruel's 'Society of
French Artists' exhibition in Bond Street in
1874. It shows St Paul's and Blackfriars Bridge
as seen, through a smoke-laden haze, from a
point along the wharves on the south bank of
the river. Men are unloading sacks, perhaps of
coal, from a row of black barges occupying the
lower third of the composition. The faith of the
Barbizon School of landscapists in the goodness
of everything rural rested upon an abhorrence of
the urban and the industrial; the city was the
antithesis to the peace, solitude and silence they
valued in the country. As we might expect from
a member of that group, Daubigny lays stress

161

dogs with sexuality and from hints of vulgarity such as the combination of blue socks with brown and white shoes. Above the sailor a ship's figurehead in the form of a bare-breasted woman looms up as if embodying his thoughts. As in Whistler's *Wapping* (no.155), the docks are presented as a place where Victorian standards of sexual morality do not apply – which seems humorous enough to us, but struck Victorian critics as a scandal.

When no.163 was shown at the Royal Academy in 1876, the *Athenaeum* considered the women to be 'ugly and low-bred', the depiction of the Pool of London a 'libel', and the picture as a whole 'thoroughly and wilfully vulgar'. The *Spectator* accused the women of being 'undeniably Parisian' and even the *Graphic*, which was generally well-disposed towards Tissot, found the work clever 'but hardly nice in its suggestions. More French, shall we say, than English ?' (see Michael Wentworth, *James Tissot*, Oxford, 1984, p. 108). The British audience often suspected that Tissot, the sophisticated Frenchman, was gently making fun of their sense of propriety in life and art, and they may well have been right.

See Colour Plate XXVIII

upon the dark side of his subject, contrasting the lowness, heaviness and materiality of the world of industry represented in the foreground with the remote and apparently fading forms of St Paul's, which reads as a symbol of higher values. *See Colour Plate XXIV*

JAMES TISSOT
French, 1836-1902

Tissot anglicised his name from Jacques to James at the outset of his career, probably in emulation of his friend James McNeill Whistler (q.v.). After an severely academic training in Paris, he developed an enthusiasm for the Belgian painter of historical scenes, Henri Leys, and for several years worked largely in Leys's manner. He achieved success from 1864 with carefully observed, modish and occasionally comic scenes from contemporary life. Tissot saw action in the Franco-Prussian War but fled to London after the collapse of the Paris Commune in 1871. He stayed in London until 1882, living in some style with his beautiful Irish

mistress Kathleen Newton in St John's Wood. Back in Paris, he found himself out of fashion and his series of large paintings of *Woman in Paris*, exhibited in 1885, was a critical and commercial failure. The following year he visited the Holy Land and began gathering material for a lavishly illustrated edition of the New Testament, which appeared to enormous acclaim in 1896-7. From 1897 onwards he lived a reclusive life in the stately Château de Buillon, near Besançon.

163. The Thames 1876

Oil on canvas, 28½ x 46½
Signed 'J.J.Tissot' (lower r.)
Lent by Wakefield Art Galleries and Museums

The single man with a pair of attractive young women was Tissot's favourite cast of characters, and in this case it is a sailor taking his girlfriends for a pleasure-boat trip through the London docks. There is an air of sexual innuendo about the group arising from the fact that the women are unchaperoned in the company of a sailor, from their closeness to him, from the presence of alcohol, from the traditional association of

164. The Trafalgar Tavern, Greenwich 1878

Etching and drypoint, 14 x 9½
Signed and dated 'J. J. Tissot 1878' (lower l.)
Lent by a private collector

The view is looking westwards along the river front of the tavern, with a corner of the Royal Naval Hospital beyond. The work also exists in a later state with dark stormclouds that add a *frisson* of foreboding to the atmosphere.

165. Waiting for the Ferry about 1878

Oil on panel, 10 x 14
Signed 'J.J.Tissot' (lower l.)
Lent by a private collector

The scene is set by the Falcon Tavern at Gravesend, on the south bank of the Thames estuary. The female figure is recognisable as the artist's mistress Kathleen Newton. The ambiguity in the subject is deliberate and quite typical of Tissot; there is clearly something going on, both on a narrative and on a psychological level, but it is left to the spectator's imagination to supply the details.

165

JAN TOOROP
Dutch, 1858-1928

Born in Java of Dutch parents, Toorop studied art at the academies of Amsterdam and Brussels. He exhibited with the avant-garde group 'Les XX' in Brussels from 1885 to 1893. Working largely as an illustrator and designer, he developed the sinuous draughtsmanship and ambiguous subject-matter for which he is best known in the 1890s; his mature style shows the influence of both the Symbolist movement and *art nouveau*. In 1905 Toorop became a Roman Catholic convert and devoted much of his art to sacred themes. His contacts with London began when he met his future wife Annie Hall, who was a fellow art student in Brussels. He visited her family in 1884 and 1885-6 and they were married in London in 1886, although afterwards they lived mostly in the Netherlands.

166. Charing Cross Bridge 1886

Oil on canvas, 14 x 18¼
Signed 'J. Toorop' (lower r.)
Lent by the Rijksmuseum Kröller-Müller, Otterlo

Toorop painted no.166 while in London around the time of his marriage to the Englishwoman Annie Hall, and showed it at the exhibition of 'Les XX' in Brussels later the same year. It shows the railway bridge leading out of Charing Cross Station across the Thames, the subject of works by Whistler and Monet in the 1890s, looking eastwards towards the factory-lined south bank. More remarkable as engineering than as architecture, the bridge appears especially imposing from this low viewpoint. The separateness of the dabs of paint suggests the influence of the 'divisionist' painters of the Parisian avant-garde, Seurat and Signac, although the use of the direction and texture of the brushwork to differentiate parts of the subject betrays a relatively old-fashioned Impressionist approach. The dabs run diagonally on the piers of the bridge, horizontally across the surface of the water and in various directions on the shore and in the sky.

166

PARK AND SUBURB

YES, THE CITY OF BANKERS, OF SHOPKEEPERS, OF MONEY-MAKING PEOPLE, IS,
TAKING IT ALL IN ALL, A CITY WITH PASTORAL PREDILECTIONS, WITH IDYLLIC
TENDENCIES. IT HAS PARKS THAT RESEMBLE MEADOWS. IT LOVES TO SEE,
STRETCHING OUT BETWEEN STREETS FULL OF NOISE AND MOVEMENT, LARGE
OPEN SPACES IN WHICH SHEEP BROWSE AND CATTLE GRAZE . . . IT IS THE
CUSTOM THEREFORE TO HAVE SOMEWHERE IN THE SUBURBS OF LONDON A
RURAL RETREAT CONTAINING THE DOMESTIC HEARTH, FROM WHICH ONE
STARTS IN THE MORNING TO RETURN TO IT IN THE EVENING, SAFE TO LOSE
TWO, THREE, OR EVEN FOUR HOURS A DAY TRAVELLING BY RAILWAY.
Louis Blanc, 1861

It was a relief for many visitors to find that, not far from the centres of industry and
commerce, there existed an alternative London of leisure, relaxation and greenery,
a *rus in urbe*. The extensive parks and salubrious suburbs provided plenty of
opportunity for the city dweller to get in touch with nature without completely
leaving town. The London parks were admired not only for their size but also for
their authentically rural appearance, and the middle-class suburbs that developed in
the mid century, fostered by the growth of the railway network, were to be
imitated throughout the world.

168

169

JAMES MCNEILL WHISTLER
American, 1834–1903

For a brief biography of Whistler and a note on his 'Thames Set' of etchings, see nos.145–59 above.

167. Chelsea Bridge and Church probably 1860-1, reworked 1871

Etching and drypoint, 4 x 6½
Lent by the Trustees of the British Museum

168. Early Morning, Battersea 1861

Etching and drypoint, 4½ x 6
Signed 'Whistler' (lower l.)
Lent by the Trustees of the British Museum

Nos.167-8 are later etchings from Whistler's 'Thames Set' showing views in Chelsea, an altogether safer, suburban locale than the dockland from which he drew the majority of his subjects. This was where his sister and brother-in-law lived, and where the artist himself settled in 1863. The delicate, atmospheric treatment of the riverscape looks forward to the *Nocturnes* of the 1870s, and no.168 in particular bears witness to the simplifying, flattening influence of the Japanese prints that Whistler so admired.

169. 'The Adam and Eve', Old Chelsea 1878

Etching and drypoint, 6¾ x 11¾
Signed with the artist's butterfly emblem (above the church)
Lent by the Trustees of the British Museum

Whistler etched and published no.169 with Messrs Hogarth and Son in a vain attempt to stave off impending bankruptcy as the costs of

170

his court case against Ruskin added to his mounting debts. It shows, in reverse, a venerable old inn on the river that had been destroyed with the building of the Embankment some six years before; the artist worked from a photograph of the site taken in 1871 by the local photographer James Hedderly. The tower of Chelsea Church is visible in the background.

170. Old Putney Bridge 1879

Etching, 8 x 11¾
Signed with the artist's butterfly emblem (lower centre)
Lent by the Trustees of the British Museum

Old Putney Bridge was another doomed landmark of old Chelsea. A new bridge was built shortly after Whistler made no.170 and the old one was demolished in 1884-6. The old bridge clearly reminded him of those highly decorative wooden bridges that feature in the 'floating-world' prints of Japanese masters such as Hokusai and Hiroshige.

171. Maunder's Fish Shop, Chelsea 1890

Lithograph, 7½ x 6¾
Signed with the artist's butterfly emblem (on shopfront)
Lent by the Whitworth Art Gallery, Manchester

Maunder's fish shop was in a converted seventeenth-century house on Lombard Street. Published in the *Whirlwind* on 20 December 1890, no.171 records its appearance shortly before demolition, again demonstrating Whistler's preservationist response to the buildings of old Chelsea.

CAMILLE PISSARRO
French, 1830-1903

This leading figure in the Impressionist movement was one of a number of French artists, including Monet (q.v.), who took refuge in London from the Franco-Prussian War. Pissarro arrived towards the end of 1870 with his common-law wife Julie Vellay. His half-sister Emma, her husband and children had settled in London some years before and had been joined by his mother. By 1870 Emma had died and Mme Pissarro was living with the children in a private school in the south London suburb of Lower Norwood. Pissarro took rented accommodation near by in Upper Norwood and stayed until the summer of the following year. He soon made contact with Monet and both began painting their new environment. 'Monet and I were very enthusiastic over the London landscapes', he later recalled. 'Monet worked in the parks, whilst I, living at Lower Norwood [sic], at that time a charming suburb, studied the effects of fog, snow and springtime. We worked from Nature, and later on Monet painted in London some superb studies of mist. We also visited the museums.'

All Pissarro's London paintings of this time show views within a couple of miles of where he was staying. Before leaving he managed to sell four of them to the dealer Paul Durand-Ruel, whom he met through Monet. On 14 June 1871 he married Julie at the Croydon Register Office and shortly afterwards returned to his home at Louveciennes, near Paris, where he found that most of his belongings had been destroyed, including some twenty years' work. He was again in London in 1890, 1892 and 1897 to visit his eldest son Lucien (q.v.). On these later trips he painted further suburban subjects in Bedford Park, as well as central London sites such as Hyde Park and Charing Cross Bridge. For fuller discussions of Pissarro's views of London, see Nicholas Reed, *Camille Pissarro at the Crystal Palace*, 1987.

172. Fox Hill, Upper Norwood 1870

Oil on canvas, 14 x 18
Signed and dated 'C. Pissarro 70' (lower r.)
Lent by the Trustees of the National Gallery

This view westwards up Fox Hill is probably the work exhibited at Durand-Ruel's 'Society of French Artists' exhibition in March 1871 as *A Snow Effect*. As a refugee from a country defeated and occupied by enemy forces, Pissarro was appreciative of the calm and security of the London suburbs. They also represented an alternative to the overcrowded and corrupt city that was modern and not merely escapist, as well as proof that the manmade need not obliterate nature. Pissarro's Norwood pictures suggest this idea by bringing nature, buildings and people together in scenes unified by light, atmosphere and 'effects' such as the snow in no.172. We are clearly in a built-up area yet there is plenty of open ground, grass, trees and bushes. The older red-roofed house on the left and the organic bend in the road suggest that the place has grown over a period of time, and the figures of the two women and a man with a walking stick, apparently meeting by chance, help convey the sense of a local community.
See Colour Plate XXXII

173. Upper Norwood, with the Crystal Palace in the distance 1870-1

Oil on canvas, 15¾ x 20
Signed 'C. Pissarro' (lower r.)
Lent by a private collector

No.173 may be the picture Pissarro showed at the 'Society of French Artists' exhibition in March 1871 under the title *View in Upper Norwood*. The view is from a point near that of *Fox Hill, Upper Norwood* (no.172) but looking north instead of west. The Crystal Palace, which appears on the horizon to the right, was the vast structure of iron and glass built by Joseph Paxton for the Great Exhibition of 1851.

After the exhibition it was dismantled on its original site in Hyde Park and rebuilt in Sydenham, where it housed a variety of historical, artistic and scientific displays. It was the most conspicuous landmark for miles around, a major attraction for both British and foreign tourists and a symbol of the modern world; it was destroyed by fire in 1936. It was topical during Pissarro's London period because 1871 was the twentieth anniversary of the Great Exhibition, and a commemorative International Exhibition was held in South Kensington from May onwards.

Not all foreign visitors admired the place, and Hippolyte Taine thought it typical of the barbarism of the British, 'a monstrous pile devoid of style and bearing witness not to their taste but to their power'. But Pissarro implies no such criticism, and seems to juxtapose the grey, looming form of the 'palace' with the modest domestic housing closer-to as a way of suggesting a happy balance of public and private; the same idea informs his other Crystal Palace view, now at the Art Institute of Chicago. This is a more obviously manmade piece of suburbia than that represented in no.172, with a terrain that bears the marks of having been cut through, dug out, banked up and fenced off at a fairly recent date. Yet there remains a sense of plentiful space, and earth, grass and trees are still allowed to make their presence felt. *See Colour Plate XXXIII*

174. Study at Lower Norwood 1870-1

Oil on canvas, 15½ x 18
Signed with initials 'C. P.' (lower l.)
Lent by Mr and Mrs Edward McCormick Blair

This study in shades of green of some rising fields or parkland is the most emphatically rural of Pissarro's views in the south London suburbs. Sunlight filters through foliage, some horses are peacefully grazing on the right, and the few buildings included are screened by rows of trees in the background. In its harmonious integration of the natural and the manmade, its overall green-ness, and the glimpses through the top layers of paint to a rust-coloured underpainting, the work bears witness to Pissarro's enthusiasm for the landscapes of John Constable. The title *Etude à Lower Norwood* was probably coined as late as in 1930 by the

cataloguers of Pissarro's work, his son Ludovic-Rodo and Lionello Venturi, and may well be inaccurate. The scene is certainly in the Norwood area, but not necessarily Lower Norwood. For a suggested identification of the site, see Nicholas Reed, *Camille Pissarro at the Crystal Palace*, 1987. No.174 was one of the pictures by Pissarro owned by his son and fellow painter of the suburbs, Lucien Pissarro (q.v.).

175. Hyde Park 1890

Tempera on paper, laid on canvas, 21 x 25½
Signed and dated '[Pissar (overpainted)] ro 1890' (lower r.)
Lent by a private collector

No.175 dates from Pissarro's visit to London to see his son Lucien in May-June 1890. By showing the view along an avenue and adding extra linear definition to the foreground tree to make it stand out against the deepest part of the composition, the artist stresses the spaciousness of the park. Like Pissarro's suburban subjects, the park was a modern environment blending the manmade and the natural; a road busy with carriages passes through a place of recreation, greenery and dappled light.
See Colour Plate XXXIV

176. The Train, Bedford Park 1897

Oil on canvas, 21½ x 25¾
Signed and dated 'C. Pissarro 97' (lower r.)
Lent by a private collector

Nos.176-7 were painted in May-July 1897 on another visit to Lucien, who had just moved to a new house at 62 Bath Road in the western suburb of Bedford Park. The view in no.176 is along a nearby stretch of railway line that no longer exists. Like Pissarro's earlier treatment of the railway theme in the *Lordship Lane Station* of 1871 (Courtauld Institute Galleries), the work makes an unashamedly solid and suburban contrast to the famous Gare St-Lazare paintings of Monet. The train was an appropriate enough subject for a painting about suburbia since the railway was one of the principal factors that brought about the rapid growth of the suburbs in the Victorian period. Several of Lucien Pissarro's London pictures celebrate the same downbeat, unpicturesque kind of scenery (see nos.183-4). *See Colour Plate XXXV*

177. Jubilee Fête, Bedford Park 1897

Water-colour, 10 x 13½
Signed 'C.P.' (lower r.)
Lent by a private collector

A leafy impression of the celebrations held on Turnham Green for Queen Victoria's Diamond Jubilee.

177

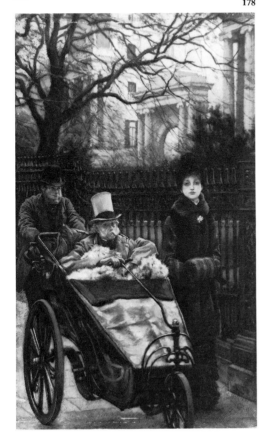

178

JAMES TISSOT
French, 1836-1902

For a brief biography, see nos.163-5 above.

178. The Warrior's Daughter about 1879

Oil on panel, 14¼ x 8¾
Signed 'J. J. Tissot' (lower r.)
Lent by Manchester City Art Galleries

The setting is Regent's Park, with Cumberland Terrace in the background. An old officer takes the air accompanied by a servant and his attractive daughter, a likeness of the artist's mistress Kathleen Newton; the spectator is placed titillatingly in the position of having caught her eye without her father having noticed.

THEODORE ROUSSEL
French, 1847-1926

Roussel became an artist relatively late in life, only abandoning a military career in 1872. He received some training but was largely self-taught. He came to London in 1877 attracted by the idea that the British art world was more open than the French. In 1879 he married an English widow, Mrs Amelia Bull; they lived first in Chelsea then from 1891 in Parson's Green. In 1885 he became friendly with Whistler, sometimes describing himself in exhibition catalogues as the older man's pupil. Roussel was an etcher as well as a painter, and contributed to the 'etching revival' inspired by Whistler's example.

179. Chelsea Palaces about 1888

Colour etching, 3½ x 5¼
Lent by Mr and Mrs P. Lyon Roussel

Roussel was technically innovative as an etcher, developing his own subtle and complex method of colour etching, of which no.179 is an example. The high-roofed building in the centre is the seventeenth-century Lindsey House, former home of the artist's mentor, Whistler. Roussel's title is a reference to Defoe's description of Chelsea as a 'town of palaces' and a compliment to Whistler, casting him as a kind of king. The image has been reversed in the process of printing so that what might appear to be a view westwards is in fact looking eastwards. As with many of Roussel's prints, it is surrounded by a broad decorative border also produced by colour etching.

180. Corner of Luna Street, Chelsea about 1888

Etching, 6½ x 5¾
Signed 'Theodore Roussel' (lower r.)
Lent by Mr and Mrs P. Lyon Roussel

By drawing directly onto the etching plate *en plein air*, Roussel achieved a spontaneity of touch that lends great freshness, atmosphere and charm to his subjects, in this case a view across the new Embankment, with women and children on the pavement looking at the boats on the river in the background.

179

180

181. Chelsea Children, Chelsea Embankment about 1889

Etching, 7½ x 5¼
Signed 'Theodore Roussel' (lower l., and again on a tab below)
Lent by the Victoria and Albert Museum

This is another Embankment scene, with a mother, or perhaps a maid, sitting on a bench surrounded by a group of six children of various ages. Roussel's view of suburban Chelsea is whole-heartedly positive, and here he seems to be stressing that it is a good place to raise children, a place where they will be nurtured and cared for like the young tree protected by fencing. The artist lived in Chelsea himself and by this time had three children and a stepson of his own, who may well feature among the 'Chelsea children' of no. 181.

LUCIEN PISSARRO
French, 1863-1944

Lucien Pissarro's parents Camille Pissarro (q.v.) and Julie Vellay brought him to London as a child to escape the dangers of the Franco-Prussian War; they spent several months in 1870-1 in Norwood, where his grandmother was already living. Later, under the influence and tutorship of his father, he became a painter and showed works at the Salon des Indépendants in Paris from 1886 to 1894. He occasionally returned to England and in 1890 settled in London for good. The Pissarros must have had some connection with Jacob and Miriam Bensusan, who had lived near Lucien's grandmother in Lower Norwood, for in 1892 Lucien married their daughter Esther. In 1897 the couple moved into 62 Bath Road in the west London suburb of Bedford Park. The artist was associated with some of the more avant-garde British painters and played an active part in the New English Art Club. His work consists mainly of English landscapes painted in a manner that recalls his father. He became a naturalised British subject in 1916.

182. Demonstration in Hyde Park 1892

Ink applied with a brush and blue crayon, 9 x 12
Stamped 'L. P.' (lower r.)
Lent by the Whitworth Art Gallery, Manchester

Lucien Pissarro shared his father's libertarian beliefs and was sympathetic towards the British labour movement. No.182 shows the scene at Hyde Park Corner on Sunday 1st May 1892 when 300,000-500,000 workers gathered to demand a statutory eight-hour day.

183. Well Farm Bridge, Acton 1907

Oil on canvas, 18 x 21½
Signed and dated 'LP 1907' (lower r.)
Lent by Leeds City Art Galleries

No.183 was exhibited at the New English Art Club in 1907. The bridge is the one carrying a north-south railway line situated a quarter of a mile to the east of the present North Acton underground station. The view is looking westwards, which means that the train would be on its way from the suburbs into town, towards Paddington Station. In treating such mundane railway scenery, Lucien was following the lead

of his father in pictures such as the *Lordship Lane Station* of 1871 (Courtauld Institute Galleries) and *The Train, Bedford Park* of 1897 (no.176). The carefully placed vertical accents are reminiscent of the latter work in particular.

184. Shunting at Acton 1908

Oil on canvas, 17¼ x 21
Signed and dated 'LP 1908' (lower r.)
Lent by a private collector

Like his father, Lucien uses a painterly technique to imbue the hard-edged forms of the railway-scape with a more picturesque, organic appearance than they actually possessed, and to integrate them with what was left of nature in the scene. No.184 was shown in 1908 at the exhibition of the Allied Artists' Association in the Royal Albert Hall.

183

184

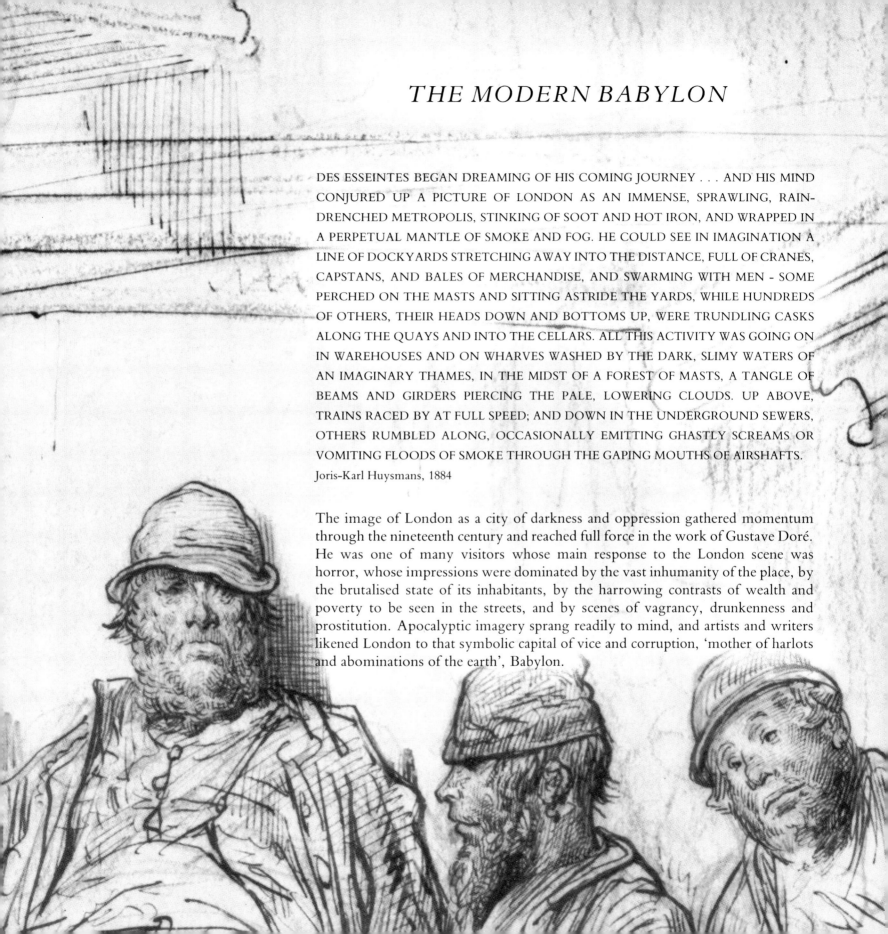

THE MODERN BABYLON

DES ESSEINTES BEGAN DREAMING OF HIS COMING JOURNEY . . . AND HIS MIND CONJURED UP A PICTURE OF LONDON AS AN IMMENSE, SPRAWLING, RAIN-DRENCHED METROPOLIS, STINKING OF SOOT AND HOT IRON, AND WRAPPED IN A PERPETUAL MANTLE OF SMOKE AND FOG. HE COULD SEE IN IMAGINATION A LINE OF DOCKYARDS STRETCHING AWAY INTO THE DISTANCE, FULL OF CRANES, CAPSTANS, AND BALES OF MERCHANDISE, AND SWARMING WITH MEN - SOME PERCHED ON THE MASTS AND SITTING ASTRIDE THE YARDS, WHILE HUNDREDS OF OTHERS, THEIR HEADS DOWN AND BOTTOMS UP, WERE TRUNDLING CASKS ALONG THE QUAYS AND INTO THE CELLARS. ALL THIS ACTIVITY WAS GOING ON IN WAREHOUSES AND ON WHARVES WASHED BY THE DARK, SLIMY WATERS OF AN IMAGINARY THAMES, IN THE MIDST OF A FOREST OF MASTS, A TANGLE OF BEAMS AND GIRDERS PIERCING THE PALE, LOWERING CLOUDS. UP ABOVE, TRAINS RACED BY AT FULL SPEED; AND DOWN IN THE UNDERGROUND SEWERS, OTHERS RUMBLED ALONG, OCCASIONALLY EMITTING GHASTLY SCREAMS OR VOMITING FLOODS OF SMOKE THROUGH THE GAPING MOUTHS OF AIRSHAFTS.

Joris-Karl Huysmans, 1884

The image of London as a city of darkness and oppression gathered momentum through the nineteenth century and reached full force in the work of Gustave Doré. He was one of many visitors whose main response to the London scene was horror, whose impressions were dominated by the vast inhumanity of the place, by the brutalised state of its inhabitants, by the harrowing contrasts of wealth and poverty to be seen in the streets, and by scenes of vagrancy, drunkenness and prostitution. Apocalyptic imagery sprang readily to mind, and artists and writers likened London to that symbolic capital of vice and corruption, 'mother of harlots and abominations of the earth', Babylon.

GUSTAVE DORE
French, 1832-83

Prolific as an illustrator and monumentally ambitious as a painter, Doré was one of the most popular artists of the nineteenth century. He began his career while still a boy, contributing comic drawings to the *Journal pour rire*. He made his name with an illustrated edition of Rabelais published in 1854 and reached the peak of his celebrity as an illustrator in the 1860s with his designs for Dante's *Inferno* (1861), the Bible, and Milton's *Paradise Lost* (both 1866). The 'Doré Gallery', which opened in London in 1869, was the main showcase for his vast paintings of epic and religious subjects. Doré's success in England led to frequent visits and in 1872 to the publication of *London. A Pilgrimage*, an intensely Babylonian vision of the London scene. In 1877 he took up sculpture, his grandest project being his monument to Alexandre Dumas père, inaugurated a few months after his early death in 1883.

DORE IN LONDON
by Samuel F. Clapp

When Doré came to London for the first time in 1868, he was already a household name for his illustrations to such classic texts as the Bible, Paradise Lost and Don Quixote, published in English editions by the firm of Cassell. The reason for his trip was not his popularity as an illustrator, however, but his ambition as a painter. The previous year he had arranged for an exhibition of his paintings to be mounted at the Piccadilly Hall, featuring the powerful Dante and Virgil in the Ninth Circle of the Inferno, and the result had been explosive. Though recognising that Doré was 'regarded in England no less than in France as, in some respects, the most remarkable book-illustrator of any age or nation', the critic of the Illustrated London News had not been alone in feeling that, with his principal picture, he had gone too far:

in the comparatively indefinite medium of what may be considered the poet's semi-mystic semi-realistic word painting, this incident is revolting enough . . . while here, pah: from the dripping red blood, from the more than fiendish cannibalism, we turn away in sickening disgust

Another artist might not have chosen this particular work as the centrepiece of his opening exhibition in Victorian London. Nevertheless Doré persevered, and the reaction of the public must have been favourable for in 1868 Messrs Fairless and Beeforth opened an exhibition of no less than forty of his pictures in the German Gallery at 168 New Bond Street. The following year the exhibition was moved to 35 New Bond Street, quarters presently occupied by Sotheby's, where it became a permanent attraction and a London landmark for over twenty years: 'the Doré Gallery'. Doré's idea of exhibiting and selling works through an independent gallery rather than the traditional forum of the Paris Salon was in keeping with a general movement away from the Salon during the Second Empire. Moreover, his sheer productivity made a gallery desirable since from 1864 the Salon strictly limited the number of works each artist could show. In view of his popularity and publishing activity in England, it is not entirely surprising that Doré should have chosen to present his cherished paintings to the London audience, and the London offices of firms such as Goupil bore witness to the demand in England for French painting.

Although the Doré Gallery was owned by Fairless and Beeforth, the artist's correspondence with them, extracts from which are published here for the first time, indicates that he exercised a close supervision over the presentation of his works. He was never happy with the original premises at the German Gallery. 'It is indeed quite clear that if I continue to show my pictures in too modest an environment, a small cluttered room where one cannot regulate the play of light,' he wrote on 22 July 1868, 'the public appreciation of the pictures will always be influenced by their ineffectual presentation.' He especially objected to the double hanging of pictures, writing on 10 November: 'I would insist on this point; it is to have, in future, only *one row*; everybody's impression, and mine too, is that a *second row* is like a voluntary depreciation.'

On 14 December Doré insisted that unless the proprietors were willing to obtain new premises permitting 'a large, beautiful, dignified and sumptuous exhibition', he would 'keep my lesser works for the German Gallery and . . . not show my best . . . to your public'. With negotiations towards the new gallery under

way, he wrote on 5 January 1869: 'remember to obtain in your transactions the right to raise the roof, if necessary, for one must anticipate that I might want to show some very large things.' This was almost an understatement: *Christ leaving the Praetorium* which was displayed from 1872, was twenty feet high and thirty across. On 13 January he renewed his complaints about the German Gallery, calling it 'a gloomy den that can only disenchant a public that expects much of me', and was adamant that in the new gallery the hanging and re-hanging of pictures must be carefully controlled, and not too many changed at any one time. 'If we go on like this, the affair will profit only as an *exhibition* but never as a *market*', he wrote on 23 June. 'In spite of their esteem for my works, people will hesitate when it comes to buying things that come out every year in batches of twenty . . . whereas with clever and well managed substitutions, the same number if not more can be submitted in succession to the public's eye.'

The Doré Gallery operated from 1869 to 1892, and it is estimated that more than 2½ million people paid the one shilling entrance fee to see the exhibition. It was less successful with the critics. Indeed, many equated its popularity with vulgarity, and the fact that a visiting housewife could see Doré's paintings for a shilling prompted John Ruskin to write in *Fors Clavigera* that 'she had better see the Devil'. But the critics did little damage to its commercial success. In addition to the entrance fee, there was a lively and profitable business in engravings of the paintings on show, which were available on plain paper for two and a half guineas and India paper for three and a half; lettered proofs cost five guineas, proofs before letters eight and artist's proofs with facsimile autograph twelve.

Doré was as sought-after in London society as he was successful in his profession. As Blanchard Jerrold wrote in his biography of the artist:

Doré delighted in his annual trips to London during the season; and was charmed by the welcome he received in society. The Prince and Princess of Wales invited him to Chiswick, and received him at a *dîner intime* . . . at Chiswick he was introduced to the Queen, and Her Majesty . . . said she hoped to see him at Balmoral . . . the Princess Louise delighted him by accepting one of his sketches. . . When he was the guest of the Lord Mayor, the ladies stood upon their chairs to look at him and wave their handkerchiefs . . . sometimes he would stay for five or six weeks, drawing and painting, first in Jermyn Street, then at Morley's Hotel, then at the Westminster Palace, and lastly at the Bath; and giving his afternoons and evenings to drives, calls, dinners and receptions (*Life of Gustave Doré*, 1891, p. 199).

But Doré never really settled himself in London. He had no residence, did not speak English, felt the climate to be injurious to his health and missed his friends and his mother, to whom he was abnormally closely attached. When Fairless and Beeforth offered to convert the ante-chamber of the Doré Gallery into a studio, he declined, writing to them on 26 January 1870: 'I am not in the least prepared to do it . . . the works that I might have to do in London would not require so complete an installation, since they would only be sketches for which the light of a room is enough.' He remained a visitor in London in many ways quite unaffected by his environment, perhaps because his work was his life and it did not matter very much to him where he was.

The most important product of Doré's English experience was his illustrations to *London. A Pilgrimage*. He and his friend Blanchard Jerrold, who wrote the text, embarked upon their 'pilgrimage' to the different parts of the city some time in 1869. 'We spent many days and nights visiting and carefully examining the more striking scenes and phases of London life,' Jerrold wrote.

We had one or two nights in Whitechapel, duly attended by police in plain clothes; we explored the docks; we visited the night refuges, we journeyed up and down the river; we traversed Westminster, and had a morning or two in Drury Lane; we saw the sun rise over Billingsgate, and were betimes at the opening of Covent Garden market; we spent a morning in Newgate; we attended the boat-race, and went in a char-à-banc to the Derby . . . we entered thieves' public-houses; in short I led Doré through the shadows and the sunlight of the great world of London (*op. cit.*, p. 151)

Doré seldom made anything more than the briefest sketch on the spot, priding himself on a photographic memory. 'J'ai beaucoup de collodion dans la tête' was one of his favourite sayings. In the evening he would return to his

hotel room and make finished sketches, normally wash-drawings heightened with gouache, on the basis of the day's observations. The artist mounted his London drawings in a large album to be shown to prospective publishers and an agreement was concluded with the firm of Grant & Co. in the spring of 1870. But the Franco-Prussian War intervened, preventing Doré from returning to London again until July 1871. This time he came with his artist friend Emile Bourdelin, who helped him

185

with the architectural parts of some of the London drawings, and later wrote an account of Doré's continuing researches for the project:

two private detectives had been placed at our disposal; and every night we spent hours in populous London districts such as Lambeth, Clerkenwell, Bayswater, and the docks . . . it was a real pleasure to watch Doré, dressed in some ragamuffin style or other, hurrying in and out of the streets and alleys, and rapidly taking notes with the rarest precision - notes which served him in the composition of his blocks. I filled in backgrounds, houses or monuments, which he afterwards animated with his glowing fanciful pencil. There is no horrible place which may be seen in London

into which he did not penetrate'. (See Blanche Roosevelt, *Life and Reminiscences of Gustave Doré*, New York, 1885, p. 368).

As Bourdelin says, the final drawings were made directly onto the blocks from which the illustrations were to be printed, and necessarily destroyed by the wood-engravers in the process of cutting. Doré subsequently dismantled the album he had prepared in 1869, the drawings of which formed the basis for many of the illustrations, and distributed its contents among his friends (see nos.187-92, below). *London. A Pilgrimage* was issued in parts from January 1872 and in a full bound edition later that year. It contains 54 full-page illustrations and 126 vignettes.

In 1876 Hachette published a French edition entitled *Londres*, which included all but six of the engravings but with a different text written by Louis Enault, author of a number of popular French travel books. No satisfactory explanation has ever been given for the change of author. Jerrold stated that 'his vanity had been his enemy here . . . he must appear before his countrymen as the sole discoverer of the hidden ways of London' (*op. cit.*, p. 205), but Doré's correspondence with the Doré Gallery suggests another reason. On 12 February 1873 the Gallery wrote to him:

We are sorry to complain of the conduct of your friend Mr Jerrold, but in the protection of our interests, it is necessary for us to inform you that we have received a formal notice that he has sold the drawing of *Christ leaving the Praetorium* which we have at present in the Gallery, and that we are to deliver it to the orders of the persons who have purchased it.

As Doré considered his painting of this subject to be his master work, and was unduly sensitive about his painting anyway, the effect of Jerrold's sale of the drawing cannot be underestimated. He replied the following day: 'the news contained in your letter of this morning concerning Mr Jerrold was for me a great and painful surprise . . . I regret bitterly having given a present to someone with so little self-respect as to sell it.'

More than any other work by Doré, *London. A Pilgrimage* has aroused comment as to its veracity. Van Gogh considered Doré to be among 'the great draughtsmen of the people' and based a painting on his illustration of

Newgate Gaol, while a more earthbound critic on the *Athenaeum* wrote the whole book off as 'utterly unlike London' (6 January 1872, p.23). There is no doubt that Doré took liberties with the letter of the London scene - his illustrations are full of exaggerations and topographical errors - but a reading of Henry Mayhew's *London Labour and the London Poor* would suggest that he was true to the spirit, at least to its darker side. His work falls squarely in the last of the categories of drawing described by Baudelaire in his Salon review of 1846:

There are several kinds of drawings, as there are of colour: the exact or silly, the physiognomic and the imaginative. The first is negative, incorrect by sheer force of reality, natural but absurd; the second is naturalistic, but idealised draughtsmanship - the draughtsmanship of a genius who knows how to choose, arrange, correct, rebuke, and guess at nature; lastly the third, which is the noblest and strangest, and can afford to neglect nature - it realises another nature, analogous to the mind and the temperament of the artist.'

In an original manifesto for *London. A Pilgrimage*, Blanchard Jerrold wrote:

We are pilgrims: not, I repeat, historians, nor antiquaries, nor topographers. Our plan is to present London in the quick to the reader - as completely as we may be able to grasp the prodigious giant, and dissect his Titan limbs, the floods of his veins, the iron beams of his muscles ! (*op. cit.*, pp. 175–6)

The aim of the book was to capture a truth that went beyond mere facts, and it is on that basis that it should be judged.

185. Outcasts: London Bridge probably 1869

Pen and sepia ink, 6 x 4½
Signed 'G Doré' (lower l.)
Lent from a private collection

No.185 is reproduced under the title given here in Blanchard Jerrold's *Life of Gustave Doré*, 1891, p. 149; the work has also been known as *Sur le Pont de Londres*. In a characteristic mixture of realism and fantasy, Doré shows some vagrants sleeping rough on London Bridge watched over by a guardian angel. He may have made this small sketch during one of the nocturnal walks he and Jerrold made around London gathering material for *London. A Pilgrimage*. 'We went, once, at midnight to London Bridge, and remained there an hour, while he meditated over the two wonderful views – that above, and that below, bridge,' wrote Jerrold. 'His heart was touched by some forlorn creatures huddled together, asleep, on the stone seats' (p. 153). Doré drew a similar scene without the angel onto a large woodblock for *London. A Pilgrimage* that was never cut (no.196), included a smaller version with more figures in the book (p. 179) and used the idea yet again later in an etching (no.197).

186. Scene in the slums, with St Paul's in the background 1869

Wash and pen and ink, heightened with white, 18¼ x 11¾
Signed and dated 'Gve Doré 1869' (lower l.)
Lent by the Cabinet des Estampes de Strasbourg

This nightmarish vision was probably drawn with *London. A Pilgrimage* in mind. It was not used for any illustration in the book as published, but, with its pathetic contrast of the beggar-woman and the general destitution of the street with the grandeur of St Paul's, would have fitted perfectly with Louis Enault's introductory words in the French edition of 1876 (no.212): 'It is not a single city that we have to show and make come alive for our readers: it is twenty cities in one, or, more exactly, it is a whole world – a world in which all extremes and excesses meet; where you are dazzled by the wonders of an extraordinary civilization and appalled by misery of a depth and poignancy unknown in any other nation.'

DORE'S LONDON ALBUM

Similar in size and in their elaborate technique, nos.187-92 are probably from the album of drawings made by Doré in 1869-70 to show to prospective publishers of *London. A Pilgrimage*. Many served eventually as the basis for illustrations in the book, although Doré introduced major alterations in the process of re-drawing them onto woodblocks for his engravers. By and large, the engraved versions in the book do little justice to the original album drawings, coarsening them and failing to reproduce their lively variations of focus and finish. The artist dismantled the album after it had served its purpose and gave away most of the drawings to friends.

187. Gray's Inn Lane – Robbers' Kitchen 1869

Sepia and grey washes, heightened with white, 13¾ x 9¾
Signed and dated 'G Doré 1869' (lower r.)
Lent from a private collection

The title is given in an inscription on the back by Blanchard Jerrold. Though possibly the most haunting of all Doré's London drawings, no.187 was for some reason not used for an illustration in *London. A Pilgrimage*. In a slum interior, some low-life characters gather around a table, perhaps excited by the arrival of a haul of stolen goods, as a man and a Maenad-like woman dance a bare-footed jig near by. Their wild gestures and expressions, and the gloom surrounding them, suggest the atmosphere of a madhouse. Jerrold mentions a visit to such a place in his biography of the artist, remembering vividly how it was 'charged with the unmistakable, overpowering damp and mouldy odour, that is in every thieves' kitchen'. No. 187 is a striking example of Doré's use of dark, smudgy washes to re-create the grime and menace of London's lower depths. With its pronounced chiaroscuro, it is like a sordid, de-spiritualised reincarnation of a Rembrandt.

187

188

188. Billingsgate Market probably 1869-70

Pen and black and sepia inks, sepia wash and pencil, heightened with white, 13¾ x 9¾
Signed 'Gve doré' (lower r.)
Lent from a private collection

An engraved version of no.188 appears as an illustration in Doré's *London. A Pilgrimage* (p. 152). With their bundled-up clothing, coarse, lumpy features, shaggy beards and sideburns, the figures are typical of Doré's idea of the proletarian Londoner. The drawing is brought up to a higher degree of finish than no.187, with some tonal variations created through hatching rather than washes, and greater definition in the clothing and faces. Doré used the time-honoured drawing method of applying broad washes to lay out the composition, bringing things into focus by the addition of increasingly crisp lines, improvising and exploiting happy accidents in the process, and leaving certain areas in their original undefined, ambiguous state. With the London drawings the unkempt result is well suited to his subject-matter.

189. Landing the Fish probably 1869-70

Pen and sepia ink, grey wash and black chalk, 14¼ x 10
Signed 'G doré' (lower r.)
Lent by a private collector

Another Billingsgate scene, with fishermen carrying baskets of fish up the steps leading to the market. By leaving the figures in the lower right part of the drawing merely outlined and ghostly, treating those on the steps more densely then returning to the ghostly manner again for the ships' rigging, Doré creates an effect of selective focus. Like many of the subtler ideas in the album drawings, this is almost entirely lost in the engraved version in *London. A Pilgrimage* (opp. p. 152).

190. Warehousing in the City probably 1869-70

Pen and ink, grey wash and black chalk, heightened with white,
14 x 10¼
Signed 'Gve doré' (lower r.)
Lent by the Victoria and Albert Museum

189

No.190 was again used as the basis for an illustration in *London. A Pilgrimage* (opp. p. 114). Doré uses perspective to the right of his composition to suggest both the mistiness of the London atmosphere and the vast scale of the warehouse, which fades into the distance like a mountainside. His warehousemen grapple with bales and barrels perched precariously over the abyss on small, unfenced and overcrowded platforms, spicing the effect of sublimity with a touch of vertigo.

191. Outside Brakemen at Barclay Perkins 1870

Pen and sepia ink, and pencil, 13 x 9¾
Signed and dated 'Gve doré 1870' (lower r.)
Lent from a private collection

The brewery of Barclay Perkins & Co. in Southwark was a perennial fascination for foreign visitors surprised to discover an establishment of such grandeur devoted to the making of beer. One was Astolphe de Custine, who reflected: 'A few centuries from now, it will be difficult for people looking at the extent of its remains to guess the purpose for which such a monument was erected. It is the

191

Colosseum of London (*Mémoires et voyages*, Paris, 1830, vol. II, p. 128). Doré features several views of the place in *London. A Pilgrimage*, including one based on no.191 but with the image reversed and a different background (opp. p. 132). The workers have the coarse and brutish faces of characteristic Doré cockneys, looking indeed like illustrations of low types from a physiognomic textbook.

192. Putney Bridge 1870

Pen and black and sepia inks, with grey and sepia washes and black chalk, heightened with white, 16 x 11
Signed and dated 'G doré 1870' (lower l.)
Lent by the Trustees of the British Museum

As a public occasion, the annual Oxford-versus-Cambridge boat race on the Thames gave Doré an opportunity to suggest the class division existing in London society. This he does by grouping some shabby malcontents together on Putney Bridge and hugely exaggerating its height to create a symbolic distance between them and the more privileged spectators on the boats below. In the engraved version that appears in *London. A Pilgrimage* (opp. p. 60), the division is less pronounced: the bridge is lower and the spectators are generally better-dressed and cheerful-looking. For Whistler's very different, spare and elegant depiction of the same bridge, see no.170.

193. The Docks probably 1869-70

Sepia and blue washes, pencil and touches of pastel, 21 x 12¼
Lent from a private collection

No.193 is too large to have been in the London Album, and no corresponding illustration appears in *London. A Pilgrimage*, but the subject is certainly the London docks. Doré shows the same fascination with the perils of winching heavy goods up and down the outsides of warehouses as in no.190, and employs a restless line to convey the idea of bustle in the street below without stating its nature or purpose too exactly. The scribbled, shadowy forms of horses, carts, beer barrels and figures half-emerge from a chaotic mass.

193

192

192 a

194. Demolition of old houses adjoining the Sanctuary, Westminster 1869-71

Pencil, pen and ink, and grey wash, 11 x 8¾
Signed 'G doré' (lower r.)
Lent by the City of Westminster Libraries

Both picturesque and emotive, the ramshackle, half-destroyed slum in the foreground is typical of the kind of London building that attracted Doré. The medieval architecture of Westminster looms up behind like a ghostly apparition.

195. London characters 1871

Sketchbook containing drawings in combinations of pencil, pen and ink, and black chalk, each 3¾ x 5¼
Lent from a private collection

No.195 was given by the artist to his friend Amelia Edwards, the well-known traveller and novelist, who published her recollections of Doré in the *Art Journal* in 1883. The sketches were clearly made as preparatory works for figures in *London. A Pilgrimage*, the date 1871 appears on a medallion around the neck of a man driving a cart or coach in one of them. The other subjects include various workmen, girls holding babies and an old man and a child seated on a bench.

196. Vagrants on London Bridge 1871

Pen and ink, sepia and grey washes and water-colour, heightened with white, on a woodblock, 7½ x 10
Signed and dated 'Gve Doré 1871 – Londres' (lower r.)
Lent by a private collector

197. Vagrants on London Bridge 1870s

Etching, 7¾ x 13¼
Lent from a private collection

Nos.196-7 have also been known by the title *A la belle étoile, sur le Pont de Londres*. Their common origin was the brief sketch of the same bridge scene with a guardian angel sitting on the parapet (no.185). No.196 is an example of the drawings Doré made on woodblocks for the illustrations in *London. A Pilgrimage*. They were normally destroyed when the block was cut by the wood-engraver but in this case, for reasons unknown, the process was stopped at the drawing stage, Doré's work left intact and

197

another, smaller variant of the design included in the book (p. 179). No.197 is so similar in composition to no.196, almost a mirror image, that it seems likely to have been derived directly from it. Though excluding the angel, no.196 retains a hint of religious imagery in the crosses formed by the ship-masts in the background, and the stars in all the variants suggest a higher presence watching over the vagrants, hope for their souls and the idea that 'in Heaven there is rest'.

198. Westminster 1871

Engraved woodblock, overall: 9¾ x 8, image: 7 x 6¾
Lent from a private collection

Another woodblock, or more precisely eight blocks joined together, but this time with the design as cut by the wood-engraver Jonnard and used to print an illustration in *London. A Pilgrimage*, the view of Westminster on page 43. The surface has since been treated to make the design more easily visible.

PROOFS OF ILLUSTRATIONS TO 'LONDON. A PILGRIMAGE'

Nos.199-207 are proofs on India paper of wood-engravings made from Doré's drawings as illustrations to *London. A Pilgrimage* They are all inscribed with their English titles and the date 1871 by Blanchard Jerrold, the author of the text, and some with French titles by Doré himself. The page on which the illustration appears in the book as published is given after the name of the engraver.

199. The Workingmen's Train

Wood-engraving by Quesnel (p. 113), 3¾ x 6¾
Lent from a private collection

200. Warehousing in the City

Wood-engraving by Pannemaker (opp. p. 114), 9½ x 7¾
Lent from a private collection

Compare with Doré's original drawing of this subject, no.190 above.

201. Over London Bridge by Rail

Wood-engraving by Pannemaker (opp. p. 120), 7¾ x 9¾
Lent from a private collection

Inscribed by Doré: 'Maisons modèles d'ouvriers – près de Bermondsey road' (Model housing for workers near Bermondsey Road)

202. Outside Brakemen at Barclay Perkins

Wood-engraving by Hildibrand (opp. p. 132), 9¼ x 7¼
Lent from a private collection

Compare with Doré's original drawing of this subject, no.191 above.

203. Brewer's Dray

Wood-engraving, anonymous (p. 134), 3¾ x 2¾
Lent from a private collection

194

Inscribed by Doré: '59 – enfans derrière un camion / rue de Londres' (59 – children behind a waggon / London street). The composition also exists in a drawing, on which no.203 was probably based, and a later etching (see Samuel F. Clapp, *Gustave Doré 1832-1883*, exhibition catalogue, Hazlitt, Gooden and Fox, London, 1983, nos. 30-1).

204. Newgate Prison Exercise Yard

Wood-engraving by H. Pisan (opp. p. 136), 9¼ x 7½
Lent from a private collection

No.204 was copied by Van Gogh in a painting of 1890 now at the Pushkin Museum in Moscow.

205. Billingsgate – Early Morning

Wood-engraving by A. Doms (opp. p. 150), 9¼ x 7½
Lent from a private collection

206. Outside the Workhouse

Wood-engraving by Levasseur (p. 142), 4 x 4¼
Lent from a private collection

207. Cremorne Gardens

Wood-engraving, anonymous, 10½ x 11
Lent from a private collection

Though clearly intended as an illustration to *London. A Pilgrimage*, no.207 was not used in the book as published.

208-9. Parts of London. A Pilgrimage 1872

Lent from a private collection

London. A Pilgrimage was published by Grant & Co. in parts from January 1872, and nos.208-9 were the first and second to be issued. For a full discussion of the genesis and publication of the work, see Samuel F. Clapp's essay, above.

210-11. London. A Pilgrimage 1872

Lent from a private collection and the Guildhall Library

Copies of the complete, bound edition that appeared later the same year.

212. Louis Enault Londres 1876

Lent from a private collection

This later edition of Doré's London illustrations with a new text in French by Louis Enault was published in Paris by Hachette.

213. London flower-sellers 1876

Etching, 7¼ x 9¾
Signed and dated 'G Doré 76' (lower l.)
Lent from a private collection

Flower-selling was closely associated with prostitution, and the pathos of images such as no.213 is that the women's beauty is like their flowers, for sale and shortly to fade. Doré places the women against a wall and on a narrow pavement as if to suggest entrapment, shows their flower-basket half in the gutter, and includes the children who will carry their poverty and squalor into the next generation.

214. London beggar-girl about 1879

Water-colour, heightened with white, 15¼ x 12
Lent by a private collector

This beautiful head-and-shoulders study could be an enlarged and coloured detail from one of Doré's London street scenes. With her blue eyes, fair skin and blond hair, the girl is every foreigner's idea of an English beauty. Only her ragged clothes, a slight darkening around her eyes and a hardness about her mouth hint at her state of destitution. Her fixed look puts us in the harrowing position of someone from whom she is begging.

215. The Violet-Seller 1881

Oil on canvas, 25 x 21
Signed and dated 'Gve Doré / 1881' (lower l.)
Lent from a private collection

The model may be the same girl as in no.214, and she wears a tartan shawl like the women in *London flower-sellers* (no.213). She gazes wearily and abstractedly into space, resting her head on her hand in a pose traditionally associated with melancholy. The silhouette of St Paul's is visible against a smog-grey sky in the background.

See Colour Plate XXX

211

213

STREET LIFE

THE GREATEST INTEREST OF LONDON IS THE SENSE THE PLACE GIVES US OF
MULTITUDINOUS LIFE.

Henry James, 1888

The many-sidedness of the image of London, the fact that it meant different things
to different artists, was never more evident than in the later nineteenth century.
Alongside the grim Babylonian picture drawn in black-and-white by Doré, there
existed an altogether more colourful alternative, a world of bustling vitality into
which Doré's 'pilgrim' might emerge blinking and wondering whether he were
still in the same city.

216

EDOUARD DETAILLE
French, 1848–1912

In 1865 Detaille became a pupil of Ernest Meissonier and, largely under his influence, went on to a career as a painter of painstakingly factual military history pictures. He enjoyed success at the Salon from the time of his debut in 1867 onwards. Detaille was capable of works on a vast scale, painting battle panoramas as well as grand mural decorations for the Hôtel de Ville in Paris in 1902 and the Pantheon in 1905.

216. Street scene at Temple Bar 1869

Pen and ink and water–colour, 7½ x 10½
Signed and dated EDOUARD DETAILLE 1869 (lower l.)
Lent by the Musée du Louvre (Département des Arts Graphiques)

Detaille made the first of a number of trips to London from 16 to 25 August 1869, and it was presumably then that no.216 was made. Temple Bar at the west end of Fleet Street was a traffic bottleneck and a suitable place to set a scene intended to convey the hubbub and colour of the London streets. Detaille attempts a Frith–like synopsis of British society, with carefully contrived contrasts of young and old, rich and poor. He reveals a marked penchant for uniforms, as we might expect from a specialist in military subjects, and there are two policemen, two soldiers and a Chelsea Pensioner. Perhaps ironically to suggest a comparison between the busy street and a field of battle, the artist shows one of the soldiers in serious danger of being run down by a cab charging out from under the arch of Temple Bar.

JAMES TISSOT
French, 1836–1902

For a brief biography, see nos.163–5 above.

217. A Procession descending Ludgate Hill 1870s

Oil on canvas, 84½ x 43
Lent by the Guildhall Art Gallery

The setting is recognisable as Ludgate Hill, with St Paul's visible in the background near the top of the composition, but the obviously splendid occasion taking place has yet to be identified. It is an unusually large canvas for Tissot but no particular reason for this is known; it is unlikely to have been a commissioned work since the artist himself gave it to the Curator of the Luxembourg Museum in Paris some time in the 1870s. It has been known as *The Lord Mayor's Show* and variations on that title, although the rosettes and cockades worn by the figures suggest a more special occasion, possibly a state visit from a foreign dignitary. Another possibility is the grand processions held on 27 February 1872 when a service of thanksgiving was held in St Paul's for the recovery of the Prince of Wales from a dangerous illness. A public holiday was declared and the Queen, the Prince and Princess of Wales and other members of the royal family proceeded in state from Buckingham Palace to St Paul's and back through streets crowded with spectators and hung with banners and flags. No.217 seems to show the Master of a City livery company and his Prime Warden, and they are moving away from St Paul's. The Masters and Wardens certainly attended the thanksgiving service in 1872 and they may well have taken part in the procession leaving St Paul's, although further evidence would be needed to associate Tissot's painting firmly with that event. The scene may even be largely imaginary. The foreground characters do conform suspiciously to certain stereotypes of Englishmen to be found elsewhere in Tissot's paintings, especially the Master and the Beadle with their Henry VIII–like features. *See Colour Plate XXVI*

218. London Visitors about 1874

Oil on canvas, 34¼ x 24¾
Signed 'J.J.Tissot' (lower l.)
Lent by the Layton Art Collection, Milwaukee Art Museum (Gift of Frederick Layton)

The couple who have just come out of the National Gallery embody the enthusiasm and the boredom that tourism can inspire. As the man hunts eagerly through his guidebook for information, his companion points languidly towards Trafalgar Square with her umbrella and gazes into space. She may be more interested in lunch than the next sight to be seen: the clock on the steeple of St Martin–in–the–Fields tells us that it is 1.53 p.m. Judging particularly from the man's ginger beard, they are probably meant to be English rather than foreign visitors, literally provincial and perhaps provincial in the pejorative sense of the word too – there are other works by Tissot where he explicitly makes fun of people from 'out of town'. The man is Tissot's version of a certain English type, as is the blue–coat boy in the immediate foreground, a scholar at Christ's Hospital, whose upturned nose and half–closed eyes make him the very picture of the young English snob. No.218 is a smaller version of the large picture Tissot exhibited under this title at the Royal Academy in 1874, which is now at the Toledo Art Museum. *See Colour Plate XXV*

219. Going to Business about 1879

Oil on panel, 17¼ x 10
Signed 'J.J.Tissot' (lower r.)
Lent by the Edmund J. and Suzanne McCormick Collection

It is a wet, grey morning and a City businessman engrossed in his newspaper is being driven to his office along the street to the south of St Paul's. His carriage is followed by an omnibus, a lower–class form of commuter transport that may well contain some of his employees; as the boss, he takes the lead, even on the way to work. *See Colour Plate XXVII*

GIUSEPPE DE NITTIS,
Italian, 1846–84

Based in Paris from 1868 until his premature death, De Nittis studied under Gérôme and made his name as a painter of street life in Paris and London. He came to London regularly from 1874 onwards, exhibited at the Grosvenor Gallery and sold pictures to Kaye Knowles and other British collectors. He was a close friend of Tissot's and, from 1876 to 1878, a fellow member of the Arts Club. But his English was poor and he seems, on the whole, to have found London a depressing place. When a young admirer remarked upon the melancholy atmosphere of one of his London subjects, he replied: 'I believe that as artists get older they draw upon feelings they had when they were young, and I have depicted London with the sadness of the restless youth I was, a dreamy and rebellious urchin to whom the cost of his desire for independence was often hunger' (see Enrico Piceni, *De Nittis. L'uomo e l'opere*, 1979, p. 18).

220. The National Gallery and St Martin–in–the–Fields probably 1878

Oil on canvas, 27½ x 41½
Signed 'De Nittis' (lower r.)
Lent by the Musée du Petit Palais, Paris

It is five minutes past five on a summer's afternoon and the heavens are about to open in a downpour. Summing up the changeability of the English climate in a single moment, De Nittis contrasts the sunlight playing on the pavement on the left with an ominous pool of deep shadow spreading from Trafalgar Square on the right, the lit and shaded areas separated by a gutter soon to be awash with rain. Perhaps distracted from the imminent change in the weather by the monocled dandy engaging her in conversation, a maid carries a parasol; the more observant young woman in the foreground puts up an umbrella. De Nittis suggests social as well as meteorological extremes, contrasting the children of the rich, attended by maids, with the children begging with their mother by the wall of the National Gallery, and the middle–class gentlemen in their top hats with the sandwich–board man in the gutter carrying an advertisement for the Oxford Street Pantheon. The framing of the scene so that figures are cut off by the edges recalls contemporary

photography and the similarly 'casual' compositions of Degas. No.220 was shown in the *Exposition Universelle* in Paris in 1878 and was probably painted that year; the same date appears on another view of Trafalgar Square, looking south rather than east, which is now in a private collection.   *See colour plate XLI*

FELIX BUHOT
French, 1847–98

Buhot's artistic training was interrupted by the Franco–Prussian War. He made a late debut at the Salon of 1875 with a water–colour and some etchings. From about that date he devoted himself almost exclusively to etching, developing a swirling, sometimes menacing manner indebted to Goya.

221. Westminster Bridge 1884

Etching and drypoint, 11¼ x 15¾
Lent by the Trustees of the British Museum

Buhot gives us London in the rush–hour. With 'Big Ben' presiding over the crowds and traffic on Westminster Bridge, his main scene is a study of time and motion in the big city. The scaffolding to the right, indicating building in progress, underlines the idea of the place as being in constant flux. Surrounding the view across the bridge are what Buhot called 'symphonic margins', a characteristic feature of his work in which he elaborated on his central subject. Here (following a clockwise direction from the left) are an assemblage of architectural forms, a riverscape, a view of St Paul's by moonlight, a staircase leading down from a bridge, and, below, an evocation of the London underground full of rushing figures. The owl was the artist's Goya–esque trademark, serving here as his signature but also conjuring up associations of night and darkness that chime in with his image of London.

WILHELM TRÜBNER
German, 1851–1917

This versatile artist began his career painting in a realist manner indebted to Courbet and Manet, although from the later 1870s he extended his range to scenes from history and myth.

221   222

222. Ludgate Hill 1884

Oil on canvas, 25¾ x 19¼
Signed 'Wilhelm Trübner' (lower r.)
Lent by Vermeer Associates (on loan to the Harvard University Art Museums, Cambridge, Mass.)

Trübner brings together varied types of transport and varied types of Londoner, including a prominent policeman with carefully studied uniform and hordes of businessmen in top hats. The scene is realised in a solid and slightly naive style that gives the place a toytown–like appearance, and much attention is paid to the lettering on signs, especially those of the famous pub The King Lud on the left.

PAOLO SALA
Italian, 1859–1924

Although he studied architecture at the Brera Academy in Milan, Sala made his career as a landscape painter, and watercolourist. His frequent travels took him to Paris, London, the Netherlands, South America and Russia. He mounted a major painting campaign in London in 1885 and exhibited a number of London subjects in Milan the following year.

223. Ludgate Circus 1885

Oil on panel, 11½ x 14¾
Signed and dated 'P Sala / LONDON 85' (lower r.)
Lent by the Trafalgar Galleries, by courtesy of a private collector

The view is northwards from Ludgate Circus looking up Farringdon Street, with The King Lud behind the row of cabs on the right. Sala's tentatively sketchy technique imparts both animation and charm to what seems to have been the recommended place for seeing London's traffic at its busiest.
See colour plate XLIII

NIELS MÖLLER LUND
Danish, 1863–1916

Lund attended the Royal Academy Schools, where he studied under Millais, and the Académie Julian in Paris. He was a painter of cityscapes, landscapes, portraits and genre subjects, and a regular contributor to the Royal Academy exhibitions.

224. The Heart of the Empire 1904

Oil on canvas, 54 x 72
Signed 'Niels M. Lund' (lower l.) and signed and dated 'Niels M. Lund pinx. / London 1904' on the back of the canvas
Lent by the Guildhall Art Gallery

A view from the roof of the Royal Exchange looking westwards and showing most prominently the Mansion House and St Paul's. Sunlight penetrates the cloud cover in shafts and creates a lively *chiaroscuro*: St Paul's is quite shadowy whereas the steeple of St Mary–le–

Bow to its right appears spot–lit. The way the spectator's attention is led from the hubbub of the streets upwards to the dramatically illuminated rooftops and away into the hazy distance recreates the flow of power and energy from heart to Empire. *See colour plate XLII*

JACQUES-EMILE BLANCHE
French, 1861–1942

Blanche was a successful portraitist whose painterly style owed much to artists of the avant–garde on both sides of the Channel. About 1882 he came to London and spent a formative period working in close contact with Whistler and Sickert. He returned frequently and from 1904 spent part of the year in London on a regular basis, painting portraits of English celebrities and members of the royal family as well as lively street scenes. He was also prolific as an author, publishing books on art, volumes of autobiography and novels. Blanche's friendship with leading painters, musicians and dancers of his time made his Paris studio a glamorous artistic meeting–place.

225. Holborn 1905

Oil on canvas, 28¾ x 36¾
Signed and dated 'J.E.Blanche 1905' (lower r.)
Lent by the Prudential Corporation plc

The view is looking eastwards along High Holborn, with Alfred Waterhouse's terracotta Prudential Building on the extreme left of the composition. Blanche's casual–looking technique brings out the rough–and–tumble quality of London street life. Like the Impressionist painters in whose stylistic

footsteps he followed, he simulates a mere glimpse of the moving scene by blurring lines and replacing detail with a complexity of colour; the facial features of the characters are hardly described at all, yet the elusive colours in shadows are lovingly observed. In the scene, and the moment he has chosen to depict, the artist offers a cross–section of types of London transportation, with a motor car, a couple of horse–drawn carts, a vegetable barrow, some green cab–drivers' shelters and two red buses.
See colour plate XLIV

226. Piccadilly Circus: London Pavilion (June Morning) 1912

Oil on canvas, 27¾ x 37½
Signed 'J. E. Blanche' (lower r.)
Lent by York City Art Gallery

Another scene of glimpsed busy–ness, shown at an exhibition of Blanche's work in Paris in 1927 under the title *Piccadilly Circus: London Pavillon (Matinée de juin)*. The view is looking north up Shaftesbury Avenue, with the Shaftesbury Memorial ('Eros') on the left.

227. Knightsbridge from Sloane Street (Beautiful December Morning) probably 1913

Oil on canvas, 33 x 39
Signed 'J. E. Blanche' (lower r.)
Lent by York City Art Gallery

We are looking across Knightsbridge to the north, and the horse–drawn buses in the centre would be heading for Sloane Square. In Blanche's Paris exhibition of 1927 the work was entitled *Knightsbridge vu de Sloane Street (Belle matinée de décembre)*.

226

NIGHT AND FOG

AND WHEN THE EVENING MIST CLOTHES THE RIVERSIDE WITH POETRY, AS WITH
A VEIL, AND THE POOR BUILDINGS LOSE THEMSELVES IN THE DIM SKY, AND THE
TALL CHIMNEYS BECOME CAMPANILI, AND THE WAREHOUSES ARE PALACES IN
THE NIGHT, AND THE WHOLE CITY HANGS IN THE HEAVENS, AND FAIRY-LAND IS
BEFORE US – THEN THE WAYFARER HASTENS HOME; THE WORKING MAN AND
THE CULTURED ONE, THE WISE MAN AND THE ONE OF PLEASURE, CEASE TO
UNDERSTAND, AS THEY HAVE CEASED TO SEE, AND NATURE, WHO, FOR ONCE,
HAS SUNG IN TUNE, SINGS HER EXQUISITE SONG TO THE ARTIST ALONE.

James McNeill Whistler, 1888

The fog was an essential ingredient of the image of London from early in the
nineteenth century, when industrial progress thickened an already vaporous
atmosphere with steam, smoke and pollution. Artists and writers of the romantic
period associated the fog with the darkness and oppression of the modern world,
and it was a commonplace to liken it to a funeral pall. But in the later part of the
century an alternative response developed in which the fog, aided and abetted by
nightfall, was regarded as an aesthetic catalyst; it brought out the grandeur and
poetry of the cityscape, and inspired whole worlds of ideas in the imagination of
the sensitive observer. The shift in attitude found its canonical form in the work
and the writings of Whistler, but underlay the London views of innumerable other
artists, including Claude Monet.

JAMES MCNEILL WHISTLER
American, 1834–1903

For a brief biography of the artist, see nos.145–59 above.

228. Nocturne in Blue and Gold about 1874

Oil on canvas, 18½ x 24½
Lent by the Corporation of Glasgow, Burrell Collection

Like many of Whistler's works, no.228 was known by a number of different titles even in the artist's lifetime, but the one given here seems to be the earliest. Whistler refers to it as 'a Nocturne in blue and gold' in a letter of 1874, and it was listed as *Nocturne in Blue and Gold, No.3* when first exhibited, at the Dudley Gallery, in 1875. The view is looking upstream from Westminster Bridge, with the southern end of the riverfront of the Houses of Parliament to the right. The subject is unique among Whistler's London *Nocturnes*; normally he painted only the stretch of the river near his home in Chelsea. But in its simple, banded composition, its expanses of river and sky separated by riverbanks with lights reflecting in the water, it is quite typical. The artist borrowed the name of the *Nocturnes* from the famous piano pieces by Chopin and intended the paintings to be 'musical' themselves, in the sense that they lack narrative or anecdotal content and are carefully composed harmonies of form and colour. As Whistler recognised, by dissolving details and poetically veiling the riverscape, the misty London evenings did half his work for him. It was a rare case, he said, of Nature singing in tune.

He made only brief sketches for the *Nocturnes*, working largely from memory and refining his impressions in the process of realising them on canvas. In no.228 the riverfront of the Houses of Parliament, one of the most intricate displays of architectural ornament in London, has been refined almost beyond recognition, appearing as a mere dark shape. Whistler was clearly less interested in recording facts than in creating beautiful pictorial effects and a satisfying completeness of design. He took a pride in painting thinly, which makes the image look as if it came easily and allows for effects such as the warm underpainting showing through to suggest the afterglow from a recently set sun,

and the way the visible weave of the canvas mimics the vibrating, granular quality of night-time vision. Although they played some part in the genesis of the later Thames subjects of Monet (q.v.), the *Nocturnes* represent quite different principles at work; the sense of drama and the technical complexity that we find in Monet's treatment of the Houses of Parliament are qualities that Whistler deliberately avoids. There is a drawing in broad washes that may have been the basis for no.228 in a private collection (see Andrew McLaren Young et al, *The Paintings of James McNeill Whistler*, 1980, pp. 88–9). *See Colour Plate XXI*

229. Nocturne: the River at Battersea 1878

Lithotint, 6¾ x 10¼
Signed with the artist's butterfly emblem (lower r.)
Lent by the Victoria and Albert Museum

Whistler's interest in the decorative flatness of Japanese woodblock prints is particularly evident in this image of his favourite nocturnal subject, the industrial riverfront of Battersea, across from his home in Chelsea. The sheer unlikeliness of such a place as a subject for art undoubtedly appealed to Whistler's sense of humour, and made its enchanted and mysterious appearance in the evening all the more fascinating. No.229 was printed from his drawing on the lithographic stone by his friend Thomas Way, who originally introduced him to the techniques of lithography, and in 1887 published in an edition of 100 proofs in *Art Notes*

230. Nocturne in Grey and Gold – Piccadilly 1883–4

Water-colour, 8¾ x 11½
Lent by the National Gallery of Ireland, Dublin

'I am bored to death after a certain time away from Piccadilly !', Whistler wrote to his sister-in-law in 1880 while staying in Venice. 'I pine for Pall Mall and I long for a hansom !' His marvellously economical suggestion of a busy West End street on a foggy evening contrasts with the serene majority of *Nocturnes* and shows him finding subject-matter away from the river, which he did increasingly in the 1880s as the Chelsea scene was disrupted and transformed by the building of the Embankment. The work was

shown in his first one-man exhibition, at Dowdeswell's Gallery on Bond Street in 1884.
See Colour Plate XXII

231. Savoy Pigeons 1896

Lithograph, 7¾ x 5¼
Signed with the artist's butterfly emblem (lower r.)
Lent by the Whitworth Art Gallery, Manchester

Nos.231–2 date from the period early in 1896 when Whistler returned to London from Paris so that his wife Beatrix, who was dying of cancer, could consult a London specialist. They stayed at the Savoy Hotel. Thomas Way prepared lithographic stones for Whistler and he drew views from the balcony outside his room, looking to the left over Waterloo Bridge and to the right over Charing Cross Bridge. Monet was to paint the same views, also from the Savoy, in 1899–1901. No.231 shows Charing Cross Bridge with the Houses of Parliament and Westminster Bridge in the distance. It was published in the *Studio* magazine.

231

232. The Thames 1896

Lithotint, 10½ x 7¾
Signed with the artist's butterfly emblem
Lent by the Whitworth Art Gallery, Manchester

The image here is back-to-front, with Charing Cross Bridge shown to the left instead of the right; the artist and his printer Thomas Way have not corrected for the reversal involved in the printing process, as they must have done with no.231 for instance. The work is none the less a technical tour-de-force. Whistler exploits the smudgy effects to which lithography lends itself to suggest the fugitive half-light of early evening.

234

233

GIUSEPPE DE NITTIS
Italian, 1846–84

For a brief biography, see no.220 above.

233. Westminster about 1878

Oil on canvas, 43¼ x 76¾
Lent by Co. Dr. Umberto Marzotto

Like no.220, this monumental tribute to the vaporousness of the London atmosphere was shown at the *Exposition Universelle* in Paris in 1878. It was bought from De Nitis by his main London patron, the millionaire collector Kaye Knowles. The view is from Westminster Bridge. The triangle of bridge across the corner of the composition contrasts in its suggestion of depth with the silhouette of the Houses of Parliament, emphasising the way the fog reduces distant objects to abstract forms as well as blurring them. The fog is assisted by steam rising up around the bridge from a passing boat. The sun in the west above the Houses of Parliament shows that it is early evening, and the workers in the foreground are resting after the labours of the day. They sound a weary note quite in tune with the grey-brown gloominess of the work as a whole. Monet was to paint similarly moody views of the Houses of Parliament some twenty years later, but without the element of human interest that was essential to De Nittis's understanding of the London scene. *See Colour Plate XXXVI*

JULES BASTIEN-LEPAGE
French, 1848–1884

In his early career Bastien-Lepage painted portraits and religious and classical subjects, but the foundation for the enormous popularity he enjoyed from around 1877 until his premature death was his earthy and humane vision of peasant life in northern France. He painted out of doors in a naturalistic manner but without the sketchiness and colouristic boldness that made Impressionism unacceptable to conventional taste. Around him grew up an international 'school' of *plein-air* painters of the rustic scene. Bastien-Lepage first visited London in 1879 and returned several times, finding a warm welcome among fellow artists and admirers

234. Waterloo Bridge probably 1882

Oil on canvas, 19 x 25½
Signed 'J. BASTIEN-LEPAGE' (lower l.)
Lent by the Musée des Beaux-Arts, Tournai

235

This single arch of the bridge takes on a desolate grandeur against the silvery mists of the Thames and frames a shimmering distant riverscape.

THEODORE ROUSSEL
French, 1847-1926

For a brief biography, see nos.179–81 above

235. Battersea under Snow probably 1890s

Oil on canvas, 28 x 35
Lent by Mr and Mrs P. Lyon Roussel

This delicate tonal study of the industrial shoreline veiled by mist bears obvious similarities to the Thames scenes of Roussel's mentor Whistler. Yet Roussel simplifies less, respecting the structural complexity of the buildings and introducing sporadic touches of definition to set off the areas of mistiness.

236. Battersea Asleep about 1905

Oil on canvas, 26 x 32
Signed 'Theodore Roussel' (lower l.)
Lent by Mr and Mrs M. Hausberg

A study of the same stretch of shoreline by moonlight and seen from a more distant viewpoint, shown under the given title at the exhibition of Roussel's work held in 1905 at Colnaghi's. With its silhouettes, dots of light and reflections, and its surface textured by the canvas weave, the work is unmistakably a tribute to Whistler's *Nocturnes*.

HENRI DE TOULOUSE-LAUTREC
French, 1864–1901

The son of aristocratic parents, Lautrec suffered accidents as a boy that fractured both his legs and stunted his growth. During long periods of convalescence he took up art as a serious occupation and finally moved to Paris to study under Léon Bonnat. By 1890 he was established amongst the Parisian avant-garde as a painter of city subjects. He frequented the Moulin Rouge and other places of entertainment, and much of his work consists of studies of performers and their audiences; he also made poster designs and mural decorations. Lautrec came to London several times in the 1890s and had an exhibition at a London gallery in 1898.

237. Oscar Wilde and Romain Coolus 1896

Lithograph, 12 x 19¼
Signed with the artist's monogram (upper r.)
Lent by the Trustees of the British Museum

No.237 is the programme for performances of Wilde's *Salomé* and Coolus's *Raphaël* at the Théâtre de l'Oeuvre in Paris. Lautrec sets portraits of the authors against backgrounds of Paris and London as if casting them as typical of the two places. Coolus looks every inch the Parisian, light, stylish and alert; Wilde appears phlegmatic and drooping. Paris is represented by a breezy day on the Champs-Elysées, London by a nocturnal pea-souper over Westminster, suggested effectively through the technique of spatter lithography. It is an appropriate enough setting for Wilde since he had written poems evoking the London fog, including an 'Impression du Matin' that begins with the Whistlerian lines: 'The Thames nocturne of blue and gold / Changed to a Harmony in grey'.

SIMON BUSSY
French, 1870–1954

A pupil of Gustave Moreau and an early friend of Matisse, Bussy had his first success with an exhibition of landscape pastels at the dealer Durand-Ruel's in Paris in 1896. He stayed in England for a time in 1903 and was a regular visitor from then on, exhibiting at the London galleries. He became associated with the Bloomsbury Group and in 1906 painted a portrait of Lytton Strachey. In 1912 he made studies at the London Zoo and began painting the stylised pictures of animals and birds against backgrounds of exotic foliage and architecture that were to be his speciality for the rest of his career.

236

237

238. The Mansion House about 1903

Oil on canvas, 36 x 29
Lent by a private collector

What might appear to be the middle of the night is in fact a foggy afternoon, with a strange orange sun hanging above the Mansion House's roof. An anonymous mass of people, cabs and buses fills the street below. No.238 was given by Bussy to his younger friend and fellow painter Duncan Grant.

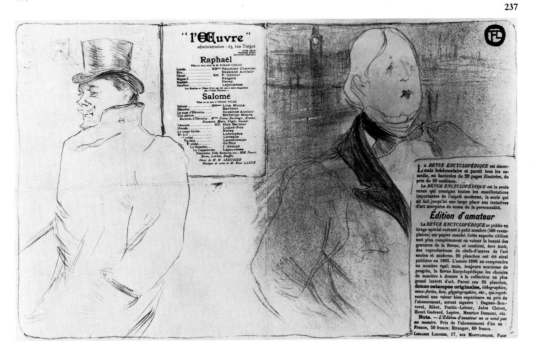

238

VILHELM HAMMERSHØI
Danish, 1864–1916

Hammershøi was a student of P. S. Krøyer and a founder member of the 'Free Exhibition' established in Copenhagen in 1891 as an alternative forum to the conservative Royal Academy. He was a widely-travelled and internationally-minded artist who lived for periods of his career in France and northern Italy as well as London. He was in London in 1897–8 and 1904. Among his artistic heroes were Vermeer and Whistler, and their influence is evident in the static, mysterious, near-monochromatic compositions that were his stock-in-trade.

179

239. The British Museum 1905–6

Oil on canvas, 20 x 17¾
Lent by the Lolland-Falsters Kunstmuseum, Maribo

240. The British Museum and Montague Street 1905–6

Oil on canvas, 17¾ x 22½
Lent by the Ny Carlsberg Glyptotek, Copenhagen

Like empty stage sets, Hammershøi's views of the British Museum have a strangely expectant silence about them. It is as if the museum containing the relics of so many ancient civilisations had itself become an awesome deserted monument.   *See Colour Plate XXXI*

HENRI LE SIDANER
French, 1862–1939

Le Sidaner studied under the academic painter Alexandre Cabanel but by 1882 had come under the aesthetic sway of Manet and the Parisian avant-garde. In that year he left Paris for Etaples on the northern coast of France, where he lived and worked until 1894, treating mainly scenes from peasant life. He developed the taste for crepuscular and moonlight subjects and the Monet-like effects of dissolution that characterize his mature work during another stay in Paris from 1894 to 1899. But he disliked the Paris art world and in the latter year moved to Bruges, then in 1900 to Beauvais, then to the nearby village of Gerberoy, where he lived for the rest of his life. Many of his subjects are taken from his own house and garden. Le Sidaner occasionally visited London, showed works at the London exhibitions and enjoyed the patronage of British collectors.

241. Trafalgar Square about 1906

Pastel on canvas, with touches of oil, 23¼ x 28¼
Signed 'Le Sidaner' (lower l.)
Lent by the Syndics of the Fitzwilliam Museum, Cambridge

The view is looking south from the terrace opposite the National Gallery, with a fountain and the statue of Major-General Sir Henry Haverstock half-emerging from the blue-green obscurity of an afternoon fog. To the right, part of the Houses of Parliament is visible down Whitehall. By leaving the scene strangely uninhabited and suggesting a light that vibrates and mystifies rather than illuminates, Le Sidaner imparts a poetic, almost fairy-tale atmosphere to his subject. Deserted squares, often with statues, were among his favourite motifs, so it is not surprising that he was drawn to Trafalgar Square when in London; he painted at least one other similar view of it, though looking east rather than south (see Camille Mauclair, *Henri Le Sidaner*, Paris, 1928, p. 56).

242. St Paul's from the River, Morning Sun in Winter 1906–7

Oil on canvas, 35½ x 46
Signed 'Le Sidaner' (lower l.)
Lent by the Trustees of the National Museums and Galleries on Merseyside (Walker Art Gallery)

The idea of St Paul's as floating ethereally over the rest of the city informs many artists' responses to the subject and Le Sidaner's is a particularly subtle example; his way of painting the dome reminded his biographer Camille Mauclair of 'a gigantic balloon ascending above the fog' (ibid., p. 132). The light of the morning sun creates magical orange glints on windows in the drum of the dome and along the riverfront below. The pencil squaring-up visible beneath the paint surface probably indicates that no.242

241

243

was elaborated from a smaller sketch. More interested in mood than truth to nature, Le Sidaner painted from memory and fairly slight preparatory drawings, and preferred to work in the studio rather than *en plein air* like the Impressionists. The title given here is the one under which no.242 was shown in his exhibition at the Goupil Gallery in London in 1908.

See Colour Plate XL

JOSEPH PENNELL
American, 1857–1926

Pennell studied art at the Pennsylvania Academy in Philadelphia, developed a particular interest in etching and admired the work of Whistler (q.v.). He lived in Europe from 1883 onwards and travelled widely, making etchings of city views, especially in Italy. He spent much time in London and in 1893 began a friendship with Whistler that led to his being co-author with his wife Elizabeth of a two-volume biography of the older artist, published in 1908. In 1917 he returned permanently to the USA, making boldly-designed lithographs of industrial subjects and teaching printmaking in New York.

243. Westminster, Evening 1909

Mezzotint, 9¾ x 14¾
Signed 'J. Pennell del sc imp' (on tab, below)
Lent by the Art Institute of Chicago

244. The City, Evening 1909

Mezzotint, 10 x 15
Signed 'J. Pennell del sc imp' (on tab, below)
Lent by the Art Institute of Chicago

In certain works of 1908-9 Pennell departed from his usual etching to experiment with mezzotint. Because the artist works from dark to light, this is a technique that lends itself well to nocturnal subjects, and the all-over grainy texture of the result suggests the vibrating imperfection of night-time vision. Pennell was living in a flat in Adelphi Terrace at this time, and nos.243–4 are night views from his own windows overlooking the Thames. As he surely realised, he was practically following in the footsteps of Whistler and Monet (q.v.), who had produced views from the nearby Savoy Hotel only a few years before. He shows more

interest in the effects of artificial illumination against the darkness than either of his celebrated predecessors, evoking the scene in velvety shades of black punctuated with spots of white light representing lamps and their reflections. No.243 features Westminster Bridge and the Houses of Parliament, with Charing Cross Bridge just cutting across the lower left corner, and no.244 takes in the Embankment, Waterloo Bridge, the City skyline dominated by St Paul's and some smoking chimneys on the south bank.

YOSHIO MARKINO
Japanese, born 1874

Markino attended the American Missionary College in Japan, studied art at the California State University in San Francisco from 1894 to 1897 and in the latter year moved to London, continuing his studies at the Goldsmith's Institute and the Central School. His work consists largely of delicately tinted water-colours and prints of London street scenes.

245. Green Park with Buckingham Palace in the background about 1911

Colour print from woodblocks, 9½ x 13¾
Signed in pencil 'Yoshio Markino' (lower r.)
Lent by the Victoria and Albert Museum

Above the row of trees appear the ghostly form of the palace, some white spray from the fountains in front and, on the far left, the gilt statue of Victory on the Victoria Memorial. Clothing these landmarks in an evening mist and choosing a viewpoint from which they are all but concealed, Markino shows a selectivity and understatement in the treatment of the London scene that may come from his Japanese background, the influence of Whistler, or both. The Japanese inscriptions give Markino's name and those of the engraver Hasegawa and the printer Nishimura.

246. W.J.Loftie
The Colour of London 1914

Lent by the Guildhall Library

247. London Pictured by Yoshio Markino 1917

Lent by the Guildhall Library

Nos.246–7 are books illustrated with reproductions of works by Markino, both published by Chatto and Windus. In addition to the text on London by W.J.Loftie, *The Colour of London* contains an appreciation of Markino by M.H.Spielmann and an essay by the artist himself. 'I am a great admirer of English ladies,' he writes. 'To me those willowy figures seem more graceful than the first crescent moon, while those well-built figures seem more elegant than peony flowers' (p. xxvi). But the principal attraction of London was the atmosphere: 'I think London without mists would be like a bride without a trousseau. I like thick fogs as well as autumn mists. Even on a summer day I see some covering veils . . . Indeed the London mist attracts me so that I do not feel I could live in any other place but London' (p. xxxviii).

ANONYMOUS
Probably Indian

248. Fog Battery 1913

Water-colour and pen and ink, 17¼ x 20¼
Signed with an indecipherable monogram and dated 1913 (lower l.)
Lent by the Guildhall Library

No. 248 is from a series of drawings entitled *Wake-Up London!* made by an unknown artist in 1913–14. They represent ideas and schemes designed to make London a brighter, cleaner, healthier and happier place in the future. It seems reasonable to infer that the artist was Indian from the special concern that is evident in the series for the welfare of Indians in London. The architectural projects, for example, include a design for an Indian centre accompanied by the inscription: 'Great numbers of our fellow subjects of India are scattered over London, living in dingy lodgings and uncongenial surroundings and associations. These people are, for the most part, polite and intellectual and law abiding. They are engaged in various occupations, in trade, and as students of different professions. But they have no social centre like other foreigners in this city.' One senses that the artist might in fact be thinking of himself. The architecture of the proposed centre and most of the other designs for buildings look distinctly Indian in their style, and are represented in a way that suggests only a partial understanding of the rules of perspective.

No.248 shows a cannon for dispersing fogs invented, according to the inscriptions, by Professor Demetrio Maggiora, and used in various cities of northern Italy. Reminding us that the 'annual loss to London caused by fogs is enormous, to say nothing of public health', the artist proposes the siting of twelve such cannons in a ring around London and assures us that 'twenty explosions from each projector would rid London of its densest fog. In twenty minutes the sky would be perfectly clear and the sun shining.'

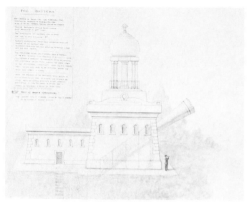

248

ANONYMOUS
German

249. Zeppeline über England 1916

Lent by the Bishopsgate Institute

This German propaganda booklet issued by Ullstein and Co. of Berlin is illustrated with photographs and drawings showing English efforts against the threat of the Zeppelins: people anxiously watching the skies, operating searchlights, and so on. One of the measures adopted to protect London was the 'black-out' – a striking instance in its way of life imitating art – and the most memorable illustration in *Zeppeline über London* shows a darkened Oxford Street at 7 in the evening.

250

LUDWIG GIES
German, 1887–1966

Gies was a sculptor and medallist. He studied at the Munich Academy under Balthasar Schmidt from 1910 to 1913, served in the German army in the First World War then taught sculpture in Berlin, becoming a Member of the Berlin Academy in 1924. He was expelled by the Nazis in 1937. After the Second World War he became Director of Sculpture at the Cologne Academy.

250. Zeppelins in London probably 1916

Medal, iron, 2 ⅜ diameter
Lent by the Trustees of the British Museum

No.250 is from a series of medals by Gies treating the theme of war in a non-propagandist and fairly critical manner. For some reason, he shows London as full of skyscrapers with telegraph wires running between them, rather as he shows Manhattan in another medal of the series that attacks American military spending; in fact, the skyscrapers in London are even taller than they are in Manhattan. This may result from mere ignorance of the actual appearance of London or from a deliberate distortion of reality for the purposes of expression, to conjure up an ultra-modern world of inhuman scale and violence.

EMILE CLAUS
Belgian, 1849–1924

Pursuing an artistic career in spite of parental opposition, Claus was a student at the Antwerp

Academy from 1869 to 1875. His early work is in a French-influenced vein of rustic naturalism, although in 1879 he had a brief flirtation with Orientalist subject-matter. During a stay in Paris in 1888 he was inspired by the work of Monet to adopt a more brilliant palette. Still painting mostly rural subjects, he developed a vibrant and joyful style particularly suited to capturing effects of sunlight, and became the leading figure in a group of Belgian painters sometimes called the 'luminists'. He came to London as a refugee during the First World War.

251. The Embankment 1918

Oil on canvas, 38 x 36¼
Signed and dated 'Emile Claus London 1918' (lower l.)
Lent by the Museum voor Schone Kunsten, Ghent

Claus found the London atmosphere uncongenial to his 'luminist' style but nonetheless painted some striking views of the Thames under various weather conditions, mostly wintery. No.251 is an example, and there are many more in the modern art department of the Musées Royaux des Beaux-Arts in Brussels. In highlighting effects such as that of the sun permeating fog, Claus's London pictures are clearly indebted to Monet, and many show Monet's favourite motif of Waterloo Bridge. But Claus affords the London street traffic a more prominent position than his predecessor and mentor, and often devotes most of his foreground to an Embankment busy with cabs and carriages.

251

THE CITY IN FLUX

SMOKE AND FOG; FORMS, ARCHITECTURAL MASSES, PERSPECTIVES, A WHOLE DULL, RUMBLING CITY IN THE FOG, COMPOSED OF FOG ITSELF; THE STRUGGLE OF LIGHT AND ALL THE PHASES OF THAT STRUGGLE; THE SUN HELD CAPTIVE IN THE HAZE OR BREAKING THROUGH THE COLOURED, IRRADIANT, SWIRLING DEPTHS OF THE ATMOSPHERE IN SEPARATE BEAMS; THE COMPLEX DRAMA OF REFLECTIONS ON THE SURFACE OF THE THAMES, INFINITELY TRANSIENT AND SUBTLE, SOMBRE OR MAGICAL, DISTURBING, DELICIOUS, BLOSSOMING OR TERRIBLE; NIGHTMARE, DREAM, MYSTERY, CONFLAGRATION, FURNACE, CHAOS, FLOATING GARDENS, THE INVISIBLE, THE UNREAL, AND ALL OF THESE TOGETHER FORMING A NATURE, THE NATURE PARTICULAR TO THIS PRODIGIOUS CITY – WHICH WAS CREATED FOR PAINTERS, BUT WHICH PAINTERS BEFORE M. CLAUDE MONET HAVE NEVER LEARNT TO SEE, HAVE NEVER BEEN ABLE TO EXPRESS.

Octave Mirbeau, 1904

Monet's London paintings are not so much views of the the city through a veil of atmosphere as views of the veil itself, an 'envelope' (to use the artist's own word) that was infinitely sensitive to changes of weather and light. Their poetry – the wealth of ideas and associations they suggest – lies not only in their mistiness but also in the state of flux that Monet evokes by painting the same subject repeatedly under different conditions. As cityscapes, they stand at the opposite extreme to Canaletto's images of order and fixity, presenting urban experience as an unseizable flow.

CLAUDE MONET
French, 1840–1926

Like his friend Camille Pissarro (q.v.), Monet first came to London as a refugee from the Franco-Prussian War, fleeing after the Prussian invasion of Paris in September 1870 and staying till towards the end of the following year. In London he was introduced by Daubigny (q.v.) to Paul Durand-Ruel, who showed his works at his 'Society of French Artists' exhibitions in New Bond Street, beginning an artist-dealer relationship that was to be important and at times crucial to Monet for the rest of his life. He met regularly with Pissarro to visit the London galleries, where they admired the work of Constable and Turner. He seems to have produced relatively few paintings during this first stay; only five are known, two views of parks, two of the Pool of London and one of the Thames and the Houses of Parliament. The bulk of Monet's work in London dates from much later in his career. In the 1880s he became friendly with Whistler (q.v.) and after a brief visit in 1887 wrote that he intended painting some views of fogs over the Thames. He realised his plan in 1899–1901, when he came for further visits and began over a hundred canvases, although he was to leave many unfinished and probably to destroy others as unresolvable. The paintings show just three views under different conditions of weather and light, Charing Cross Bridge and Waterloo Bridge as seen from the artist's room in the Savoy Hotel, and the Houses of Parliament as seen from St Thomas's Hospital. Monet showed 37 of those he considered exhibitable as finished works at Durand-Ruel's gallery in Paris in 1904, under the title *Vues de la Tamise à Londres*.

MONET'S 'VIEWS OF THE THAMES IN LONDON'

Monet travelled to London in September-October 1899 to visit his son Michel, who had come to perfect his English, but also took the opportunity of beginning paintings of the views towards Charing Cross and Waterloo bridges from his room at the Savoy. He returned for a more solitary and productive stay in February–April 1900, mentioning in a letter of 18 March that he had 'something like 65 canvases covered with colours'. It was on this stay that he seems

254

to have begun painting the Houses of Parliament, from a vantage point on the terrace of St Thomas's Hospital, as well as continuing with the two bridge subjects. His third campaign was the last and the longest, from January to April 1901; he seems to have worked more this time on his Waterloo Bridge and Houses of Parliament subjects, and less on Charing Cross Bridge. He continued to work on his London canvases at home in the studio at Giverny, bringing them before the public for the first time at Durand-Ruel's gallery in May–June 1904; the exhibition contained eighteen views of Waterloo Bridge, eleven of the Houses of Parliament and eight of Charing Cross Bridge.

Like his serial paintings of grainstacks and Rouen Cathedral, Monet's London pictures were meant to be seen together to recreate the sensation of changeability in the motif. He was interested not only in the bridges and Parliament in themselves, but also in the way their appearance was affected by changes in the weather conditions; the word 'effet' occurs in about a third of the titles Monet gave his works in the Durand-Ruel exhibition. The main attraction of London was that it was constantly in a state of meteorological flux. To see lights and colours transformed, he had no need to wait for the sun to move to a different position in the sky since the weather would do the job far more rapidly. 'My practised eye has found that objects change in appearance in a London fog more and quicker than in any other atmosphere', he said in 1901.

Monet came to London in the winter months when he was sure of getting fogs. In order to obtain dramatic silhouettes and gleaming and

256

struggle of light') to the concrete ('conflagration' or 'floating gardens'), and it is surely with this kind of multiple resonance that the artist intended them to work.

252. Waterloo Bridge: overcast weather
finished 1900

Oil on canvas, 24½ x 39½
Signed and dated 'Claude Monet 1900' (lower r.)
Lent by the Hugh Lane Municipal Gallery of Modern Art, Dublin

No.252 was shown in the 1904 exhibition under the title *Temps couvert* and bought from Durand-Ruel by Hugh Lane the following year.

253. Waterloo Bridge: effect of sunlight
finished 1903

Oil on canvas, 24½ x 39½
Signed and dated 'Claude Monet 1903' (lower l.)
Lent by the Helen Dill Collection, Denver Art Museum

This mistier treatment of the Waterloo Bridge motif appeared in the 1904 exhibition under the title *Effet de soleil*. The 'effect' is at its most striking in the brilliant gleam on the water set off by the dark form of the barge near the lower edge of the canvas. *See Colour Plate XXXVIII*

254. The Houses of Parliament: effect of sunlight finished 1903

Oil on canvas, 31½ x 36¼
Signed and dated 'Claude Monet 1903' (lower l.)
Lent by the Brooklyn Museum (Bequest of Grace Underwood Barton)

No.254 was also shown under the title *Effet de soleil* in the 1904 exhibition. The cold light and mist of a late winter's afternoon turn the Houses of Parliament into a remote and imposing silhouette. *See Colour Plate XXXVII*

255. The Houses of Parliament: the seagulls finished 1903

Oil on canvas, 31½ x 36¼
Signed and dated 'Claude Monet 1903' (lower r.)
Lent by the Art Museum, Princeton University

sparkling reflections on the Thames, he viewed all three of his London motifs against the light, looking south-east towards Waterloo Bridge in the mornings, south-west towards Charing Cross Bridge in the afternoons and west towards the Houses of Parliament in the hours before sunset. The paintings suggest changeability both because they are in series and because of the shifting, unseizable nature of Monet's colours; his compositions are simple, but the many-layered texture of brushwork across each elemental block of river, building or sky is so intricate that there seem to be no colour areas, only transitions.

It is important to remember that for Monet at this stage in his career, the capturing of atmospheric effects was a means to an emotional end. His London paintings are not meant merely to show what London happened to look like,

but to stimulate feelings and ideas in the mind of the spectator. Most obviously, their mistiness serves as a metaphor of mystery. Monet himself said: 'London wouldn't be beautiful without the fog, which gives it its marvellous breadth. Its regular, massive blocks become grandiose in that mysterious cloak.' Like Monet's brushwork, the meaning of his pictures is complex and many-layered. We may take him at his word and associate the buildings in his London pictures with grandeur and the fog with mystery, yet they seem equally open to association with the ideas, respectively, of permanence and change, the manmade and the natural. If we follow the lead of Monet's friend Octave Mirbeau in his introduction to the 1904 exhibition catalogue, we will allow them to suggest a kaleidoscope of different ideas, from the abstract ('mystery') to the metaphorical ('the

Nos.255–6 show the view a little to the left of that in no.254, with the tallest part of the building, the Victoria Tower, to the right of the composition. No.255 did not feature in the 1904 exhibition but was sold by the artist to Durand-Ruel the following year as *Le Parlement, les mouettes*. The flitting gulls add to the sense of changeability in the scene and help to suggest a body of atmosphere – a medium – between spectator and motif.

256. The Houses of Parliament: effect of fog
finished 1904

Oil on canvas, 31½ x 36¼
Signed and dated 'Claude Monet 1904' (lower r.)
Lent by the Museum of Fine Arts, St Petersburg

Another of the works in the 1904 exhibition, where it was given the title *Effet de brouillard*.

257. Waterloo Bridge probably finished after 1904

Oil on canvas, 24½ x 31½
Signed 'Claude Monet' (lower r.)
Lent by the Lowe Art Museum, University of Miami, Coral Gables (Gift of Ione T. Staley)

No.257 was not shown in the 1904 exhibition. Monet only sold it to the dealers Durand-Ruel and Bernheim-Jeune in 1920, which may be when he added the signature. The canvas is the usual height for the Waterloo subjects but considerably narrower, which suggests it may have been cut down at some point. The framing of the motif is also unusual in that it excludes the buildings on the south bank of the river that are normally visible above the bridge.

See colour plate XXXIX

257

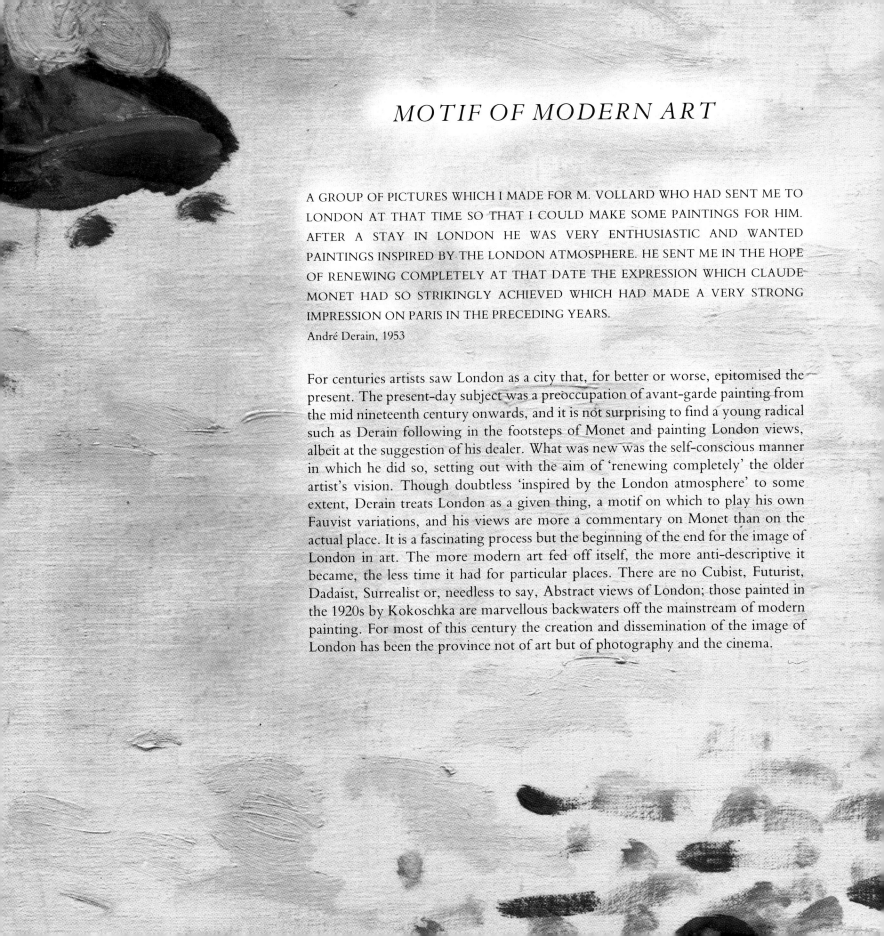

MOTIF OF MODERN ART

A GROUP OF PICTURES WHICH I MADE FOR M. VOLLARD WHO HAD SENT ME TO LONDON AT THAT TIME SO THAT I COULD MAKE SOME PAINTINGS FOR HIM. AFTER A STAY IN LONDON HE WAS VERY ENTHUSIASTIC AND WANTED PAINTINGS INSPIRED BY THE LONDON ATMOSPHERE. HE SENT ME IN THE HOPE OF RENEWING COMPLETELY AT THAT DATE THE EXPRESSION WHICH CLAUDE MONET HAD SO STRIKINGLY ACHIEVED WHICH HAD MADE A VERY STRONG IMPRESSION ON PARIS IN THE PRECEDING YEARS.
André Derain, 1953

For centuries artists saw London as a city that, for better or worse, epitomised the present. The present-day subject was a preoccupation of avant-garde painting from the mid nineteenth century onwards, and it is not surprising to find a young radical such as Derain following in the footsteps of Monet and painting London views, albeit at the suggestion of his dealer. What was new was the self-conscious manner in which he did so, setting out with the aim of 'renewing completely' the older artist's vision. Though doubtless 'inspired by the London atmosphere' to some extent, Derain treats London as a given thing, a motif on which to play his own Fauvist variations, and his views are more a commentary on Monet than on the actual place. It is a fascinating process but the beginning of the end for the image of London in art. The more modern art fed off itself, the more anti-descriptive it became, the less time it had for particular places. There are no Cubist, Futurist, Dadaist, Surrealist or, needless to say, Abstract views of London; those painted in the 1920s by Kokoschka are marvellous backwaters off the mainstream of modern painting. For most of this century the creation and dissemination of the image of London has been the province not of art but of photography and the cinema.

ANDRE DERAIN
French, 1880–1954

Along with Henri Matisse and Maurice Vlaminck, Derain was a leading member of the group of painters known as the Fauves, who developed a radical style inspired by the work of Van Gogh and Gauguin. Their experiments with vividly unnaturalistic colour and raw brushwork reached joyful fruition in the landscapes painted by Derain and Matisse at Collioure on the French Mediterranean coast in the summer of 1905. Later that year they exhibited their works together at the Salon d'Automne in Paris and were dubbed 'Fauves', or wild beasts, by the critic Louis Vauxcelles. Derain had been to England on a number of occasions but had never visited London. When he finally came, towards the end of 1905 and again in the spring of 1906, it was at the suggestion of Ambroise Vollard, the dealer and friend of many Parisian artists of the avant–garde. He painted a number of London subjects in the Fauvist manner for Vollard, mostly views on the Thames. From 1908 he turned away from Fauvism towards a more structural style influenced by Cézanne, the Cubists and 'primitive' art, for which he had developed an enthusiasm after seeing the examples at the British Museum. Derain served in the French army during the First World War, after which his ideas on art became more and more conservative and his painting self–consciously traditional, looking back to Corot and various masters of the Renaissance and Baroque periods. From 1919 he was a successful and innovative designer of sets and costumes for the ballet.

DERAIN'S LONDON VIEWS

Derain came to paint in London the year after the London pictures of Monet (q.v.) were shown at Durand–Ruel's gallery in Paris. It was the idea of Ambroise Vollard, who presumably sensed that following Monet would be good for Derain's reputation and saleability; it would ally him with a living old master of the avant–garde and at the same time help establish the originality of the Fauve vision as against Impressionism. He also persuaded Vlaminck to come, but he seems to have responded less prolifically to the London scene than his friend. Derain certainly set about 'renewing' Monet's

260

London (to use his own word), dispensing with the fog, heightening and contradicting actual colours, conveying few facts but an intense visual excitement, recreating his subjects rather than describing them. The landmarks of London are recognisable in his London views, but how much difference being in London as opposed to Paris or Collioure made to their mood is open to question. Vollard wrote in his *Recollections of a Picture Dealer*: 'I was bitterly reproached at the time for having taken these artists "out of their element" by diverting them from their usual subjects. Now that time has done its work it is easy to see, on putting the French paintings beside those done in England, that a painter "who has something to say" is always himself, no matter in what country he is working' (translated by Violet M. Macdonald, 1936, p. 201).

Derain's London views are all taken from different positions, unlike Monet's, and he painted at least twenty – mostly during his second visit of spring 1906. They include the

occasional street or park scene, but the majority show bridges, barges and riverfront buildings along the Thames; he had painted similar views on the Seine in Paris. Their chronology is difficult to establish, although the views with the choppier 'divisionist' brushwork probably pre–date those with flatter, Gauguinesque colour areas.

258. Waterloo Bridge 1905–6

Oil on canvas, 31¾ x 39¾
Signed 'a derain' (lower l.)
Lent by the Thyssen–Bornemisza Collection, Lugano

We are looking eastwards from a viewpoint on the opposite side of the subject from that taken by Monet, probably somewhere along Blackfriars Bridge. A cascade of yellow light showers down from the late afternoon sun and creates a glittering path across the surface of the river. Towards the horizon it turns to pink, against which the bridge and riverfront buildings stand out in shades of blue and green. The separateness of the dabs of paint, which suggests this was one of Derain's earlier London compositions, creates an effect of intense vibration. London appears energised and dazzling. *See colour plate XLVII*

259. The Houses of Parliament by Night
1905–6

Oil on canvas, 31 x 39
Signed 'a derain' (lower r.)
Lent by the Metropolitan Museum of Art, New York (Robert Lehman Collection)

Derain's concession to the night is to make his colours cooler rather than darker, allowing blue to dominate. The Houses of Parliament were another of Monet's favourite subjects, and nowhere is the invitation to compare Derain's London views with those of the older artist more clearly implied. In place of mist and mystery, Derain gives us a carefree celebration of colours and shapes, some inspired by the subject, others of his own invention.
See colour plate XLV

260. On the Thames probably 1906

Oil on canvas, 29 x 36¼
Signed 'a derain' (lower r.)
Lent by the National Gallery of Art, Washington

An example of the more relaxed, fluent brushwork and emphasis on contour that Derain seems to have developed in his later London works. The ships and barges of the Pool float against a lighter–toned background as simple rhyming shapes, presided over by an abstracted version of Tower Bridge.

261. The Thames and Tower Bridge
probably 1906

Oil on canvas, 26 x 39
Lent by the Fridart Foundation

Another view of the Pool. The bright reds of the ships and barges and the green of the river create a strongly articulated foreground, paling into pinks and yellows in the distance. In spite of his liberated and playful approach to picture–making, Derain never sacrifices space, often contriving his own unorthodox but none the less effective system of colouristic perspective.
See colour plate XLVI

262

262. St Paul's from the Thames probably 1906

Oil on canvas, 39¼ x 32¼
Signed 'a derain' (lower l.)
Lent by the Minneapolis Institute of Arts (Bequest of Putnam Dana McMillan)

Again Derain achieves a strong effect of depth through colour, here by alternating warmth and coolness. A halo of pink sky throws into relief a blue St Paul's, which in turn throws into relief the pink warehouses along the riverfront; the pink–topped barges in the foreground stand out emphatically against a luminous yellow–green river.

LIST OF LENDERS

PHOTOGRAPHIC ACKNOWLEDGEMENTS

The publishers of the catalogue and Barbican Art
Gallery would like to thank all the lenders of works
from both private and public collections who have
kindly supplied photographic material for the
catalogue and exhibition, or who have given
permission for its use.

Thanks must also extend to the following people and
organisations:

The Addison Gallery of American Art, Andover
Boston, Museum of Fine Arts
J E Bulloz, Paris
Courtauld Institute Galleries (Courtauld Collection)
Fogg Art Museum, Harvard University, Cambridge,
Mass.
Freer Gallery of Art, Smithsonian Institution,
Washington DC
J G Links
National Museum of Wales
Philadelphia Museum of Art
Tate Gallery
John Webb

We are also most grateful to the following
photographers who undertook considerable
photographic work for catalogue reproduction use:
Annie Gilbert, Jonathan Morris-Ebbs, Nick Warwick

Copyright for the following artists: Derain ©
A.D.A.G.P. 1987; Le Sidaner © D.A.C.S. 1987; J. E.
Blanche © D.A.C.S. 1987.